COUNTRY INNS *of* *California*

JACQUELINE KILLEEN

Photograph on cover: The Spreckels Mansion on Buena Vista West in San Francisco. This splendid example of Colonial Revival architectecture was built in 1898 for Richard Spreckels, a nephew of sugar baron Claus Spreckels. In 1979 the historic house in the city's Haight Ashbury District was transformed into one of San Francisco's first luxury bed-and-breakfast inns.

For more information about staying at the Spreckels Mansion, see the review that appears on page 114.

Photographer: Saxon Holt

PUBLISHER
Robert J. Dolezal
EDITORIAL DIRECTOR
Christine Robertson
PRODUCTION DIRECTOR
Ernie S. Tasaki
SYSTEM MANAGER
Katherine L. Parker
PROJECT COORDINATOR
Laurie A. Steele
MAP DESIGNER
Marti Walton Design
SERIES FORMAT DESIGN
Pentagram Design
PRODUCTION
Studio 165
PRINTING
W. A. Krueger Company

Library of Congress Catalog Card Number: 88-72346
ISBN: ISBN 0-89721-184-7

Published by 101 Productions and distributed by Ortho Information Services, Box 5047, San Ramon, CA 94583.

Previously titled *Country Inns of the Far West: California*, 5th edition

COUNTRY INNS *of* California

AUTHOR
Jacqueline Killeen

ILLUSTRATOR
Roy Killeen

PROJECT DIRECTOR
Karin Shakery

PUBLISHED BY 101 PRODUCTIONS DISTRIBUTED BY ORTHO INFORMATION SERVICES

PREFACE

California these days is rife with country inns, ranging from quaint B&Bs to historic hotels to luxury resorts. The traveler has an abundance of choices, but this wasn't always the case. When we compiled the first edition of *Country Inns of the Far West* twelve years ago, we found only thirty-one hostelries in California that we felt were worth writing about. And these weren't easy to find. There were no books on the subject in those days, so we took to the road, searching small towns, back roads, and even big cities for the quintessential country inn.

In compiling this latest edition we again took to the road, traveling over four thousand miles up, down, and across the state to locate the best of the plethora of inns that have opened in recent years. Unlike some guidebook writers who never venture beyond their word processors, we personally inspect each inn before including it in the book. We also abhor the deplorable practice of requiring payment from an inn in return for a listing in a guidebook. We charge no fees nor "membership dues," we require no purchase of books, and we accept no free lodgings, except in rare cases in which the innkeepers, over the years, have become our friends.

What are our criteria? We strive to present a wide range of accommodations from an inexpensive four-bedroom B&B to a two-hundred-room luxury hotel. And we expect each to be the best of its kind—a special place with a unique character. In the small inns, the personality of the innkeeper is a key factor; in the larger resorts, the quality of the service and the quantity of the amenities are scrutinized. We are partial to places with interesting histories, unusual architecture, spectacular sites, enchanting decor, fabulous food, a variety of recreational activities, and extras such as fireplaces, decks, and in-room spas. (Would you believe that we actually found some places with *all* these attributes?) Whether the rates are forty dollars a night or four hundred, we ask: Are you getting what you pay for? And the bottom line, as always, is: Would we want to stay here? We hope you enjoy this edition of *Country Inns of the Far West: California* as much as we have enjoyed researching it for you.

—Jacqueline and Roy Killeen

RULES OF THE INN

Rates: Due to price fluctuations, specific rates are not quoted in this book. Instead we have classified the rates for one room shared by two people as follows: under $60, inexpensive; $60–$100, moderate; $100–$140, expensive; over $140, very expensive. When dinner is included in the price, we have adjusted the scale to reflect this. These price classifications were based upon rates in effect at the time of publication and are subject to change. Many inns also have lower off-season and midweek rates, as well as group rates; inquire.

Reservations, Deposits, Cancellations, and Refunds: Reservations are advised, especially during peak travel periods. For holiday and weekend stays, inns are often booked months in advance. Most require a deposit of at least one night's fee and a minimum stay of two nights on the weekends. In most cases, your deposit will not be refunded if you cancel at the last minute; sometimes even a week's notice is required. Call or write in advance to ask about the current requirements, rates, and refund policies.

Children: Many of the smaller inns are not suitable for children: they may lack adequate soundproofing or play areas; there is often an abundance of breakable objects and furnishings; and many innkeepers want to provide a place for people who are taking a vacation from their own children. We have indicated where children are welcome; many other inns will accept children under special circumstances. But when traveling with children, always inquire first.

No-Smoking Policies: Most of the smaller inns do not allow smoking within the building, although in most cases guests are free to smoke outdoors on porches, patios, or in the gardens. These inns have adopted this policy for important reasons: consideration of other guests and fear of fire or damage to priceless antiques.

Facilities for the Handicapped: "Wheelchair access" means only that one or more rooms may be reached with no stairs from a parking area. "Fully equipped for the handicapped" means wheelchair access plus extra-wide doors and bathrooms specially designed with grab bars and other safety features as prescribed by local building codes, which vary. It is advisable to inquire about your particular needs when making reservations.

CONTENTS

LAND
OF THE SUN

THE SOUTH COAST
FROM SAN DIEGO TO LOS ANGELES
ARROWHEAD AND BIG BEAR
IDYLLWILD
RIVERSIDE
PALM SPRINGS

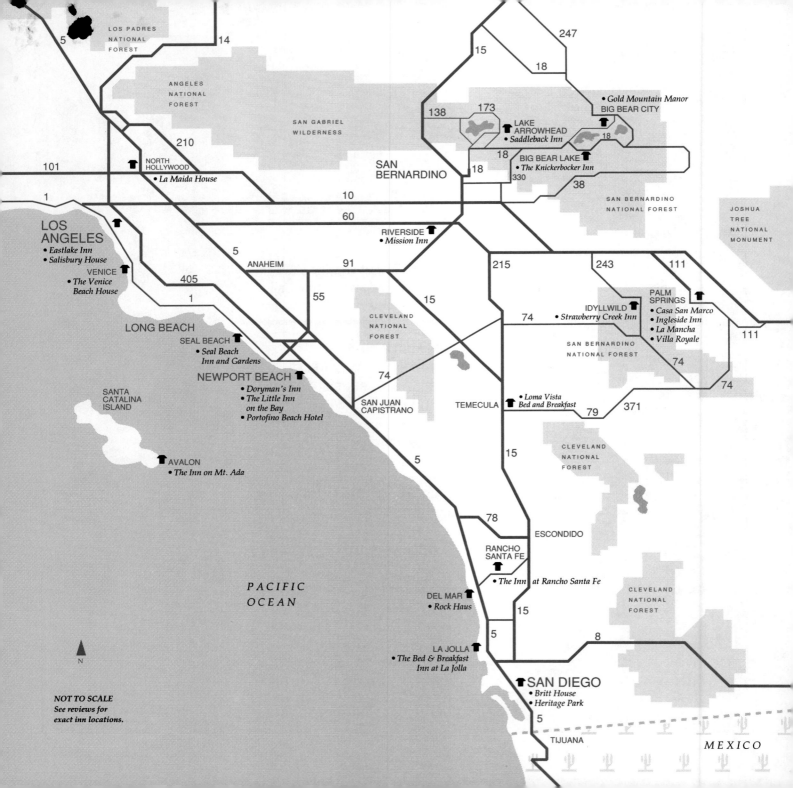

SAN DIEGO

In 1542 the Spanish explorer Juan Rodríguez Cabrillo sailed into San Diego Bay. The first white man to set foot on California soil, he claimed the area for Spain, which proceeded to ignore its new territory for over two centuries. The Spanish were looking for gold and, ironically, could see no potential in this wilderness inhabited only by Indians, a wilderness that one day would provide the biggest gold strike in history. Finally, in 1769, Father Junípero Serra led a group of Franciscan padres to California and founded the state's first mission at San Diego. These priests became California's first innkeepers, building a string of twenty-one missions along the coast. The missions were spaced a day's journey apart so that travelers could find food and lodging each night.

Today San Diego is the third-largest and one of the fastest-growing cities in the state. Besides being a major commercial and educational center (nine institutions of higher learning are located here), the city and its adjacent communities are a year-round vacationland. Water sports—from swimming at the sun-drenched beaches to deep-sea fishing off the coast—are popular diversions. San Diego also boasts one of the finest zoos in the country, as well as Sea World, the largest oceanarium in the world. Sightseeing opportunities include Old Town (the original Spanish settlement with many of the old adobes intact) and the Mission San Diego de Alcala. A short drive whisks you across the border to Mexico.

It seems fitting that the city where California's string of missions began should also be the site of southern California's first bed-and-breakfast inn. In 1979 designer Robert Hostick and home-economics teacher Daun Martin opened this inn in a three-story Queen Anne Victorian with a circular tower and gabled roof. Attorney Eugene Britt had built the house circa 1887, but for many years it was owned by newspaper publisher E. W. Scripps.

The most dramatic feature of the Britt House is a monumental entrance hall with intricate paneled wainscoting and an oak stairway. Three stained-glass windows rise from floor to ceiling, and a filigree of spoolwork arches over the entrance to the parlor, which contains a baby grand piano. Afternoon tea, accompanied by a large variety of sweet and savory goodies, is served here.

Robert Hostick designed the interiors, opting for country charm rather than authenticity. In the ten bedrooms, furnishings from several periods are mixed with considerable grace. Marble-topped Eastlake dressers and old platform rockers

BRITT HOUSE

406 Maple Street,
San Diego, California 92103

Telephone: (619) 234-2926

Accommodations: ten rooms with twin or queen-size beds; one room with private bath, other rooms share four baths with tubs or showers; one room with wheelchair access; telephone jacks; television on request.

Rates: moderate to expensive, breakfast and tea included. Children welcome. No smoking.

Cards: AE, MC, V

Open all year.

mingle with wicker and rattan and with comfortable queen-size beds with quilted spreads. Gilt-framed "family portraits" adorn the dressers, and Hostick's own bright, contemporary graphics hang on the walls. Rag dolls and stuffed animals recline around the bedrooms, where you'll also find bouquets of fresh and silk flowers, bowls of fruit, and homemade cookies. Two rooms have private balconies, and a garden cottage has a kitchenette and private bath. In the main house, four community baths offer some intriguing choices: One has two ("his and hers") claw-foot tubs, complete with bubble bath.

Each day, Daun or her assistant bakes individual loaves of a different yeast bread—nine grain, orange, or carrot, for example. The bread is served on bedroom trays along with fresh-squeezed orange juice, shirred eggs, and Viennese-roast coffee. After breakfast it's time for a stroll. Britt House is only two blocks from the famed Balboa Park and San Diego Zoo, and it's only a ten-minute walk to the beach and the harbor.

Getting There: From Highway 5, take Washington Street exit, proceed east to Fourth Street, and turn right on Fourth to Maple.

On a hillside above historic Old Town, a meticulously landscaped eight-acre park—complete with cobblestone walkways and nineteenth-century street-lights—preserves some of San Diego's finest examples of Victorian architecture. Heritage Park is owned by the County of San Diego, which moved eight landmark houses here from other parts of the city, restored their exteriors, and leased them for commercial ventures ranging from gift shops to law offices. Lori Chandler, an avid antiques collector and former teacher, converted one of the buildings—a splendid 1889 Queen Anne—into a bed-and-breakfast inn.

Before opening her inn in 1985, Lori spent some fifteen years researching the B&Bs of America. She took an authentic approach to the decorating, leaving the lacquered redwood moldings in the high-ceilinged rooms, installing William Morris papers on the walls, and filling the house with turn-of-the-century antiques and bric-a-brac. It's hard to describe the furnishings, however, because what you see to-day may be gone tomorrow: The Victoriana is all for sale. Three of the bedrooms contain the original tile fireplaces, now filled with plants; a turret room commands a view of downtown San Diego.

Breakfast is substantial at Heritage Park B&B—juices, fruit, the inn's award-winning strawberry jam on freshly baked breads, and a hot egg dish—and is either brought to your room on an antique tray or served outside on the wide veranda. For

HERITAGE PARK BED & BREAKFAST INN

2470 Heritage Park Row, San Diego, California 92110

Telephone: (619) 295-7088

Accommodations: nine rooms with double or queen-size beds; three rooms have private baths, six rooms share three baths; showers or tub/showers; one room fully equipped for the handicapped; telephones on request; no television.

Rates: moderate to expensive, breakfast included. No smoking.

Cards: MC, V

Open all year.

Heritage Park Bed & Breakfast Inn

other meals you can stroll down the hill to Old Town or drive a few miles to San Diego's numerous fine restaurants. If you're in the mood to stay home in the evening, Heritage Park provides some unusual amenities. Every night a vintage film is shown on the VCR, which is the only modern device in the inn's old-fashioned parlor. And with advance notice, the innkeeper will arrange for a country-style barbecue supper or a five-course dinner to be served in your room at a candlelit table.

Getting There: From Highway 5, just north of downtown San Diego, take Old Town exit to San Diego Avenue. Turn left on San Diego, then turn right on Harney, which leads into Heritage Park.

A few miles north of San Diego, a hilly peninsula forested with Torrey pines juts into the Pacific. On its northern slopes, extending down to the beaches, lies the affluent community of La Jolla with its showplace homes and fine shops and restaurants. John Philip Sousa lived here in the 1920s, in a house built in 1913 in a Cubist-southwestern style surprisingly contemporary for that era. This house has now been elegantly refurbished as an exquisite B&B.

The sixteen bedrooms are decorated in a variety of styles ranging from a Laura Ashley country look with white wicker furniture to a more traditional mode with wing chairs and canopied beds. Throughout, dhurrie rugs are scattered over polished pine floors, gracing each bed there is a heap of pillows topped with a fortune cookie, and bowls of fresh fruit and flowers are placed in each room. Three guest rooms have wood-burning fireplaces, and several have partial or full views of the ocean.

A sunny second-floor common room, stocked with lots of books and a television set, opens onto a big deck. Downstairs a pretty, formal dining room looks out on a brick patio and a lawn surrounded by trees and gardens. You may choose to have your breakfast of juice, rolls, and coffee here in the dining room, on the upper deck, or in your room.

From The Bed & Breakfast Inn it's an easy walk to La Jolla's shops and restaurants, and municipal tennis courts are just across the street. Next door is St. James Church, where every fifteen minutes during the day the bells toll for guests at the inn.

Getting There: From Highway 5, north of San Diego, take La Jolla Village Drive exit and turn left on Torrey Pines Road. Proceed for two and one-half miles to Prospect, turn right and, when in town, turn left on Draper. Off-street parking behind the inn.

THE BED & BREAKFAST INN AT LA JOLLA

7753 Draper Avenue,
La Jolla, California 92037

Telephone: (619) 456-2066

Accommodations: sixteen rooms with twin or queen-size beds; all but one have private baths with showers or tub/showers; one room with wheelchair access; telephones on request; no television.

Rates: moderate to very expensive, breakfast included. Children over twelve welcome.

Cards: MC, V

Open all year.

At the century's turn Henry W. Keller developed the beautiful beach resort of Del Mar just north of San Diego. In 1910 he built a large summer home for his family on a hill overlooking the village and the Pacific. Constructed of stone and wood and surrounded by Torrey pines, the house is an elaborate example of the Craftsman style. In the 1920s the hillside mansion became a private club and hosted almost every illicit activity imaginable. During the 1960s it was used as a safe house for smuggling Mexicans into California.

In 1982 attorney Tom Hauser and his wife, Carol, bought the mansion and turned it into a lovely inn. This is indeed a new era for the handsome building, which sits on an acre of groomed lawn and gardens. Carol has decorated the ten bedrooms to look the way the rooms in a 1910 summer home should: lots of wicker and rattan, flowery comforters, mounds of ruffled pillows, some beds with canopies, and little antique writing tables. Most of the upstairs rooms have fabulous ocean views; four downstairs rooms, one with a fireplace, have private entrances.

Probably the most interesting guest room is the Whale Watch Room, a good place to bone up on the migration of the great gray whales that can be spotted all along the California coast during winter months. The Hausers have placed *Moby Dick* and other works on "whaleology" in the room, along with an 1861 chart of the whale migration and a replica of an old whalers' lodging sign, a reminder that San Diego was once a major whaling port. There's also a reminder of the inn's shady past: a paneled and mirrored headboard that once served as a false front for the area off the living room where the gambling tables were hidden.

Today this living room, with its beamed ceiling, stone fireplace, and Oriental rugs on the hardwood floors, contains more wholesome amenities: a player piano, backgammon set, and comfortable couches and chairs where you might want to curl up with a book from the Hausers' large library. Refreshments are served here in the evening. A sun porch with a clear view of the Pacific is the setting for a light breakfast of fresh fruit, juice, and muffins or coffee cake.

The beach and the village shops are the chief attractions of Del Mar, except in the summer months, when the racetrack, built by Bing Crosby and Bob Hope in 1937, brings some fifty thousand horse-racing fans to town. The many diversions of San Diego are only a short distance away.

Getting There: From San Diego, take Del Mar Heights exit off the San Diego Freeway and head west to Camino Del Mar, turn right to Fifteenth Street, and turn right again. From Los Angeles, take Via de la Valle exit off the San Diego Freeway and head southwest along Jimmy Durante Boulevard to the village of Del Mar; turn left on Fifteenth Street. Courtesy pickup at the Amtrak station in Del Mar.

ROCK HAUS

410 Fifteenth Street,
Del Mar, California 92014

Telephone: (619) 481-3764

Accommodations: ten rooms with twin, queen-, or king-size beds; six upstairs rooms share three baths with showers or tubs; four downstairs rooms have private baths with showers; no telephones; no television.

Rates: moderate to expensive, breakfast included. No smoking.

Cards: AE, MC, V

Open all year.

Rock Haus

The very exclusive community of Rancho Santa Fe consists of elegant tile-roofed houses set among dense eucalyptus groves in the hills inland from Del Mar beach. The hub of the area is a tiny village containing exquisite shops and an inn. This place was just a barren stretch of land, however, until 1906, when the Santa Fe Railroad purchased the site for the purpose of raising Australian eucalyptus for railroad ties—one of the most colossal agricultural follies in California history. Over three million seedlings were planted before Santa Fe officials realized that the gnarled eucalyptus wood was totally unsuitable for ties. They recouped their investment by planting the remaining acres with citrus and by selling off the eucalyptus forests for home sites. To house prospective purchasers, they constructed a lovely Spanish-style adobe building, which is now the nucleus of the inn.

The adobe and clusters of guest cottages occupy twenty acres of woods, lawns, ivy-bedded walkways, and gardens rife with bougainvillea, roses, magnolias, and palms. The Royce family has owned the inn since 1958, and Daniel Royce now manages it in a very personal fashion. Family antiques, including a large collection of old sailing-ship models, adorn the walls and tables of the living room. Here massive beams support a wooden ceiling that pitches some eighteen feet above the richly carpeted floor, and comfortable couches surround a fireplace. The choice of dining areas (there are four) ranges from an al fresco terrace to a cozy book-lined library. And on balmy summer weekend nights there is dancing under the stars.

The wide range of accommodations here will fit almost any budget. Most rooms in the main building have private lanais and are furnished simply with white wicker. Many of the cottage units have living rooms with fireplaces, and some have kitchenettes; most also have private patios, terraces, or decks. These cottages were also designed with flexibility in mind; rooms can be opened to each other to accommodate groups or families of various sizes.

The Inn at Rancho Santa Fe has all the amenities of a fine resort hotel: Three tennis courts, a swimming pool, and a croquet court are located on the grounds. Guest privileges are available at two private eighteen-hole golf courses nearby. And if you seek the beach, the inn maintains a seaside cottage with dressing rooms and showers at Del Mar, which is only a few minutes away.

Getting There: From the San Diego Freeway, take the Lomas Santa Fe Drive exit or the Via de la Valle exit and head east. Both roads lead to the inn. For a nominal charge and with advance notice, the inn will pick up guests at the Amtrak station in Del Mar or at Lindbergh Field in San Diego.

THE INN AT RANCHO SANTA FE

Box 869,
Rancho Santa Fe, California 92067

Telephone: (619) 756-1131

Accommodations: seventy-five rooms, most with twin beds and some with king-size beds; private baths with stall showers or tub/showers; telephones; television.

Rates: moderate to very expensive, no meals included. Dining rooms open for breakfast, lunch, and dinner; room service available. Children welcome. One dog allowed in certain rooms for an extra fee.

Cards: AE, CB, DC, MC, V

Facilities for weddings and conferences. Open all year.

The Inn at Rancho Santa Fe

Rancho California, an hour's drive from San Diego, is a planned community of ranches, vineyards, orchards, estates, and even a man-made lake. It covers sixty square miles of rolling hillsides east of Temecula, an 1890s stagecoach stop. In the late 1960s the developers of Rancho California started marketing ready-made vineyards and even provided the viticultural care. One of the takers was Ely Callaway, president of Burlington Industries. Callaway's wines were first released in 1975 and have subsequently become regarded as some of the finest bottlings to come from California. A few years later the Mount Palomar Winery opened, and others followed. Today some dozen wineries are located in the Temecula Valley, offering tastings and tours; many also have restaurants and picnic areas.

Knowing that every wine region needs a country inn, Dick and Betty Ryan—inveterate worldwide B&B travelers—built a tile-roofed, mission-style hacienda in 1987 on a hilltop overlooking the vineyards of Temecula Valley. Half the house is their home; the other half comprises the inn. The wines of the region are poured each evening by the fireside in the spacious living room, which is well stocked with other diversions such as books, games, and television. French doors open from here and the adjoining dining room to lawns and a terrace with a magnificent view of the vineyards. Betty serves a full breakfast, perhaps eggs Benedict or huevos rancheros or even ham and eggs.

Six guest rooms occupy the second floor, each named for a varietal wine and decorated with a different theme. Sauvignon Blanc is done up in desert hues with southwestern-style sandblasted pine furnishings. Champagne has the Art-Deco look of the 1940s with framed photos of Mae West and Fred Astaire. Fumé Blanc is frilly and feminine with white wickerware; Merlot has a masculine aura with cherrywood furniture and duck decoys. Chardonnay has a Laura Ashley country look, and Zinfandel is traditional with Queen Anne furnishings. Take your pick. Four of the rooms open to private balconies, all offer fantastic views, and in each you'll find a bowl of fresh fruit and a decanter of Mount Palomar port.

In addition to wine touring and tasting, this area provides a range of activities from antiques shopping in Temecula to hot-air ballooning over the countryside. Several championship golf courses are nearby, as are lakes for boating and fishing. And a scenic mountain road brings you to San Juan Capistrano and the beaches of Orange County.

Getting There: From San Diego, take Highway 15 north to Temecula; exit to the east on Rancho California Road. Just after you pass the Callaway Winery (and before you reach the Piconi Winery), turn left on La Serena Way. To reach the coast from Temecula, go north on Highway 15 to Highway 74, which leads over the hills to Coast Highway 1.

LOMA VISTA BED AND BREAKFAST

33350 La Serena Way,
Temecula, California 92390

Telephone: (714) 676-7047

Accommodations: six rooms with twin, queen-, or king-size beds; private baths with tub/showers; no telephones; no television.

Rates: moderate, breakfast included. No smoking in bedrooms.

Cards: MC, V

Open all year.

NEWPORT BEACH

The resort towns of Newport Beach and Balboa are built on a finger of land that juts from the coast to shelter a colorful harbor. Dotted with hundreds of pleasure boats and tiny picturesque islands connected by bridges, this is one of the major yachting centers on the California coast. If you're not a sailor, you'll still enjoy swimming beaches, some of the southland's best shopping, and restaurants galore. And for the kiddies—of all ages—Disneyland is thirty minutes away.

Getting There: From the San Diego Freeway, take the Harbor Boulevard or Costa Mesa Boulevard exit west. These roads eventually become Newport Boulevard, which crosses Highway 1 and then leads into Newport Beach.

B ring along your yachting cap and you'll feel right at home here. Sited on the edge of the harbor, this winsome inn even has its own boat to take guests on a complimentary cruise of the bay. Everything is oriented toward the water: Most guest rooms have views of the harbor and channel; a bayside terrace provides tables and lounges for sitting, sunning, and admiring the passing parade of boats; even the swimming pool is a few steps from the docks. Bicycles for exploring the area may be checked out.

When owners Herrick and Janice Hanson refurbished this small hotel in the mid-1980s, they envisioned a New England–style inn near the Pacific shores. Yet despite the Early American furnishings, the ambience is more Newport, California, than Newport, Rhode Island. The small standard rooms are lovely and lovingly appointed, but the suites are sensational. Sitting areas with sliding glass doors open to decks, and each suite has a wet bar and microwave oven.

The New England tradition, however, is strongly felt in the hospitality department. Some type of refreshment almost always awaits guests in the lobby— fruit, coffee, and pastries; iced tea, wine, and cheese; or milk and cookies—at various appropriate times of the day. And staffers here really care about living up to their motto: "Where old-fashioned innkeeping is still in keeping."

Getting There: From Highway 1, take Newport Boulevard west. At first stoplight, turn left onto Via Lido. Drive two blocks and turn right on Lafayette. At second boulevard stop, turn left on Lido Park.

THE LITTLE INN ON THE BAY

617 Lido Park Drive,
Newport Beach, California 92663

Telephone: (714) 673-8800

Accommodations: thirty rooms with one or two queen-size or one king-size bed; private baths with tub/showers; telephones; television.

Rates: moderate to expensive, breakfast and bay cruise included. Children welcome.

Cards: AE, DC, MC, V

Open all year.

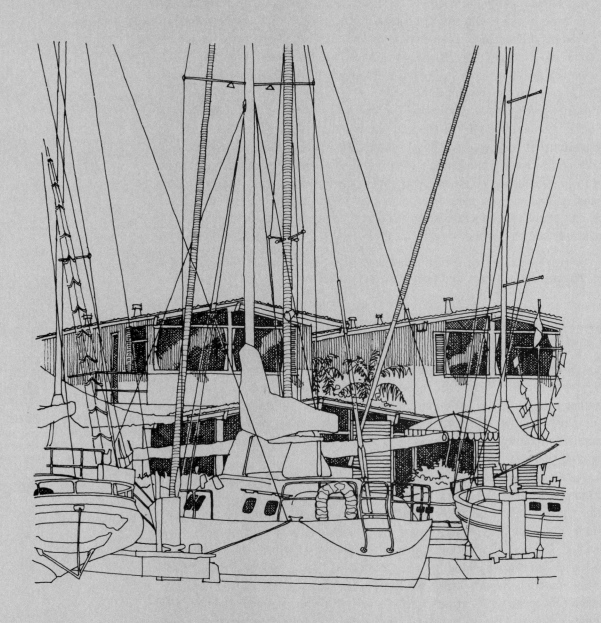

The Little Inn on the Bay

P iero Serra had long dreamed of owning a small oceanside hotel reminiscent of those in the Mediterranean coastal towns of his native northern Italy. In 1986 his dream came true when he restored this small beachfront hotel just down from the Newport Pier. Downstairs there's a wine and beer bar where complimentary hors d'oeuvres are served to guests in the evening and a Continental breakfast is provided in the morning.

Upstairs, twelve guest rooms line the long hall, and at one end a pretty little parlor offers a panoramic view of the sea. The two front rooms share this view; you can even admire it from your whirlpool tub for two. Many of the other rooms, some with tiny patios, have partial ocean views. And some have single whirlpool tubs, too. Serra has furnished the rooms with wool Oriental rugs, antique dressers and bedsteads, quilted spreads, mounds of lace-edged pillows, French lithographs, fresh flowers, and plants. And if you wish to stroll across the street to the beach, the hotel provides beach chairs and towels.

Getting There: From Highway 1, take Newport Boulevard to Newport Peninsula, turn right on Twenty-second Street, and turn right on Ocean Front.

PORTOFINO BEACH HOTEL

2306 West Ocean Front,
Newport Beach, California 92663

Telephone: (714) 673-7030

Accommodations: twelve rooms with queen-size beds; private baths with showers and tub/showers, some with whirlpool tubs; telephones; television.

Rates: expensive to very expensive, breakfast included.

Cards: AE, DC, MC, V

Open all year.

O n the ocean side of the Balboa Peninsula, the Newport pier thrusts into the Pacific from a popular surfing beach. Across from this beach, real estate developer Rick Lawrence spent two million dollars to transform an old rooming house into a classy little inn. Doryman's looks for all the world like a Barbary Coast bordello, but one patronized by bankers and silver barons rather than boat handlers. Actually, it's patronized by a bevy of celebrities, including a number of Hollywood superstars.

A restaurant occupies the first floor and offers room service to the inn's guests. Luminaries need not worry about being spotted by the public; patrons of the inn enter through a private side door and are whisked by elevator to the second floor. Here in the hallway, skylights are hung with plants and shiny brass wall sconces adorn the oak wainscoting, which is polished to a mirrorlike finish. Each of the ten rooms has a gas-burning fireplace, controlled by the flick of a wall switch, with antique mantels imported from Europe. Bathrooms are outfitted with skylights and sunken tubs faced with Carrara marble, some with whirlpool jets. And of course everything is soundproofed so you won't be disturbed by noise from the beach.

The rooms are papered with reproductions of 1880 patterns, some with hand-stenciled friezes around the top. Matching floral drapes and quilted bedspreads, lace

DORYMAN'S INN

2102 West Ocean Front,
Newport Beach, California 92663

Telephone: (714) 675-7300

Accommodations: ten rooms with queen- or king-size beds; private baths with tub/showers, some with whirlpool tubs; telephones; color television.

Rates: very expensive, breakfast included.

Cards: AE, CB, DC, MC, V

Open all year.

curtains, down comforters, and pillows trimmed with eyelet ruffles add to the romantic aura. Furnishings are mostly European antiques: Carved headboards, canopied four-posters, armoires, needlepoint chairs, rockers, and gilt-edged mirrors abound. Six of the rooms have unobstructed views of the Pacific and several have French doors opening onto a tiled balcony.

Most guests prefer the privacy and luxury of breakfast in bed—a tray of orange juice, fresh fruit, soft-boiled eggs, and such treats as pumpkin or banana bread. Breakfast is also served in the little sitting room or on the balcony. But the prime public spot is the rooftop sun deck with its 180-degree view of the Pacific and Balboa Bay.

Getting There: From Highway 1, take Newport Boulevard to Thirty-second Street and turn right; turn left on Balboa Boulevard and right at the sign to Newport Pier.

During the 1920s Seal Beach was a popular playground for the wealthy residents of Hollywood and Pasadena. The resort was the last stop on an electric railway that later extended to Newport Beach, and during the town's heyday gambling palaces, wooden bathhouses, and small hotels flourished. The only hotel remaining from that era is the Seal Beach Inn, which Jack and Marjorie Bettenhausen have transformed into a charming Mediterranean-style hostelry. The rooms surround a brick-paved courtyard ablaze with roses, geraniums, jasmine, camellias, hibiscus, and oleander. Fountains, statues, and benches from France are scattered about, along with ornate old street lamps from Long Beach. The second-floor veranda is trimmed with filigreed ironwork entwined with flowering vines.

Since purchasing the place in 1977, the Bettenhausens have never stopped improving it, shipping back truckloads of antiques and objets d'art from their frequent travels throughout the United States and Europe. The result is a potpourri of furnishings ranging from Early Americana to Renoir prints, from Victoriana to Art Nouveau. Hollywood also gets into the act: A headboard from John Barrymore's bed occupies one room, and a stained-glass door from Universal Studios opens to a bridal suite bedecked with lace and rose-colored satin. The accommodations range from tiny rooms (about ten by twelve feet) to suites with sitting areas and completely equipped kitchen bars. A penthouse suite has a flower-filled private deck, a large living room, a full kitchen with a breakfast nook, and two old-fashioned sleeping porches.

"The look of an inn is important," Marjorie says, "but loving people and being hospitable are even more important." And she does these things well. Plenty of

SEAL BEACH INN AND GARDENS

212 Fifth Street,
Seal Beach, California 90740

Telephone: (213) 493-2416

Accommodations: twenty-three rooms with twin, double, queen-, or king-size beds; private baths with showers or tub/showers; telephones; color television.

Rates: moderate to expensive, breakfast included. Children welcome. No smoking.

Cards: AE, MC, V

Open all year.

reading material is found in the downstairs library (as well as in the rooms), along with chess sets, Scrabble boards, and puzzles to enjoy by the fire. In the adjoining tea room, an elaborate breakfast buffet is served—fresh fruit, house-made jams and jellies, Seal Beach's own granola, boiled eggs, and a variety of pastries and breads. Both common rooms open to a patio with another touch of Hollywood—a kidney-shaped swimming pool.

The many diversions of Seal Beach are nearby. The ocean is only a block from the inn; amenities there include a pier, boat excursions, fishing, and a windsurfing school. The inn will even pack a picnic for your day's excursion. The Long Beach Marina and its Seaport Village are just five blocks away. And many shops, boutiques, and restaurants are located in the area.

Getting There: From the San Diego Freeway, take Seal Beach Boulevard exit to Highway 1; head north and turn left on Fifth Street.

So you want to escape to a tropical isle for a romantic holiday in a palatial mountaintop hideaway. Consider The Inn on Mt. Ada on Catalina Island, just twenty-two miles off the California coast. The history of this lovely isle in some respects mirrors the saga of the Golden State. Friendly Indians inhabited Catalina when Juan Rodríguez Cabrillo discovered it in 1542. Later, the abundance of sea otters around the island lured American and Russian fur traders, and the secluded ports attracted smugglers of Chinese immigrants and other illicit cargoes. Catalina was even the site of a mining boom in the 1860s.

Since 1848 the island has been privately owned, but it was not really developed until 1919 when industrialist William Wrigley, Jr. (of chewing gum and Chicago Cubs fame) acquired it. On the highest point above Avalon Bay, he built a spectacular Georgian Colonial mansion as a summer home and played host to the rich and famous of the 1920s, including the Prince of Wales, who later became Edward VIII. In the summer of 1923, Wrigley painted the house white in honor of the impending visit of President Harding, who died in San Francisco en route to the island. His successor, Calvin Coolidge, however, did use the mansion on Mt. Ada as a summer retreat.

In 1978 the Santa Catalina Land Company gave the Wrigley mansion to the University of Southern California, which used it as a conference center for a time and then in 1985 leased it to a group of local residents for use as an inn. The Inn on Mt. Ada is now elegantly restored, furnished with exquisite antiques, and repainted

THE INN ON MT. ADA

**1 Wrigley Road (Box 2560),
Avalon, California 90704**

Telephone: (213) 510-2030

Accommodations: six rooms with double or queen-size beds; private baths with showers or tub/showers; no telephones; television on request.

Rates: very expensive, breakfast and golf cart included. No smoking.

Cards: MC, V

Facilities for weddings and conferences. Open all year.

The Inn on Mt. Ada

its original gray. Its broad decks and terraces have awe-inspiring views of the surrounding mountains, the town and port of Avalon far below, and—on clear days—the California coast across the channel.

The spacious rooms on the first floor include a seventy-foot-long formal drawing room that boasts a fireplace, a grand piano, and French doors leading out to a terrace. A more casually furnished den is well stocked with games and complimentary soft drinks. There's also a cozy study and a plant-filled sun room where a telescope helps you to admire the view of the town. A lovely dining room is the setting for breakfast, served on small tables colorfully set with California pottery and flowered china. A typical menu might include orange juice, blueberries with cream, a mushroom, onion, and cheese omelet, and English muffins. In a pantry off the kitchen, freshly baked cookies, fruit, and an assortment of coffee and teas are set out night and day.

The six guest accommodations on the second floor range in splendor (and price) from Wrigley's former quarters (a grand suite with a large living room, fireplace, and private terrace) to a tiny sun room surrounded by windows. In between, there's Ada Wrigley's room, which has a fireplace and a small sitting room with a chaise, and the corner guest room once occupied by Coolidge, also with a fireplace. All the rooms have incredible views—even the bathrooms.

Two of the inn's leaseholders, Susie Griffin and Marlene McAdam, serve as innkeepers and are happy to advise on the island's offering of activities. These include tennis, golf, horseback riding and, of course, swimming, snorkeling, and scuba diving in the sapphire-clear waters of the bay. The inn even provides a golf cart with each room for getting around the island. Curio shops and mobs of tourists have tarnished the picturesque town of Avalon, but most of the island—some forty-two thousand acres—is an untouched wilderness preserve for nature lovers to explore.

Though Avalon has a number of restaurants, none share the inn's world-class status. But not to worry. On certain nights the Inn on Mt. Ada serves a four-course dinner of "American Pacific Cuisine" befitting the elegant style of this hilltop showplace.

Getting There: Catalina may be reached from the mainland by seventeen-minute helicopter and thirty-minute airplane service, or ideally by boat. The fastest boat service is a ninety-minute crossing from San Pedro on comfortable 149-passenger vessels operated by Catalina Express, Box 1391, San Pedro, California 90733; telephone (213) 519-1212. Visitors are not permitted to take automobiles to Catalina, but car and bike rentals are available.

LOS ANGELES

Los Angeles is the largest city in California and is rapidly overtaking Chicago as the second largest in America. Actually Los Angeles is a megalopolis, a giant octopus whose freeways have reached out to embrace communities from the port of San Pedro northward to the beach towns of Venice and Santa Monica, and then slithered over the Hollywood Hills into the San Fernando Valley. Los Angeles today is also a galaxy of many worlds: the world of show biz, movies, and television; the world of stretch limousines moving sedately from the mansions of Bel Air to the shops of Rodeo Drive; the world of commerce and high finance enshrined in the glass-walled towers that have risen downtown; the world of culture that richly blossoms in the Center for the Performing Arts and the Museum of Art; and many other worlds, too.

Founded in 1781 by Don Felipe de Neve, the Mexican governor of Alta California, El Pueblo de Nuestra Señora la Reina de Los Angeles remained a sleepy agricultural community and later a lawless frontier town until the late nineteenth century, when oil was discovered in southern California. Then, early in this century, the City of the Angels struck its own form of gold when its sunny, moderate climate helped it to become the moviemaking capital of the world. Today, despite all the growth and glitter, one may glimpse the aura of the California pueblo that existed here in a historic area downtown where the adobe buildings have been preserved.

This Mediterranean-style villa, surrounded by luxuriant lawns and gardens, would be a sensational setting for any inn. But the creativity and boundless energy of owner Megan Timothy make a stay at La Maida an exquisite experience that would be difficult to match anywhere. Megan's artistry is reflected in every aspect of the inn, from the ninety-seven stained-glass windows, which she designed and executed, to the sculptured pat of butter on the breakfast plate.

Italian-born Antonio La Maida built the villa in 1926 on a large estate that has since been subdivided. The mansion is typical of those built in Hollywood during that era: white stucco walls, red-tiled roof, arched windows, and lavish use of fine woods and wrought iron. The high-ceilinged living room boasts a Carrara marble fireplace and an 1881 grand piano that once belonged to bandleader Horace Heidt. An adjoining den is lined with tiers of wall-to-wall studio couches of various heights, massed with pillows; one side of this unique room opens to an enclosed tiled patio, where light filters through a stained-glass ceiling onto scores of tropical plants.

LA MAIDA HOUSE

11159 La Maida Street,
North Hollywood, California 91601

Telephone: (818) 769-3857

Accommodations: twelve rooms or suites with twin, double, queen-, or king-size beds; private baths with tub/showers or stall showers, some with whirlpool tubs; direct-line telephones; television on request; air-conditioning.

Rates: moderate to very expensive, breakfast included. No smoking.

No credit cards.

Facilities for weddings.

Open all year.

Glass doors open to the lovely gardens, where fountains tinkle under the shade of a magnolia tree, flowers bloom year round, and black swans glide on a secluded pond.

Four upstairs bedrooms are stunningly decorated. In the largest a canopied king-size bed is framed with rough-hewn wood, and a rattan chaise, table, and chairs provide an inviting spot to enjoy the pre-breakfast tea or coffee that is brought each morning. Another room features turn-of-the-century furnishings, a third is done in white wicker, and the fourth opens to a balcony. All rooms contain plants, cut flowers, complimentary toiletries, terry cloth robes, and knee robes crocheted by Megan's mother, Helen, who helps manage the inn.

But the villa is only half the story of La Maida. Megan has transformed three nearby bungalows into clusters of magnificent suites. Most have sitting rooms with fireplaces and many have private patios, whirlpool tubs, and kitchenettes. In one cottage, two doors down the street from the villa, a rear garden contains a swimming pool and a small gym that are for the use of all La Maida guests, as is the gazebo in the garden of one of the bungalows across the street. Likewise, those staying in the cottages may enjoy all the facilities of the main house.

Breakfast—or lunch or dinner by appointment—is served in one of the villa's three dining areas. If the group is small and the weather is fine, the setting might be a little second-floor balcony overlooking the garden. For eight, Megan sets the glass-topped table in a small dining area next to the enclosed downstairs patio. Finally, a large formal dining room, lit by candles and a crystal chandelier, provides seating for thirty-two at round tables.

Megan's culinary talents are remarkable, and everything—even the croissants and jams—is made from scratch. The custom-planned suppers range from a simple repast of soup and salad to an elaborate four-course feast served on gold-rimmed Limoges dinnerware.

La Maida House is only minutes away from the Hollywood Bowl. It's also close to Universal Studios and the NBC television studios, both of which conduct tours throughout each day. A twenty-minute drive takes you to Hollywood, Beverly Hills, and downtown Los Angeles.

Getting There: La Maida House is located near the intersection of the Hollywood and Ventura freeways. From the Hollywood Freeway (Highway 170), take the Magnolia exit, turn east to Tujunga Boulevard and turn right; then turn left on Camarillo Street and left on Bellflower to La Maida. From the west on the Ventura Freeway (Highway 101), take the Tujunga exit, turn right on Camarillo and proceed as above. From the east on the Ventura Freeway (Highway 134), take the Lankershim Boulevard exit north several blocks to La Maida and turn left.

La Maida House

At the century's turn, Abbot Kinney bought a stretch of coastal marshland just outside Los Angeles with the dream of re-creating Venice, Italy. Skeptical Californians nicknamed this beach area Abbot's Folly, but nonetheless Kinney proceeded to build canals, bathhouses, elegant hotels, boardwalks, long piers, and an amusement park. He also encouraged the staging of art exhibitions and other cultural events. By 1906, when Sarah Bernhardt played to a full house for three nights in Venice, Angelenos had stopped scoffing at Kinney and were flocking to his new resort. In 1911 one of these converts, Warren Wilson, wealthy publisher of the *Los Angeles Daily Journal*, built a spacious house in the California Craftsman style half a block from the beach. Two of Wilson's daughters married Kinney's sons.

The Wilson-Kinney family owned the property for some forty years, but meanwhile Venice was heading downhill. Oil was being drilled offshore, many of the canals were filled in, the old houses were cut up or torn down to make room for cheap apartments, the amusement park was demolished, and in the 1960s hippies virtually took over the town. Kinney's dream had indeed become a folly. But today the pendulum has swung in Venice's favor. The Marina del Rey, a fancy apartment complex, was built next door; the oil derricks are gone, leaving the beach clean and fine for swimming; and the seaside properties are now predominately upper-middle-class residences.

Among those who rediscovered Venice was attorney Philip Boesch, who restored the old Wilson house as an inn. Now the handsome gray-shingled house is surrounded by manicured lawns and gardens. In the wood-beamed living room, the soft gray, rose, and mauve hues of an enormous Oriental carpet orchestrate the color scheme for the rest of the house. Comfortable chairs and a sofa are set around the large brick fireplace. An adjoining sun room offers an ocean view and a breakfast buffet, which can be eaten inside at little tables or out on the wide veranda that fronts the house.

Bedroom walls are covered with padded fabrics, an ingenious soundproofing device. Upstairs, the most expensive room—which has a fireplace, ocean view, and private sun porch—is tailored in gray wool tweed with accents of mauve. In another, the walls and a canopied bed are dressed in frilly Laura Ashley prints; a contrasting, very masculine room is resplendent with wool tartan plaids. Even the bathrooms are romantic here: one has double shower spigots, one is outfitted with a whirlpool tub for two, and another contains two old-fashioned tubs with gilded claw feet.

THE VENICE BEACH HOUSE

15 Thirtieth Avenue,
Venice, California 90291

Telephone: (213) 823-1966

Accommodations: nine rooms with twin, two doubles, queen-, or king-size beds; some private and some shared baths with tub/showers; telephones and cable television available on request.

Rates: moderate to very expensive. Children over ten welcome. No smoking.

Cards: AE, MC, V

Open all year.

Whether you come to Los Angeles to play or to work, Venice is a convenient location. The inn provides bicycles for pedaling along the beach trail, which extends from Santa Monica to Long Beach. There's night life aplenty in the bustling bars and bistros of neighboring Marina del Rey. Beverly Hills and Century City are about fifteen minutes away, downtown Los Angeles about half an hour.

Getting There: From the San Diego Freeway, take the Washington Boulevard exit south of Santa Monica and head west. Where Washington forks, follow Washington Street to the beach and turn right on Speedway, the last street before the boardwalk. At Twenty-ninth Avenue, turn right into the inn's parking area.

The advent of the railroads brought a building boom to Los Angeles in the 1880s. The city's first suburb was Angeleno Heights, built by a real estate speculator on a hill just west of town. The land hustlers met incoming trains with buckboards, a band, and jugs of whisky, and took the newcomers up the hill to see "their place." The area is now a historic preservation zone.

One of these Victorian houses, now the Eastlake Inn, was built in 1887 for two women. A forerunner of the present-day duplex, the house has a common entrance flanked by twin double parlors and even twin staircases leading up to the bedrooms.

When innkeeper Murray Burns restored the building, he decorated it as authentically as possible with marble-topped dressers, Eastlake-style parlor sets, some Empire pieces, platform rockers, and antique dolls. He even replaced the bathroom fixtures with claw-foot tubs and other relics like a Pullman-car sink. He left the acid-etched windows intact, of course, and added some typical Victorian touches, such as wall stenciling and embossed leather wainscotings.

Accommodations range from a three-room downstairs suite (parlor, master bedroom, and a glassed-in sun room with a day bed overlooking the garden) to a tiny upstairs room with a wall mural of the California coast. Two of the nicest bedrooms have large, sunny bays and queen-size beds set in lace-draped niches. Fresh flowers, fruit, and fluffy chenille bathrobes are placed in the rooms. The inn serves a full breakfast: orange or grapefruit juice made from fruit just picked in the garden, seasonal fruits, eggs, cheeses, and freshly baked breads and muffins.

Eastlake Inn offers various forms of recreation appropriate to the Victorian era: lemonade on the porch, a jigsaw puzzle and a Mah-Jongg set in the parlor. About half of the inn's clientele are business travelers; downtown is within walking distance. But to attract the weekend trade, Murray has put together some intriguing

EASTLAKE INN

1442 Kellam Avenue,
Los Angeles, California 90026

Telephone: (213) 250-1620

Accommodations: eight rooms with twin, double, or queen-size beds; some private and some shared baths with tubs and showers; phone jacks in some rooms; no television.

Rates: inexpensive to moderate, breakfast included. No smoking.

Cards: AE, MC, V

Facilities for small conferences. Open all year.

packages: hot-air balloon flights, gondola cruises, murder-mystery nights, and even an Amelia Earhart search party.

Getting There: From the north on the Hollywood Freeway (Highway 101), take Glendale and Union exit. Follow the exit ramp to Temple and turn left. Continue one-half mile and turn left on East Edgeware, crossing back over the freeway to the top of the hill. Turn left on Carroll, right on Douglas, and left on Kellam. From the south, exit at Glendale Boulevard, make a sharp right turn, go to the first stop sign and turn left on East Edgeware, then proceed as above.

In the early twentieth century, the affluent citizens of Los Angeles, separated from the Pacific by ranches and citrus groves, started their move westward. One of the early residential areas was Arlington Heights, where the houses were predominately in the woodsy Craftsman style. This area began to decline after World War I and was further damaged when the Santa Monica Freeway cut through the middle of it. But in recent years, with the redevelopment of downtown, Angelenos have begun to appreciate the heritage evoked by these fine old houses, and the district is being restored.

Here on a quiet residential street, interior designer Kathleen Salisbury opened Los Angeles' first B&B. Betsy Henderson purchased the inn several years later but retained the name, the furnishings, and Kathleen's traditions of hospitality—now carried on by innkeepers Alice and Si Torvend.

The two-story Salisbury House topped with a gabled attic, was built in 1909. The downstairs is notable for the dark fir woodwork, leaded-glass windows, and beamed ceilings so typical of the Craftsman style. The rooms have an old-fashioned country look with flowered wallpapers in the Laura Ashley mode. The living room is homey, with Oriental rugs, lace café curtains, a wood-burning fireplace, and over-stuffed couches covered with floral prints. The upstairs bedrooms are also abloom with floral-print wallpaper, curtains, comforters, and ruffled pillows. Furnishings are European and American wood and wicker pieces. One room has an adjoining sun room with a trundle bed; it's a sitting room by day and a twin-bedded sleeping room by night. Under the quadruple-gabled roof, the pine-paneled attic unit also has a sitting area and a claw-foot bathtub set out in the room.

Many of the Salisbury guests are business travelers, and the innkeepers do not send them off to work hungry. Breakfast, served in the formal dining room, is a hearty meal: orange juice, a fruit dish such as apple dumpling, homemade muffins

SALISBURY HOUSE

2273 West Twentieth Street,
Los Angeles, California 90018

Telephone: (213) 737-7817

Accommodations: five rooms with double, queen-, or king-size beds; three private baths and one shared bath with tubs, tub/showers, or stall showers; no telephones; television available on request.

Rates: inexpensive to moderate, breakfast included. Children over ten welcome. No smoking.

Cards: AE, MC, V

Facilities for small conferences. Open all year.

or fruit breads, and a main course, which varies from quiche to frittata to sherried crab in a pastry shell. Long-staying guests appreciate this variety, as well as the proximity of downtown, which is only minutes away.

Getting There: The inn is off the Santa Monica Freeway, which connects downtown Los Angeles with the San Diego Freeway. Take the Western Avenue exit, go one block north, and turn left on Twentieth.

SAN BERNARDINO MOUNTAINS

Once upon a time, before Palm Springs became fashionable, Hollywood celebrities found summer solace and sunshine at Arrowhead and Big Bear lakes in the pine-forested San Bernardino Mountains northeast of Los Angeles. But it was gold—not blue skies—that brought the first settlers here.

In 1859 William F. Holcomb, a prospector who had encountered bad luck in the gold fields of northern California, heard a rumor that precious ore aplenty was buried in the San Bernardino Mountains. He discovered a valley rich with the glittering specks, and in 1860 the gold rush began. The most famous miner in these parts was one of the last: the notorious Elias J. "Lucky" Baldwin, who employed 180 men to work his Gold Mountain Mine in the 1870s. Today, remnants of these mines and frontier towns still remain in Holcomb Valley.

Later in the century, another resource—water—attracted Californians to these mountains. In 1884 a dam was built across the mouth of Big Bear Valley to provide irrigation to the arid plains below. This formed Big Bear Lake, and another dam was later constructed to form Lake Arrowhead. The latter is privately owned and still ringed by imposing estates. At the lake's south end is Lake Arrowhead Village, a sedate complex of restaurants, smart shops, and conference facilities. There are public beaches and a marina here, too. By contrast, Big Bear Lake swarms with masses of vacationers and much activity. Public facilities are available for fishing, waterskiing, sailing, and windsurfing; hiking trails wind through the surrounding forests. Snow is the latest draw of the San Bernardino Mountains; a number of ski resorts have opened in recent years.

Getting There: From Los Angeles, take San Bernardino Freeway east to Highway 15E; head north to Highway 30 east. To reach Lake Arrowhead, turn north on Highway 18. To reach Big Bear Lake, continue on to Highway 330.

On a pine-forested hillside just above Lake Arrowhead Village, woodsy cottages cluster around a handsome Alpine-style lodge. Built in 1917 and originally named The Raven, this inn hosted the elite of southern California for several decades: Mae West, Charles Lindbergh, W. C. Fields, and Howard Hughes were among the guests. In 1953 the place was enlarged and was known as Arrowhead Inn for the next thirty years. In 1983 new owners gutted the hotel and restored it as a romantic hideaway with a new name: Saddleback Inn.

Ten of the guest rooms are located in the three-story lodge, which also houses a full-service restaurant and bar. Inn guests are served a complimentary drink here on arrival, a Continental breakfast on weekdays, and a full breakfast on weekends. Another two dozen one- and two-story units are located in the cottages, which are connected by brick walkways bordered with rhododendrons and periwinkle vines. Amid the cottages sits a gazebo—a popular spot for sunning, and for weddings, too.

The guest rooms have a country look—stone fireplaces, pine furnishings, café curtains and valances, Laura Ashley prints, quilted spreads, and lots of pillows. They also contain some non-countryish amenities like whirlpool baths, hair dryers, heated towel racks in bathrooms, remote-control television, and direct-dial phones.

Getting There: From Highway 18, take turnoff to Lake Arrowhead Village. The inn is on the left just before the village.

SADDLEBACK INN

Lake Arrowhead Village, (Box 1890), Lake Arrowhead, California 92352

Telephone: (714) 336-3571

Accommodations: thirty-four rooms and suites with queen- or king-size beds; private baths with whirlpool tubs and showers; direct-dial telephones; remote-control television.

Rates: moderate to very expensive, breakfast included; lower rates midweek. Restaurant open for breakfast, lunch, and dinner. Children welcome in cottages.

Cards: AE, CB, DC, MC, V

Facilities for conferences and weddings. Open all year.

Removed from the lakeside hurly-burly, this large house sits on a hillside at the edge of the San Bernardino National Forest. Bill Knickerbocker, Big Bear's first damkeeper, constructed the building entirely of pine logs in the early 1920s as a home for his family. Knickerbocker was notorious in the valley for the six-shooters he usually carried and for his wild poker games. Bullet holes in the walls of the house remain as a testament.

Phyllis Knight, a psychologist from Orange County, now owns and operates the house as a country inn and the site of occasional metaphysical and stress-reduction seminars. Everything about the place invites you to relax: the croquet court laid out on the manicured lawn, the table-tennis set and the spa on the broad wooden deck, the comfortable couches by the native stone fireplace in the living room, the hammocks strung up on the wide rear balconies, the coffee and cookies set out in the kitchen, and the silence broken only by wind chimes and the breeze in the trees.

The upstairs bedrooms in the main house are paneled in knotty pine and furnished with calico quilts, flowered dust ruffles, wicker chairs, and lots of fluffy

THE KNICKERBOCKER MANSION

869 South Knickerbocker (Box 3661), Big Bear Lake, California 92315

Telephone: (714) 866-8221

Accommodations: eleven rooms or suites with twin, queen-, or king-size beds; some shared and some private baths with tub/showers; no telephones; cable television.

Rates: moderate to expensive, breakfast included. Older children welcome. No smoking.

No credit cards.

Facilities for weddings and small conferences. Open all year.

Saddleback Inn

pillows and paperback books. Bathroom caddies are provided for the trip to the shared facilities. A third-floor suite commands a view of the lake and boasts a whirlpool tub, potbellied stove, and huge television with VCR. Across the lawn, a carriage house contains four Victorian-style rooms with private baths, as well as a suite that sleeps six.

Phyllis serves a full breakfast: juice, fruit, home-baked breads and muffins, and a main course such as crêpes or huevos rancheros. She also has a fondness for stuffed teddy bears and live kitty cats. You'll find both around the house.

Getting There: When you reach Big Bear Dam, take the fork to the right marked Big Bear Lake. Continue on Big Bear Boulevard to the four-way intersection; continue straight ahead to Knickerbocker Road and turn right.

I n the 1920s entrepreneur Harry Kiener built the Peter Pan Woodland Club on the north shore of Big Bear Lake. His dream was to make Big Bear the most luxurious resort in the West, and he equipped the lodge with a movie theater, a ballroom, and many guest rooms. Soon movie stars and southland socialites were clamoring for membership, and Kiener constructed a log mansion for the exclusive use of his rich clientele. The lodge is long gone, but the manor still stands, renovated as a B&B by screenwriter Lynn Montgomery and artist Richard Kriegler.

Most of the seven guest rooms have fireplaces, and each is decorated in a different theme that reflects the history of the area. The Wildcat Room is dedicated to the Seranno Indian tribe that once inhabited this land, and is decorated in an Indian and Old West motif. The hearth in the Lucky Baldwin Room is built with stones from the site of his Gold Mountain Mine. The Clark Gable Room boasts a Franklin stove that came from the nearby cabin where he and Carole Lombard spent their honeymoon. And the ultrafeminine Bouquet Room—decorated with floral patterns and flower-painted tiles around the fireplace—was the favorite room of the bride of a wealthy film financier who once owned the house.

Wood-burning fireplaces also cheer the parlor and breakfast room, where guests are served a hearty meal: baked pears or apples, quiche, and freshly baked breads and muffins. And if you're game for an after-breakfast round of billiards, you'll find a pool table in the family room. More strenuous exercise? Free guest privileges are available at the Big Bear Athletic Club.

Getting There: When you reach Big Bear Dam, turn left toward Big Bear City. Continue on North Shore Boulevard seven miles beyond the town of Fawnskin to Anita; turn left.

GOLD MOUNTAIN MANOR
1117 Anita (Box 2027),
Big Bear City, California 92314

Telephone: (714) 585-6997

Accommodations: seven rooms with double or queen-size beds; shared and private baths or half baths with tub/showers; no telephones; no television.

Rates: moderate to expensive, breakfast included. No smoking.

No credit cards.

Open all year.

A mile high in the San Jacinto Mountains, cradled in a pine- and cedar-forested valley rimmed by granite peaks, lies the resort community of Idyllwild. Originally settled as a logging area, the town today attracts primarily nature and culture lovers. It's best known as the site of the non-profit Idyllwild School of Music and the Arts, which has conducted summer classes and workshops since 1950 and offers concerts and special programs the year around. Surrounding the town are 275 miles of trails for riding, hiking, rock climbing, and birdwatching; 186 types of birds have been spotted in the area. Excellent fishing is found in nearby lakes and streams.

One of these streams is Strawberry Creek, which runs through the property of its namesake inn. The rustic, shingled house was originally built as a vacation retreat, served for a while as a restaurant, and in 1985 became Idyllwild's first B&B. Owner-innkeepers Diana Dugan and Jim Goff are former San Diego city planners who did most of the renovation work themselves.

Diana is an avid quilt collector, and the bedrooms are strewn with both antique quilts and those she has made herself. Five of these rooms are located in the main house, and another four are in a new cedar unit, which the innkeepers built in back. The newer rooms have skylights over the beds, fireplaces (some built of river rock), and open to a big sunny deck. Each is decorated in a different style—southwestern, Victorian, Queen Anne, or mountain rustic. The rooms in the main house are also picture-pretty and cozy, with loveseats placed in dormer windows.

The living room looks the way a mountain lodge should, with a large stone fireplace, games, lots of reading material, and a piano in an alcove. A glassed-in porch wraps around two sides of the lodge, and a sumptuous breakfast is served here at tables for six. "All the guests eat at one time so they get to know each other," Jim explains. The menu is varied: perhaps German-style french toast served with bratwurst, a ham-and-cheese soufflé, or frittatas made from zucchini and tomatoes grown in the inn's garden; strawberries garnish the plates.

Behind the house a hammock is strung up on a shady deck so you can watch the birds and squirrels. At this writing, the innkeepers are planning to install a spa under the pines. And you can fish down the hill in Strawberry Creek or stroll along its banks into town. If you drive in the area, though, heed this warning: gray squirrels have the right-of-way on Idyllwild's roads.

Getting There: From Los Angeles, take San Bernardino Freeway (Highway 10) beyond Riverside to Banning. Head south on Highway 243. The inn is on the left side of the highway beyond the village of Idyllwild. From San Diego, take Highway 15 north to Murietta, Highway 79 north to Hemet, and Highway 74 east to Highway 243.

STRAWBERRY CREEK INN

26370 Banning-Idyllwild Highway (Box 1818), Idyllwild, California 92349

Telephone: (714) 659-3202

Accommodations: nine rooms with queen-size beds; private baths with tub/showers or stall showers in most rooms, two rooms share a bath with tub/shower; one room fully equipped for the handicapped; no telephones; television on request in new rooms.

Rates: inexpensive to moderate, breakfast included. No smoking.

Cards: MC, V

Open all year.

T his magnificent example of Spanish-style architecture is Riverside's municipal treasure. At the end of the last century, Frank Miller bought his parents' thirteen-room adobe boardinghouse and, until his death in 1935, devoted his life to making it one of the great resort hotels of the West. He determinedly added wing after wing, walkways, courtyards, fountains, bell towers, domes, galleries, and chapels, all embellished with ornately carved wood and stone, Tiffany glass, painted tiles, and religious statuary. Miller returned from his frequent travels with treasures for his inn: valuable paintings, antique bells, carved Belgian pews, a Della Robbia wall shrine, and an eighteenth-century gold-leafed altar from Mexico, around which he built a chapel dedicated to St. Francis.

Eventually the hotel grew to over two hundred rooms, encircling fabulous gardens and a beautiful swimming pool. Its illustrious guests included Amelia Earhart, Henry Ford, John D. Rockefeller, Sarah Bernhardt, and Lillian Russell. The Richard Nixons were married in the St. Francis Chapel, as were Bette Davis and the Humphrey Bogarts; Ronald and Nancy Reagan honeymooned at the inn.

The Mission Inn remained commercially viable until the 1950s, when a succession of owners allowed it to deteriorate. In 1976 the hotel was about to be demolished when the city of Riverside rescued its most beloved landmark and, joined by individual citizens and civic groups, spent the next ten years trying to restore the place. But the funds needed were too great for a medium-sized city. Enter the Carley Capital Group of New York, which bought the inn and turned its management over to Omni Hotels. The forty-million-dollar renovation, which required over 300,000 hours of work, was completed at the end of 1988.

The inn's intricately ornamented exterior was not changed, but the wings containing guest rooms were gutted inside and completely rebuilt. What was lost in individuality, though, was gained in comfort—deluxe baths and luxurious furnishings and amenities. Many of the bedrooms in the Spanish wing, some with filigreed cast-iron balconies, face an interior court where a large fountain splashes and hummingbirds dart among the flowers, lemon trees, palms, and magnolias. Meals are served here, as well as in several dining rooms.

Two presidential suites are located on the inn's rooftop; one opens onto a tiled courtyard where plants surround a long reflecting pool. They are furnished with some of Miller's priceless antiques and objects of art. And presidential they are indeed. Former occupants included Theodore Roosevelt and William Taft.

Getting There: From Los Angeles, take Pomona Freeway to Riverside. Take Market Street exit and follow the signs to Mission Inn.

MISSION INN

3649 Seventh Street,
Riverside, California 92501

Telephone: (714) 784-0300

Accommodations: 240 rooms with one or two queen-size or one king-size bed; private baths with tubs and showers; direct-dial telephones; remote-control color television.

Rates: expensive to very expensive, no meals included. Restaurants open for breakfast, lunch, and dinner. Children welcome.

Cards: AE, CB, DC, MC, V

Facilities for weddings and conferences. Open all year.

Mission Inn

PALM SPRINGS

This palm-fringed desert oasis at the base of the San Jacinto Mountains has for centuries been the home of the Agua Caliente Indians, who derived their name from the hot water that comes from the area's many mineral springs. The Indians believed that the waters had magical healing powers. Much of the surrounding land is still owned by the Indians, making them one of the richest tribes in America.

As early as the 1870s, the magical waters attracted white settlers to Palm Springs. But the boom began in 1933 when Hollywood actors Ralph Bellamy and Charlie Farrell built the Palm Springs Racquet Club, whose early members included Clark Gable, Ginger Rogers, and Spencer Tracy. Soon the rich and famous were flocking to this glamorous resort, as they still do. Bob Hope is the honorary mayor and Sonny Bono is the elected mayor; Frank Sinatra and Gerald Ford are citizens.

The restaurants and boutiques along Palm Canyon Drive are as elegant as their clientele. The area boasts some of the best golf courses in the country and over a hundred miles of hiking and equestrian trails. Sightseeing options range from touring celebrities' homes to visiting the Indian canyons and trading post to an aerial tram ride up Mount San Jacinto, where there is cross-country skiing in winter.

Getting There: From Los Angeles, take San Bernardino Freeway (Highway 10) east and follow the signs to Palm Springs. You will enter town on North Palm Canyon Drive.

This sprawling enclave of tile-roofed adobe buildings set among tropical gardens rife with palms and bougainvillea was once the estate of Pierce Arrow magnate Humphrey Birge. But for the last three decades it has been a second home to an impressive number of celebrities—Andre Kostelanetz, Greta Garbo, Salvador Dalí, Greer Garson, Marlon Brando—as well as less famous people who enjoy privacy and pampering.

And you will be pampered here. Whether you're staying in a moderately priced room or in a luxury suite, a chauffered Rolls Royce or stretch limousine will meet you at the airport. Check into your room and you'll find a fridge stocked with fruit, cheese, and soft drinks. Want to unwind with a steam or whirlpool bath? All bathrooms have both and a telephone, too. Care for a swim? You'll find a lovely pool in the garden, along with shuffleboard and darts. Shopping? A limousine will take you to town. Entertainment? You don't even have to leave the inn. And come the morning, a tray of juice, fruit, and croissants will be delivered to your door.

INGLESIDE INN

200 West Ramon Road,
Palm Springs, California 92264

Telephone: (619) 325-0046

Accommodations: twenty-nine rooms with twin, double, queen-, or king-size beds; private baths with steam baths and whirlpool tubs; direct-dial telephones; remote-control television; air-conditioning.

Rates: moderate to very expensive, breakfast included; lower rates in summer. Restaurant open for breakfast, lunch, and dinner.

Cards: AE, MC, V

Facilities for weddings, bridal consultant available. Open all year.

The Ingleside Inn has an Old World aura. Many of the antiques are priceless, such as a vestment chest used by fifteenth-century priests and a commode used by Mary Tudor. Several of the rooms contain Louis XV furnishings; Lily Pons lived in one of these suites for thirteen years. Many have fireplaces or private patios, and some of the suites have wet bars and *two* bathrooms, one with an oversized whirlpool tub. Four of the less expensive rooms are on the second floor with views of the mountains. These "penthouses" are decorated in Early American style with wood paneling, patchwork quilts on four-posters, and rag rugs on the wooden floors.

The inn is presently owned by Melvyn Haber, for whom the popular and very chic Melvyn's restaurant is named. It's located in the inn, as is the Casa Blanca Lounge, which offers dancing and entertainment.

Getting There: Drive through town on North Palm Canyon Drive to Ramon and turn right. Complimentary limousine pickup at Palm Springs airport.

Chuck Murawski, co-owner of this most picturesque inn says: "We want our guests to feel like they're in Europe, not Palm Springs." Each room is decorated in the style of a specific country, and even the menu in the inn's small restaurant focuses on a different European cuisine each night. Nevertheless, it's hard to imagine that you're in Scotland or Germany, with the profusion of royal palms, bougainvillea, and oleander that fills the inn's three acres. But visions of Spain or Morocco *are* enhanced by the Mediterranean-style villa, the fountains bubbling away in little patios, and the views of the arid mountains.

Murawski was formerly a designer for Broadway productions, and he has used his considerable talents to stage a setting for romance at the inn. At night, little brass lanterns twinkle in the trees as you take an evening dip in the large spa or one of the inn's two pools. On your return to your room, pause to listen to taped classical music that emanates from around a fountain in a little hidden patio. Have a drink at the wine and beer bar in the outdoor living room, where a fireplace takes the nip out of the cool desert night. If you want to dine on the premises, the candlelit restaurant offers a wide choice of à la carte items, in addition to the ever-changing European dinner. And when you retire to your room, you might think you're in France or Italy—or maybe heaven.

When Murawski and his partner, Bob Lee, created the inn out of a 1930s hotel, they didn't just decorate the rooms, they reconstructed each one in the architectural style of a particular country—terra-cotta floors in the Portuguese room and hand-painted tiles around the fireplace in Hispania, for example. Many of the rooms

VILLA ROYALE

1620 Indian Trail,
Palm Springs, California 92264

Telephone: (619) 327-2314

Accommodations: thirty-three rooms or suites with twin, queen-, or king-size beds; private baths with showers and/or tubs; some rooms with wheelchair access; telephones; color cable television; air-conditioning.

Rates: moderate to very expensive, breakfast included; lower rates in summer. Restaurant open for lunch and dinner.

Cards: AE, MC, V

Open all year.

Villa Royale

have fireplaces as well as private patios, some containing small spas. The partners spent six years in Europe buying the furnishings—antiques, carvings, sculptures, woven hangings, and a potpourri of artifacts just for the inn.

In the morning the *Los Angeles Times* is delivered to your door, and breakfast awaits at little tables by a pool. In addition to orange juice and grapefruit from the inn's own trees, some type of frittata is offered, along with ingenious breads, such as corn muffins with almond slices. Lunch is also served in a poolside café, though many of the rooms do have kitchenettes. And if you want to go into town to eat, a ten-speed bike is at your service.

Getting There: Take North Palm Canyon Drive through town until it becomes East Palm Canyon Drive. Turn left on Indian Trail.

Located behind the Racquet Club in an exclusive residential area, Casa San Marco offers the charm and quiet of a lovely home. But hosts Charles Long and Leonard Grotta won't intrude on your privacy. One wing of this contemporary house is exclusively for the guests' use. The rear is entirely walled with glass, offering a view of a twenty-by-eighty-foot swimming pool with a bubbling fountain at one end. Chaises and umbrella-topped tables are set around so you can admire the view of the mountains over the oleander hedge. There's a paddle tennis court, too.

You will know that these innkeepers have been there, though, when you find your bed turned down at night and a mint on your pillow. And in the morning they set out a buffet on the bar that separates the kitchen from the roomy living-dining area. Help yourself to orange juice, fresh fruit, coffee, croissants, and cereal. This kitchen is solely for the guests' use; no cooking is allowed, but you can stash your snacks and cold drinks in the fridge.

Long and Grotta have decorated the entire place with exquisite understated taste. The color schemes in the four bedrooms, and elsewhere, are subdued—white walls, pale peach quilted spreads on the beds. You'll find no clutter here, but they do know what amenities guests appreciate: wall-mounted hair dryers, bathrobes, *big* bars of soap, and a clock radio in every room.

Getting There: On the northern outskirts of town, turn left off Highway 111 onto Racquet Club Drive. Go one block and turn left on Indian Avenue. San Marco Way is the first left off Indian Avenue, just past the Palm Springs Racquet Club.

CASA SAN MARCO

187 San Marco Way,
Palm Springs, California 92262

Telephone: (619) 325-8600.

Accommodations: four rooms with queen- or king-size beds; private baths with showers or tub/showers; no telephones; color cable television; air-conditioning.

Rates: moderate, breakfast included.

No credit cards.

Open all year.

If your fantasy of Palm Springs life conjures a luxurious private villa with your own tennis court and swimming pool, you can fulfill it at La Mancha. You can even have your own private chef and a guitarist to serenade you at dinner. "If it can be done, we will arrange it," says the concierge. Of course, you will pay to live like a millionaire—about six hundred dollars a day for the pool-and-tennis villa, and more for the extras. But this exclusive resort also has luxurious units that cost no more than a first-class, big-city hotel room: Mediterranean tile-roofed villas with living and dining rooms, kitchenettes, and secluded patios, some with spas. Some mini-suites and guest rooms are quite reasonably priced, considering everything La Mancha offers.

Privacy is one of the main features. The magnificently landscaped resort complex is enclosed by walls and guarded by an electronic gate. Chrysler Le Baron convertibles may be used for three hours at a time at no charge, or used exclusively for a modest rental fee. A limousine will pick you up at the airport or take you wherever you want to go in town, and ten-speed bikes are available—all compliments of the house. A large swimming pool with a waterfall at one end, croquet courts, a nine-hole putting green, and a gym with Nautilus equipment await the pleasure of all guests; there is a nominal charge for use of the tennis courts.

The rooms are individually decorated in styles ranging from traditional to high-tech, looking as though they were waiting to be photographed by *Architectural Digest.* You'll find a big basket of fruit in your room on your arrival, as well as hair dryers, robes, and pool slippers in the baths. All units have video disc players, and there's a film library in the lobby.

Meals are served on the clubhouse patio or in its dining room, which is embellished with stained-glass windows depicting Don Quixote de la Mancha, for whom this inn is named. La Mancha's owners, Ken and Suzanne Irwin, built the resort for those in quest of "the impossible dream."

Getting There: Take North Palm Canyon Drive to Alejo Road. Turn left, then turn right on Avenida Caballeros.

LA MANCHA

444 Avenida Caballeros (Box 340), Palm Springs, California 92263

Telephone: (619) 323-1773, inside California (800) 255-1773, outside California (800) 854-1298

Accommodations: sixty-six units with one to three bedrooms and queen- or king-size beds; private baths with tub/showers, some with whirlpool tubs; some units fully equipped for the handicapped; direct-dial telephones; remote-control cable television.

Rates: expensive to very expensive, no meals included; special rates for extended visits and midweek packages. Restaurant open for breakfast, lunch, and dinner. Children welcome.

Cards: AE, MC, V

Facilities for conferences and weddings. Open all year.

THE CALIFORNIA RIVIERA

THE OJAI VALLEY
SANTA BARBARA TO BIG SUR
COALINGA

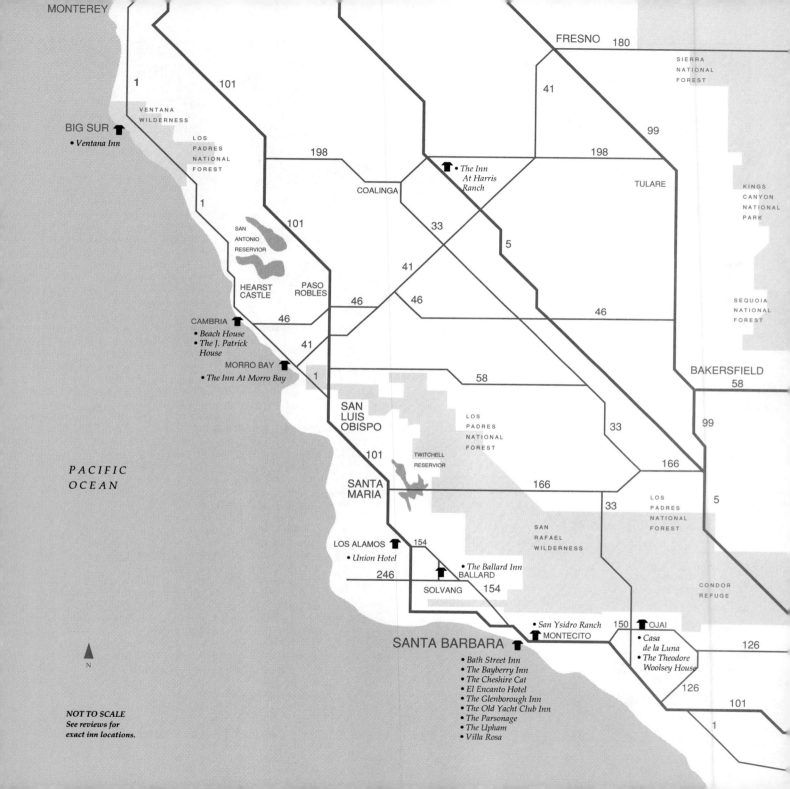

MONTEREY

PACIFIC OCEAN

BIG SUR
• Ventana Inn

VENTANA WILDERNESS

LOS PADRES NATIONAL FOREST

1

101

198

COALINGA

• The Inn At Harris Ranch

FRESNO 180

SIERRA NATIONAL FOREST

41

99

198

TULARE

KINGS CANYON NATIONAL PARK

33

41

5

SAN ANTONIO RESERVOIR

HEARST CASTLE

PASO ROBLES

46

46

46

SEQUOIA NATIONAL FOREST

CAMBRIA
• Beach House
• The J. Patrick House

46

41

MORRO BAY
• The Inn At Morro Bay

1

58

LOS PADRES NATIONAL FOREST

33

BAKERSFIELD

58

99

SAN LUIS OBISPO

TWITCHELL RESERVOIR

101

166

5

SANTA MARIA

166

33

LOS PADRES NATIONAL FOREST

SAN RAFAEL WILDERNESS

CONDOR REFUGE

LOS ALAMOS
• Union Hotel

154

246

• The Ballard Inn
BALLARD

SOLVANG

154

N

NOT TO SCALE
See reviews for exact inn locations.

• San Ysidro Ranch
MONTECITO

150

OJAI
• Casa de la Luna
• The Theodore Woolsey House

126

SANTA BARBARA
• Bath Street Inn
• The Bayberry Inn
• The Cheshire Cat
• El Encanto Hotel
• The Glenborough Inn
• The Old Yacht Club Inn
• The Parsonage
• The Upham
• Villa Rosa

126

101

1

THE OJAI VALLEY

Ojai means "the nest" in the language of the Chumash Indians, who lived in this idyllic valley before the Spaniards came. In recent times, the area in the mountains behind Santa Barbara has indeed been a nest, nurturing the minds, spirits, and bodies of both the young and the world-weary. Educators and spiritual leaders of various faiths have sought out this valley since 1889, when the Thacher School was founded. It thrives today along with Happy Valley School (cofounded by Aldous Huxley), the Oak Grove School (founded by J. Krishnamurti), the Augustinian Villanova Preparatory School, and the Krotona Institute of Theosophy. And if this lovely valley seems like Shangri-La, that's no coincidence. Ojai was depicted as the mythical paradise in the Ronald Colman film, Lost Horizon.

In the past four decades the Ojai Music Festival has brought to the valley music directors such as Igor Stravinsky and Aaron Copland. The fifty-two-year-old Ojai Valley Art Center offers little theater productions, poetry readings, dance recitals, and exhibitions of arts and crafts. But by no means is all the activity here intellectual. The Ojai Valley Tennis Tournament is the oldest in America; stars from Bill Tilden to Billie Jean King have competed on these courts. Ojai is equestrian country, too, home to some three thousand horses and the site of excellent trails and numerous riding competitions. The valley is also a paradise for bikers and hikers, and nearby Lake Casitas offers bass, blue-gill, and trout fishing.

Getting There: From Los Angeles, take Highway 101 north to Ventura and Highway 33 east to Ojai; this leads into Ojai Avenue, the town's main street. From Santa Barbara, take Highway 101 south to Highway 150 and head east over Casitas Pass to Ojai.

I n 1833 the Mexican government gave the entire Ojai Valley to Don Fernando Tico in return for his loyal service. Today, you would swear that the tile-roofed hacienda and lush gardens of Casa de la Luna were remnants of the Mexican Colonial era, probably the home of the don himself. The truth is that this home was built in 1977 by Miles "Bud" Scott, a local dentist, and his wife, Doris. The seven acres of gardens and orchards are a big part of the pleasure of staying here. Beneath giant Meiners oaks, meandering walkways lead past beds of azaleas and more than a thousand varieties of plants. Flaming bougainvillea vines climb over graceful Spanish arches, and beyond the attractive gardens are luxuriant groves of oranges, macadamias, peaches, apricots, cherries, and other fruits.

CASA DE LA LUNA

710 South La Luna,
Ojai, California 93023

Telephone: (805) 646-4528

Accommodations: three rooms with twin or king-size beds, one suite with queens; private baths with tub and shower or stall showers; no telephones; no television.

Rates: moderate, breakfast included. No smoking. No credit cards. Open all year.

The Scotts built the 6,000-square-foot hacienda as a home, a place where their children and grandchildren could come to visit. "I was caring for a houseful of guests anyway," Doris recalls, "so I thought I might as well get paid for it." Thus they moved into a wing of the house and opened the living area, three bedrooms with private baths, and a suite in an outbuilding for bed and breakfast. One of the bedrooms has a fireplace set in a raised hearth, and opens into a plant-filled sun room that also connects with the living room. The suite has a fireplace, too.

Doris and Bud decorated Casa de la Luna with eclectic abandon. The foyer floor is faced with Italian ceramic tiles, an old pump organ sits in the living room, and Victorian furnishings mix with European paintings and carved Mexican pieces throughout. The Scotts' daughter Carol Barr, a professional artist, has painted the dining room ceiling with an exquisite mural of roses. Here guests are treated to breakfast at a twelve-foot refectory table flanked by twelve hand-carved chairs. Unlike most B&B innkeepers, Doris offers a number of menu choices: waffles or french toast or eggs any style with country-fried potatoes. These are served with a fresh fruit salad and juice freshly squeezed from oranges just picked from the Scotts' own trees.

Getting There: Just west of Ojai, Highway 150 from Santa Barbara joins Highway 33 from Ventura. From Highway 33, turn left on Highway 150 (Baldwin Road) and then turn right at the second street, which is La Luna. If you are entering on Highway 150, turn left on La Luna, which is the first street after Rice Road.

Among the noted educators who came to Ojai in the 1800s was Theodore S. Woolsey, professor of international law at Yale, where his father had served an illustrious twenty-five-year term as president. Although the younger Woolsey spent only four years in California, in 1887 he built a two-story house of stone and clapboard in the Ojai Valley. (The going price for an acre of land at that time was between forty-five cents and a dollar.) In 1985, when Ana Cross purchased the house and its surrounding seven acres, the place was in shambles. After eighteen months of renovation, doing most of the work herself with the help of friends and her five children, Ana opened the doors of the old Woolsey estate as a B&B. Her remodeling goals were to remove earlier misguided attempts at modernization and to restore the house to its nineteenth-century condition, with one exception: a recently built swimming pool was left intact.

Surrounded by lovely gardens and ancient oaks, the house is just outside the town of Ojai, with views of the majestic eastern mountains—filmland's Shangri-La.

THE THEODORE WOOLSEY HOUSE

1484 East Ojai Avenue,
Ojai, California 93023

Telephone: (805) 646-9779

Accommodations: five rooms with double, queen-, or king-size beds; private and shared baths with tub/showers; no telephones; television in some rooms.

Rates: incxpensive to moderate, breakfast included. No smoking in public areas indoors.

No credit cards.

Open all year.

A wide veranda shades the front of the house, and in back a sunny garden room and terrace overlook the pool. In the large living room, rag rugs are tossed on the bare pine floors, and by the stone fireplace are couches and chairs where you can curl up with a book. (If you left yours at home, you'll find plenty of reading material around the house.) There's a piano here, too, as well as a jukebox stocked with oldies. Tables are set for four in the adjacent dining room, but most guests prefer to take their buffet breakfast out to the terrace or to the umbrella-topped tables around the pool. Ana sets out a morning spread of fruit, hot oatmeal or cold cereals, and a variety of breads—muffins, pastries, croissants, bagels.

Two of the five bedrooms have private baths; one of these rooms has its own terrace off the pool area, and the other boasts a wood-burning cast-iron stove. In her quest for authenticity, Ana even replaced the 1940s plumbing fixtures with claw-foot tubs and toilets with overhead, pull-chain tanks. A third bath is shared by three guest rooms, two of which open to rear balconies overlooking the pool. Here, as elsewhere, the furnishings are comfortable but not frilly. "This is not a Victorian house," Ana reminds you, "it's a country house where velvet, lace, and bric-a-brac would be out of place."

Getting There: Take Ojai Avenue (Highway 150) through town to the inn.

SANTA BARBARA

In 1786 the Spanish padres founded their tenth mission at the base of the Santa Ynez Mountains, which rise from the bay at Santa Barbara. After the earthquake of 1812, the mission was rebuilt and became known as Queen of the Missions for the beauty of its Moorish-Spanish architecture and the affluence of the surrounding ranches, orchards, gardens, and vineyards. The resort city of Santa Barbara still retains the aura of its Spanish heritage. Red-tile-roofed buildings and old adobes, many enclosing inner patios, grace the palm-lined streets. There are splendid beaches, sportfishing, and botanical and zoological gardens. Excellent restaurants abound. The Santa Barbara Museum of Art houses a number of international collections; other museums focus on local and natural history. And a visit to the mission, one of the most beautiful and well preserved in the state, recalls the days when the padres were this city's only innkeepers.

Getting There: From San Francisco or Los Angeles, Highway 101 leads to Santa Barbara, which is also serviced by Amtrak.

San Ysidro Ranch

Among the vast holdings of Mission Santa Barbara was San Ysidro, a citrus and cattle ranch high in the Santa Ynez Mountains, with views of the oak-studded hills sloping to the Pacific far below. Later in the nineteenth century, secular owners of the ranch built rustic stone-and-wood cottages among the groves of orange trees, eucalyptuses, and palms, and alongside a meandering creek. By 1893 San Ysidro had become a guest ranch. The old adobe, built by the Franciscans in 1825, still stands, and guests dine today in a stone building once used as a citrus-packing house.

San Ysidro's first illustrious era was in the 1930s and 1940s, when Ronald Colman and state Senator Alvin Weingand jointly owned the ranch. The guest book from those years reads like a combination of *Burke's Peerage* and *Who's Who* in politics, literature, and show business. Sir Winston Churchill wrote part of his memoirs here in a house shaded by a large magnolia tree. William Somerset Maugham produced several short stories in a cottage banked by geraniums. John Galsworthy sought seclusion here to work on the *Forsythe Saga*. David Niven, Merle Oberon, and Rex Harrison found life at the ranch a respite from the glitter of Hollywood. Laurence Olivier and Vivien Leigh were married in the gardens. And later, John F. Kennedy brought his bride to an ivy-covered stone cottage at San Ysidro for their honeymoon.

The second illustrious era at San Ysidro began in 1976, when Jim and Susie Lavenson bought the ranch and rescued it from several decades of neglect. They rebuilt the old units and added new ones, most featuring soaring ceilings, fireplaces, and private decks; many also have wet bars and private hot tubs. Susie decorated the rooms with a mix of priceless family antiques and refinished artifacts collected in the Santa Barbara area.

Then in 1987 the Lavensons retired, selling the ranch to Claude Rouas, owner of Auberge du Soleil in the Napa Valley and the famous L'Etoile restaurant in San Francisco. Not surprisingly, Rouas' major change was in the culinary department. He redesigned San Ysidro's dining room, installed Bryan Carr as chef, and introduced a menu that combines classic French cooking techniques with innovative approaches to showcase the produce and seafood of California.

But the accommodations and meals are only half the story of San Ysidro. The cottages are surrounded by lovely gardens, abloom with marigolds, daisies, roses, and geraniums, and the orchards are spangled with oranges, which guests are free to pick. The stables shelter fine riding horses, and the mountains that rise behind the inn offer 550 acres of isolated hiking trails. Back at the ranch, three tennis

SAN YSIDRO RANCH

900 San Ysidro Lane,
Montecito, California 93108

Telephone: (805) 969-5046

Accommodations: forty-three cottages with twin, queen-, or king-size beds; private baths with tub/showers; telephones; cable television with HBO.

Rates very expensive, no meals included. Restaurant open for breakfast, lunch, and dinner. Children welcome. Facilities for boarding pets and horses.

Cards: MC, V

Facilities for conferences and weddings. Open all year.

courts surround a large swimming pool. And in the main hacienda, those wishing to socialize will find a bar, game tables, and a chess board.

Some people, however, come to San Ysidro for the privacy it can provide. The cottages are so self-contained that, with room service provided, guests need never emerge—and some never do.

Getting There: From Santa Barbara, take Highway 101 south to Montecito; take San Ysidro Road east through Montecito Village to San Ysidro Lane.

Over a century ago, Amasa Lincoln, a transplanted Boston banker and distant cousin of Abraham Lincoln, decided that Santa Barbara needed a New England–style boardinghouse for homesick easterners. He hired the best architect in town to erect a two-story structure flanked by a columned veranda and topped with a cupola and widow's walk. In the early days, when the schooners arrived in town, a cook used to stand up here to receive flag signals from the dock as to how many new guests would be at dinner that night. Over the years a series of owners added two other two-story buildings and four garden cottages to The Upham, which is southern California's oldest continuously operated hotel.

In 1982 developer Carl Johnson bought and restored The Upham. The first-floor public rooms have been reconstructed to house a cheerful sun porch furnished with rattan, where wine is poured in the evening, and a large lobby with a fireplace surrounded by velvet-covered love seats. Along one side a row of tables, skirted with a flowered-print fabric, looks into the gardens. A Continental breakfast is served to hotel guests here, and Louie's restaurant, alongside the veranda, is open to the public for lunch and dinner.

In the guest rooms and cottages, antiques (four-posters, old writing desks, and armoires from England) are mixed with bold, sophisticated color schemes, quilted spreads with contemporary patterns, and white wide-louvered shutters. Earth colors—sand, brick, and chocolate brown—contrast with the navy-blue carpeting found throughout. Some of the cottages have sitting rooms, fireplaces, private decks, and whirlpool tubs. These units are reached by pathways through gardens abloom with roses, camellias, and birds of paradise. The setting is countrylike, yet The Upham is only a block away from the smart shops and restaurants of State Street.

Getting There: From the north, take Mission Street exit from Highway 101 and head east to De la Vina; turn right and proceed to Sola; turn left on Sola and drive one-half block to the hotel's carriage entrance. From the south, exit from Highway 101 at State Street; turn right and proceed to Sola; turn left on Sola to carriage entrance.

THE UPHAM

1404 De la Vina Street,
Santa Barbara, California 93101

Telephone: (805) 962-0058

Accommodations: forty-three rooms with two double beds or queen- or king-size beds; private baths with tubs or tub/showers; telephones; color televisions concealed in armoires.

Rates: moderate to expensive, breakfast included. Restaurant open for lunch and dinner. Children welcome.

Cards: AE, DC, MC, V

Open all year.

The Upham

The mere mention of Santa Barbara architecture brings to mind white Spanish-style buildings embellished with ornate wooden balconies, wrought-iron grillwork, red-tiled roofs, arched windows, and interior patios filled with fountains and tropical foliage. The Villa Rosa is a classic of this style, and it's only half a block from the beach. Four Santa Barbarans—architect Mark Kirkhart, builder Robert Young, and their wives—are responsible for the half-million-dollar renovation that transformed an old apartment house into a jewel of a small hotel.

The inside was virtually rebuilt and strikingly decorated in a contemporary southwestern fashion. Desert hues of slate, sand, and rosy terra-cotta are used throughout, as is sturdy mission-style furniture from Santa Fe. Couches and chairs are upholstered in handsome wool tweeds, beds are covered with woven spreads and rosy sheets, and Navajo blankets are hung on many of the walls. Some of the eighteen guest units are one- or two-story suites, several with beehive fireplaces and kitchenettes. Other rooms have mullioned glass doors opening to private balconies—some with an ocean view—or to the large interior courtyard.

A swimming pool and spa are set among a mélange of palm trees, banana groves, and pots of colorful flowers in the courtyard. Also opening to the patio is the lovely living room with its high, beamed ceiling and wood-burning fireplace faced with tile. Adjoining is a cozy lounge where a Continental breakfast is served and refreshments are offered in the evening. The Villa Rosa bids each guest good night by placing a long-stemmed red rose on the pillow of the turned-down bed.

Getting There: Take Chapala exit from Highway 101 and head toward the beach.

VILLA ROSA

15 Chapala Street,
Santa Barbara, California 93101

Telephone: (805) 966-0851

Accommodations: eighteen rooms with queen- or king-size beds; private baths with tub/showers; telephones; no television.

Rates: moderate to very expensive, breakfast included.

Cards: AE, MC, V

Open all year.

Innkeeper Susan Brown preserved the vintage charm of this 1873 three-story, gabled Queen Anne while rebuilding the back of the inn to focus on the lovely gardens and views of the Santa Ynez Mountains. Some Victorian overtones remain in the attractive living room, where she serves evening refreshments in front of a big fireplace; leaded-glass doors open from here to a shady side garden. In the morning, you have a choice of spots to enjoy your breakfast of juice, fruit, granola, and homemade breads: a sunny deck and garden behind the house or a formal dining room seating twelve, which is also used for small conferences.

There are books and flowers in all the bedrooms. Four rooms occupy the second floor, and three other bedrooms nestle under the top-floor eaves, the beds set in alcoves draped with floral patterns that match the spreads and window curtains. The third floor also has a library and TV room equipped with games and puzzles—

BATH STREET INN

1720 Bath Street,
Santa Barbara, California 93101

Telephone: (805) 682-9680

Accommodations: seven rooms with twin, queen-, or king-size beds; private baths with tubs or stall showers; no telephones; no television.

Rates: moderate, breakfast included.

Cards: AE, MC, V

Facilities for small conferences. Open all year.

nothing fancy, but as Susan says, "It's a place where you can relax and put your feet on the table." The Bath Street Inn really should be classified as a BBB&B: bed, breakfast, bath, and bicycles. The baths are very special, with basins set into Victorian dressers, and two have gigantic claw-foot tubs where you can soak and enjoy a view of the mountains after a bike tour of town. Bicycles are provided, compliments of the house.

Getting There: From Highway 101, take Carrillo exit and head east to Bath; turn left.

B uilt in 1912, this two-story bungalow near the beach houses Santa Barbara's oldest B&B. Once it served as temporary headquarters for the Santa Barbara Yacht Club after its clubhouse washed out to sea in a storm. Thus the inn's name, though nothing else is nautical here. The inn is decorated with homey, country-style furnishings. The large living room and dining area boasts a fireplace and a bookcase stocked with a set of the Harvard Classics. Big windows look out onto a wide front porch, lawn, and gardens. Innkeeper Nancy Donaldson loves to cook and puts a lot of effort into the breakfasts. She usually serves an omelet (perhaps zucchini or spinach) or french toast, in addition to home-baked breads, fruit, and juice. With advance notice she will also cook a five-course dinner on weekends for her guests.

The four upstairs bedrooms are decorated primarily in warm shades of rose and gold, with print spreads and matching draperies edging the lace-curtained windows. Fresh flowers are set on the tables. In the two front rooms, French doors open to a private balcony where you can hear the ocean, though it's obscured from view. A fifth bedroom with a sitting area and private bath is located downstairs.

A few years after the Old Yacht Club Inn opened, its four owners acquired the house next door and each decorated one guest room there to reflect her own background, using family memorabilia. The Hitchcock House, as it is called, might be preferred by those looking for privacy: Each bedroom has its own bath and outside entrance.

Getting There: From Highway 101, take Cabrillo Boulevard exit toward the beach; just past the Sheraton Hotel, turn right on Corona Del Mar.

THE OLD YACHT CLUB INN

431 Corona Del Mar,
Santa Barbara, California 93103

Telephone: (805) 962-1277

Accommodations: five bedrooms within the inn with double, queen-, or king-size beds; one with private bath, four rooms with sinks share two baths with tub/shower or stall shower; four rooms in Hitchcock House with queen- or king-size beds and private baths with tub/showers or showers; no telephones; no television.

Rates: moderate to expensive, breakfast included. No smoking.

Cards: AE, MC, V

Open all year.

El Encanto Hotel

High in the hills above Santa Barbara's mission, this gracious Mediterranean-style hotel offers breathtaking views of the city, the Pacific Ocean, and the Channel Islands. The main building was constructed in 1915 to provide student and faculty housing for the University of California campus that was originally across the street. Over the years, bungalows and stucco villas were built in the surrounding ten acres of lush gardens. El Encanto has been operated as a hotel since the 1930s, but Eric Friden, who bought it in 1977, has imparted the enchantment of an auberge on the French Riviera.

El Encanto's gardens are planted with bougainvillea, hibiscus, banana trees, pines, and palms. Birds of paradise and petunias border the brick walkways that lead to the guest cottages. All of the units have been extensively remodeled and contain modern tiled baths and new carpeting. Many have kitchens or wet bars and refrigerators, and the most lavish have fireplaces and private balconies or patios, some with tiled fountains. To show that children are really welcome here, one suite now includes a nursery with a crib and an old-fashioned wicker high chair. In 1978 Friden constructed a two-story building of contemporary design that contains another twenty two-room units. These have corner fireplaces, wet bars, and balconies or patios, but the bedrooms are smaller than in the older buildings. Part of the enchantment of El Encanto is a turned-down bed at night and a small decanter of Armagnac placed on the nightstand.

The public rooms in the main building are a visual symphony, orchestrated with many different fabrics in shades of forest green and mauve, natural woods, and an abundance of plants. A spacious lounge is filled with wicker and rattan chairs with cushions in a variety of patterned fabrics. Fireplaces and love seats upholstered in floral prints grace a cozy living room and adjoining library. And in the dining room, flowered wallpaper harmonizes with provincial-patterned chinaware, ceiling fans slowly revolve overhead, and large windows frame the dramatic view. Meals are also served outside under colorful umbrellas on two levels of terraces.

The hotel has a tennis court and a lovely swimming pool, but one of the greatest pleasures here is strolling the beautiful grounds, where swinging love seats are scattered about the lawns and an ancient grape arbor encloses a lily-filled reflecting pool. Whether a guest at El Encanto or not, every visitor to Santa Barbara should at least come here for a drink at sunset. Looking down on the tile-roofed town and the sea beyond, you could truly think you were on the Côte d'Azur.

Getting There: From Highway 101, take Mission Street exit east; when road ends at Laguna, turn left at the Mission, then turn right on Los Olivos; where road forks, take right fork, Alameda Padre Serra. From here follow signs to El Encanto.

EL ENCANTO HOTEL AND GARDEN VILLAS

1900 Lasuen Road,
Santa Barbara, California 93103

Telephone: (805) 687-5000, for reservations (800) 346-7039

Accommodations: one hundred rooms with two double beds or a king-size bed; private baths with tub/showers; telephones; color television.

Rates: expensive to very expensive, no meals included; midweek packages at reduced rates; restaurant open for breakfast, lunch, dinner, and Sunday brunch. Children welcome.

Cards: AE, MC, V

Conference facilities. Open all year.

JoAnn Bell and Pat Hardy opened Santa Barbara's second B&B in a residential district close to the downtown shops, restaurants, and museums, and an easy bike ride from the mission. Before long, a number of inns were clustered in the area. Glenborough is a turn-of-the-century house decorated in an old-fashioned style. From the beginning, this inn was distinguished by the small personal touches it provides: flowers, plants, and decanters of purified water in the rooms; beds turned down at night with a mint on the pillow; towels changed twice daily. And over the years, Glenborough has become a role model for other B&Bs. Pat and JoAnn even co-authored a book on the subject (*So You Want to Be an Innkeeper*), publish a how-to newsletter (*innkeeping*), and have conducted seminars for B&B owners or aspiring innkeepers nationwide. They now have a third partner, Pat Morgan, who minds the inn when they're involved with other projects.

The four upstairs bedrooms are furnished mostly with antiques: brass or oak or four-poster beds, patchwork or velvet quilts, marble-topped chests, wickerware, and curtains of old textiles, crochet, knitting, or lace. The pièce de résistance, though, is the new downstairs suite all done up in Art Nouveau with a cast-iron stove in the parlor, a canopied bed, and a private deck and garden. Glenborough also offers quarters across the street in a restored 1880s Victorian cottage with spacious gardens. Each unit here has a private entry, two have sitting rooms with fireplaces, and one has its own deck.

Breakfast is very special at Glenborough. Both Pats love to cook, and pamper their guests' palates as well as their health. Their meals are prepared without salt and with low-fat, low-cholesterol ingredients, and their menus vary. A favorite is "Santa Barbara Spanish": huevos rancheros, crispy flour tortillas sprinkled with cinnamon sugar, sliced grapefruit, and fresh berries. In the main house breakfast is delivered to your room (or the garden, if you like) on trays set with china and sterling silver. For guests in the cottage, breakfast is delivered in a basket on handmade California pottery.

Behind the rear lawn of the main house is a spa, completely fenced for privacy, which may also be used by guests staying in the cottage. All guests are also invited for beverages and homemade hors d'oeuvres each night in Glenborough's parlor, where a velvet-upholstered settee is pulled up to a Franklin stove, and an old Victrola is supplied with records.

Getting There: From Highway 101, take Carrillo Street exit and head east to Bath; turn left.

THE GLENBOROUGH INN

1327 Bath Street,
Santa Barbara, California 93101

Telephone: (805) 966-0589

Accommodations: nine rooms with double or queen-size beds; two shared baths with tub/showers in main house, other rooms have private baths; no telephones; no television.

Rates: moderate to expensive, breakfast included. Children over twelve welcome. No smoking in main house.

Cards: MC, V

Open all year.

British-born Chris Dunstan has infused two adjoining Victorians with the aura of her homeland in one of Santa Barbara's newer B&Bs. She brought many of the antiques in the handsomely restored mansions from England. The bedrooms are all done up in Laura Ashley prints and papers, and named, as is the inn, after characters in Lewis Carroll's *Alice in Wonderland.* Alice's own suite has a sitting room and a private patio, as do the suites named after the White Rabbit and Caterpillar. Eberle and Dormouse boast brick fireplaces, and the elegant Cheshire Cat suite offers a whirlpool tub for two set in the room, as well as a VCR and television.

Breakfast at the Cheshire Cat is served in the formal dining room or on the brick patio between the two houses. In the English tradition, it's a substantial meal with juices, fruit, homemade granola, yogurt, coffee cake and croissants, and a main dish such as pastryless quiche with peppers and sausage. Behind the patio, a gazebo festooned with begonias shelters a spa and looks out to a lawn and lovely gardens in the rear. And if you want to pedal into town, bicycles are provided.

Although the Cheshire Cat's brochure says "Bed & Breakfast," Chris doesn't like the term. "In England that means taking guests into your home," she explains. "We operate this place as a professionally run inn."

Getting There: From the north on Highway 101, take Mission exit, turn right on De la Vina, and turn left on Valerio. From the south, take Arrellaga exit, turn left at Chapala to Valerio.

THE CHESHIRE CAT

36 West Valerio Street,
Santa Barbara, California 93101

Telephone: (805) 569-1610

Accommodations: eleven rooms or suites with twin, queen-, or king-size beds; private baths with showers, some with whirlpool tubs; telephones; one room with television. No smoking.

No credit cards.

Facilities for small conferences. Open all year except for several days before and after Christmas.

Built in 1886, this handsome house was once a girls' boarding school, later a sorority house, and for a while a B&B known as Valerio Manor. Then in the early 1980s Keith Pomeroy and interior designer Carlton Wagner bought the place and, over a period of some four years, transformed it into one of the most luxurious little inns in southern California.

Wagner has created a designer's showcase. In the dining room, for example, the walls are covered in silk; the high-backed chairs upholstered with Italian tapestry are from a villa on Lake Como; the carpeting was hand woven in England; and overhead, framed by mirrors, is a ceiling of shirred silk—a Wagner signature. Over the beds in most of the guest rooms, a canopy of shirred silk surrounds a wreath of berries from which a crystal chandelier hangs; the velvet-draped beds are heaped with down pillows. Perfectionism extends to the tiniest details, such as hand-ironed sheets. Many of the bedrooms have fireplaces, too.

THE BAYBERRY INN

111 West Valerio Street,
Santa Barbara, California 93101

Telephone: (805) 682-3199

Accommodations: eight rooms with queen-size beds; private baths with tub/showers; telephones in some rooms on request; television on request.

Rates: expensive, breakfast included. No smoking.

Cards: AE, MC, V

Open all year.

The Parsonage

The berries in each wreath vary according to the name and theme of the bed-room. Raspberry's wallpaper was hand printed in Paris with *framboises.* Gooseberry has mirrored walls, and Blueberry boasts a bathroom you could give a party in: The tub is on a sun porch decked out with rattan loveseats, plants, and even refreshments. The only room without a canopy wreath is Thimbleberry; here you can gaze at the stars through a skylight over the bed and soak in a whirlpool tub.

Breakfast, served on Royal Doulton china with heirloom sterling flatware, is a formal affair at The Bayberry Inn. It's also a substantial affair with a main course of omelets or frittatas or perhaps a Roquefort soufflé. In the evening refreshments are served at fireside in the large living room, where multipaned windows look into the garden. Throughout the day, coffee, soft drinks, and cookies are available in the enclosed sun porch. If you want some exercise, you'll find croquet and badminton equipment in the garden, and bikes to ride into town.

Getting There: From Highway 101, take Mission exit, turn right on De la Vina and left on Valerio.

In 1892, on a hillside above Santa Barbara, the Trinity Episcopal Church built a splendid Queen Anne residence to serve as a parsonage. The good reverend must have worshipped the sun along with his professed deity, because—unlike most Victorians—the house is splashed with light through a multitude of large windows of both clear and leaded glass. When interior designer Hilde Michelmore bought the inn in 1981, her decorating talents and an impressive collection of Chinese rugs made the sunny rooms truly sparkle.

Each room derives its theme and color scheme from its rug. In the living room, for example, a green-and-lilac floral motif is echoed in the upholstery of an oversized couch. On days when the sun is not pouring in from corner windows, a fire burns in the hearth and also in the formal dining room with its large glassed-in bay. Here or on a large outside deck, Hilde serves an ample breakfast that includes scrambled eggs, french toast or quiche, and nut or date breads.

Two of the upstairs guest rooms offer fine views of the city and ocean. One of these adjoins a private solarium with three walls of glass and an enormous bathroom. The bedrooms contain turn-of-the-century furnishings: armoires, draped or canopied beds, marble-topped pieces, and, as downstairs, the handsome rugs.

Getting There: From the north, take Mission Street exit from Highway 101 east to Laguna Street and turn right, proceed one block, and turn left on Olive. From the south, take Milpas Street exit to Olive and turn right.

THE PARSONAGE

1600 Olive Street,
Santa Barbara, California 93101

Telephone: (805) 962-9336

Accommodations: six rooms with twin, queen-, or king-size beds; private baths with tub/showers or stall showers; no telephones; no television.

Rates: moderate to expensive, breakfast included. Smoking discouraged.

Cards: MC, V

Open all year.

The beautiful Santa Ynez Valley, north of Santa Barbara, has long been the headquarters for southern California's horsey set, but today it's also a destination for wine bibbers. Nine small wineries are located in the area, offering tastings and tours. Other recreational activities include glider rides, hot-air ballooning, golf, tennis, and horseback riding. In the nearby mountains, Cachuma Lake provides facilities for boating and fishing. And for snoopy types, guided tours advertise a peek at the ranch of the area's best-known citizen—Ronald Reagan.

Among the valley's prime tourist attractions are Los Olivos, site of the historic Mattei's Tavern, and Solvang, a re-creation of a Danish village with a maze of windmills, smorgasbord restaurants, gift shops, and bakeries. The Mission Santa Inés on the edge of town is the only reminder that this is California.

Between these two towns, amid farms and horse ranches, is Ballard, which contained only a church, a schoolhouse, and a general-store-turned-restaurant until the Ballard Inn was built in 1985. Though new, the inn fits into the pastoral picture, looking somewhat like a Victorian farmhouse behind its white picket fence. The interior, though, is sophisticated country elegance at its best, with each of the light-splashed rooms decorated to commemorate persons or events that were significant to the valley's history.

Fifteen guest rooms occupy the second floor, offering views of the countryside through multipaned windows. Seven rooms have fireplaces, and most have hand-made patchwork quilts on the beds plus interesting little touches of western Americana, such as night tables made from school desks and old-fashioned sewing-machine tables. Amenities include a welcoming basket of fruit, chocolates, and cheese; the bathrooms are stocked with soaps made from wine.

Down a grand staircase are four spacious common rooms, used exclusively by inn guests. A full breakfast is served at individual tables in the handsome dining room, where a fire burns in a large hearth. Besides fresh fruit and juices or frappés, the menu includes entrées such as omelets and french toast. In the late afternoon the inn offers wine and a high tea that features such goodies as steak tartare and tiny quiches. You can enjoy this by the fireplace in the elegant drawing room or in the informal game room, where a television is set up to catch the evening news.

Getting There: From San Francisco, take Highway 101 to the Los Olivos turnoff five miles north of Buellton; in Los Olivos turn right on Alamo Pintado Road, then turn left on Baseline. From Santa Barbara, take Highway 101 to Buellton, head east on Highway 246 through Solvang, turn left on Alamo Pintado Road and then right on Baseline. For a scenic route from Santa Barbara, take Highway 154 over the mountains; beyond the first turnoff to Santa Ynez, turn left on Baseline.

THE BALLARD INN

2436 Baseline,
Ballard, California 93463

Telephone: (805) 688-7770

Accommodations: fifteen rooms with twin or queen-size beds; private baths with tub and shower; one room fully equipped for the handicapped; no telephones; no television.

Rates: expensive to very expensive, breakfast and tea included.

Cards: MC, V

Facilities for weddings and conferences. Open all year.

The Ballard Inn

In the sleepy little agricultural town of Los Alamos, Dick Langdon has re-created the spirit of 1880. The Union Hotel was built that year and served as a Wells Fargo stage stop until it burned down in 1886. In the early 1900s, the hotel was reconstructed and later modernized. When Dick bought the place in 1972, he dismantled twelve old barns and rebuilt the hotel's facade exactly as it appeared in an 1884 photograph. Inside, decades of paint were stripped to reveal the original woodwork and brass, and rooms were papered with colorful Victorian prints.

Dick spent a year traveling the United States in search of antiques. In the high-ceilinged parlor, a pair of 2,000-year-old Egyptian burial urns found in Alabama flank an intricately chiseled fireplace mantel from a mansion in Pasadena. There's an 1885 Singer sewing machine, along with chandeliers from Lee J. Cobb's home and the hotel's original safe, blackened on one side from an early shooting. Swinging doors from a bordello in New Orleans lead into a saloon with a 150-year-old bar of solid African mahogany. Some of the beds in the fifteen upstairs rooms could be museum pieces: a 200-year-old Australian brass and cast-iron bedstead with insets of cloisonné, and an original Murphy bed concealed in a mahogany armoire.

The large dining room contains furnishings and gaslights from a plantation in Mississippi. Tables are set with lace cloths and an array of old mismatched chinaware. Meals are family-style country fare: for dinner, tureens of soup, corn bread, salad, platters of beef and country-baked chicken with all the trimmings, and dessert; for breakfast, apple pancakes and sausage, or bacon and eggs served with potatoes and cinnamon rolls.

In and out of the hotel, Dick has created a flurry of old-time activity for his guests. An upstairs parlor houses a Brunswick pool table inlaid with ivory. The yard is now an 1880s park equipped with old-fashioned streetlights, park benches, and (with a nod to the present) a spa concealed under the floor of a Victorian gazebo and a swimming pool. After dinner, guests gather in the saloon for table tennis, shuffleboard, and complimentary popcorn. And after breakfast, Dick shows his guests the sights of Los Alamos in a 1918 touring car.

The area around Los Alamos has its own attractions. Many guests enjoy touring the twenty-two local wineries or taking a picnic basket to nearby Zaca Lake. Solvang and the Santa Ynez Valley are not far away. And if the 1880s become too much, you can always slip back another century by visiting the area's two missions: La Purisima Concepción and Santa Inés.

Getting There: Take Los Alamos exit from Highway 101, fourteen miles north of Buellton and seventeen miles south of Santa Maria. You can't miss the hotel.

UNION HOTEL

362 Bell Street (Box 616), Los Alamos, California 93440

Telephone: (805) 928-3838 or (805) 344-2744

Accommodations: sixteen rooms with twin, double, or king-size beds; some private baths with tub/showers, shared baths with stall showers; no telephones; no television.

Rates: moderate, breakfast included, dinner (open to the public) extra.

No credit cards.

Facilities for weddings. Open only on Friday, Saturday, and Sunday, all year.

HEARST CASTLE LAND

From the 1920s through the 1940s, publisher William Randolph Hearst devoted a considerable portion of his fortune and energies to creating La Cuesta Encantada, his hilltop estate above the Pacific, midway between Los Angeles and San Francisco. For this fairy-tale castle, he dismantled and then reassembled entire rooms and even buildings from Europe and imported priceless furnishings. Next to the pool is a Grecian temple, and the guest houses are rebuilt French châteaux. For three decades, Hearst and Marion Davies held court at the castle, entertaining notables from Hollywood in particular and the world in general.

In 1958, after Hearst's death, the castle was turned over to the state of California, which operates daily tours for the public. Though Hearst Castle is the area's principal tourist attraction, it is by no means the only reason for visiting this beautiful section of California. As Highway 1 winds up the coast from the fishing town of Morro Bay, it passes by the seaside resort of Cayucos, the quaint hamlet of Harmony, and the picturesque village of Cambria.

Getting There: From Los Angeles, take Highway 101 to San Luis Obispo and Highway 1 north through Morro Bay to San Simeon. From San Francisco, take Highway 101 south to Paso Robles, Highway 46 west to the coast and Highway 1 north to San Simeon.

Two-hour tours of the castle and grounds depart at least once an hour from eight o'clock to three o'clock daily, except Thanksgiving, Christmas, and New Year's Day. Four itineraries are offered, each one showing various parts of the estate, but for first-time visitors Tour One (which concentrates on the downstairs rooms) is recommended. Reservations are strongly advised and are available from any MISTIX tour agency.

Telephone: (800) 444-7275 within California, (619) 452-1950 outside California.

Cards: MC, V

Built at the water's edge, this charming resort overlooking the fishing harbor provides a luxurious base for exploring the Hearst Castle area. The Friden Hotel Company (owner of El Encanto in Santa Barbara) recently renovated this 1950s inn, installed lush gardens, and commissioned the noted designer Mabel Shultz to redecorate the rooms in French country fashion. A majority of the units have private decks or patios and sweeping views of the bay; many have fireplaces, too, and one suite has a large whirlpool tub.

From the glass-walled dining room and deck, you are treated to an aerial ballet by the seagulls flying over the harbor; their movements seem to follow the tempo of the classical music piped through the inn. Other forms of recreation include golf at an adjacent eighteen-hole course, swimming in the inn's pool, and bicycling in the surrounding area. In addition to trips to Hearst Castle and shopping in San Luis Obispo, winery tours and tastings are popular diversions.

Getting There: From Highway 1, take Main Street exit at Morro Bay and follow Main south through the gates of the state park. The inn is on the right.

THE INN AT MORRO BAY

Morro Bay, California 93442

Telephone: (805) 772-5651, in California (800) 321-9566

Accommodations: ninety-six rooms with two doubles or queen- or king-size beds; private baths with showers or tubs and showers; telephones; television.

Rates: moderate to very expensive, no meals included. Dining room open to the public for breakfast, lunch, and dinner. Children welcome.

Cards: AE, DC, MC, V

Facilities for conferences and weddings. Open all year.

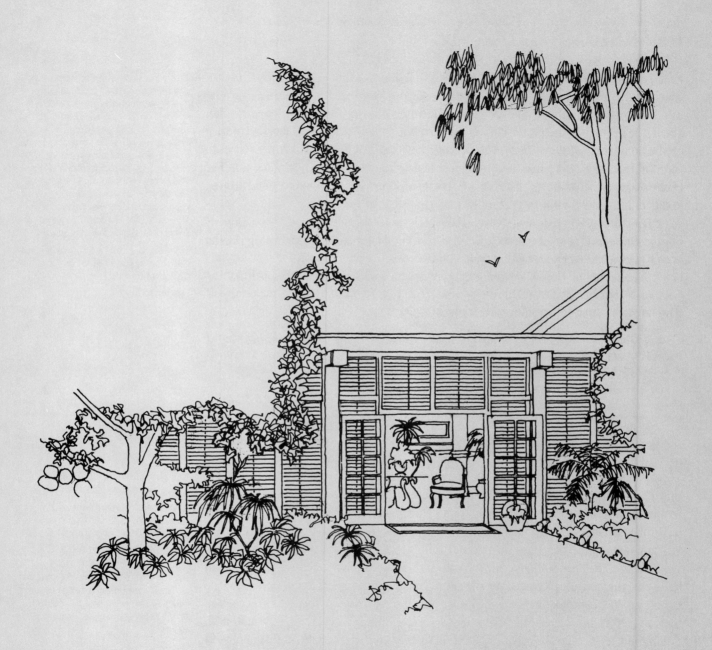

The Inn at Morro Bay

The B&B craze arrived surprisingly late in artsy-craftsy Cambria. In fact, none were located here in the early 1980s when Molly Lynch came to Cambria from southern California to open an inn. She purchased a two-story house built of pine logs on a wooded hill above the village, and behind it constructed another two-story unit containing guest rooms. Molly named the inn in honor of her father, J. Patrick Lynch, whose family came from County Cork, and gave the rooms Irish county names like Limerick and Donegal.

Beverages and appetizers are served in the evening in the pine-walled living room where a brick fireplace sits on a raised hearth. Here, and elsewhere in the inn, you'll find lots of books and magazines, along with comfortable couches and chairs in which to curl up and read. In the rear breakfast area four tables, set with crocheted cloths and blue china, look into the garden. Molly bakes the morning breads, which are accompanied by fresh fruit and granola.

The bedrooms have the same Early American country look, with wood-burning fireplaces, lots of cedar and flowery papers, and beds lavishly piled with pillows. The inn is surrounded by pines, but only minutes away from the beach or village.

Getting There: From Highway 1, turn east on Burton, which is between the two main exits to Cambria.

THE J. PATRICK HOUSE

2990 Burton Drive,
Cambria, California 93428

Telephone: (805) 927-3812

Accommodations: eight rooms with queen- or king-size beds; private baths with showers or tub/showers; no telephones; no television.

Rates: moderate, breakfast included. No smoking.

Cards: MC, V

Open all year.

Moonstone Beach, rimmed by a row of ocean-view motels, is one of Cambria's newest and nicest areas for lodgings. Amid these motels, but set off by surrounding fields, is the Beach House, a pretty little B&B. This inn, owned by Penny and Tom Hitch, who live nearby, is a family affair: The Hitch's six grown children and Tom's mother all help run the place.

The hub of the house is a spacious second-floor living room with an A-frame cathedral ceiling, a tiled fireplace, and a huge deck overlooking the ocean. The Hitches have provided a selection of games and a telescope to spot vessels far out to sea. In the rear of the room is an open kitchen, where the coffee pot is always full, and in the mornings a breakfast of fruit, juices, pastries, cereals or boiled eggs, and quiche is set out.

The bedroom furnishings are simple, befitting a beach house: down quilts and ruffled pillows atop queen-size beds, circa-1890 oak dressers (from a hotel in Vermont). You'll also find citified comforts such as private baths and television with HBO. And, most importantly, in many of the rooms you'll find ocean views. Two of the first-floor rooms face the beach directly, and are also outfitted with

BEACH HOUSE

6360 Moonstone Beach Drive,
Cambria, California 93428

Telephone: (805) 927-3136

Accommodations: seven rooms with queen- or king-size beds; private baths with showers; no telephones; television with HBO.

Rates: moderate to expensive, breakfast included. Children welcome, but room occupancy is limited to two persons. No smoking.

Cards: MC, V

Open all year.

fireplaces. But perhaps the best lodging is in a second-floor room with a king-size bed, pitched knotty-pine ceiling, skylights, and an ocean view; from the private deck, you can glimpse the ornate bell towers of Hearst Castle, just six miles away.

Getting There: From the north, take Moonstone Beach Drive west from Highway 1. From the south, turn left on Windsor Boulevard and right on Moonstone Beach Drive.

Between San Simeon and Monterey, the Santa Lucia Mountains rise precipitously above the incessantly pounding Pacific surf. Today Highway 1 traverses this rugged terrain across high bridges and along niches blasted out of the cliffs. The Spanish missionaries found this section of the coast impassable and detoured inland. But this very remoteness appealed to one of the first settlers, a Yankee sea captain with the unlikely name of Juan Bautista Roger Cooper, who landed his cargoes at the mouth of Big Sur River to avoid paying customs duties to the Mexicans in Monterey. The struggles of the homesteaders who later tried to farm this rocky land inspired the poet Robinson Jeffers. But it was another writer who shaped the destiny of Big Sur. Henry Miller moved here in 1944, seeking the serenity of the coastal mountains after his expatriate days in Paris. Other artists followed, and for the next decade or so Big Sur was a hardworking bohemian community.

Only recently has the traveler been able to enjoy the beauty of Big Sur while sleeping in style. In 1975 the Ventana Inn was built on a meadow twelve hundred feet above the Pacific. The contemporary architecture of the buildings is spectacular: soaring ceilings, giant beams, unexpected angles and planes. Every room offers views of the mountains, the meadow, or the ocean far below. The rooms are paneled in knotty cedar and handsomely appointed with wicker furniture, hand-painted headboards, patchwork quilts, and window seats tucked into alcoves. All have private balconies or patios, and many have fireplaces or Franklin stoves and individual hot tubs. Two-story units have wet bars and living rooms.

In 1988 Ventana was significantly enlarged with the construction of another cluster of units up the mountainside. These contain a common room called The Library, a perfect spot to while away the foggy mornings that are typical in this part of the coast. A fire burns in an enormous stone fireplace that rises dramatically to the peak of the cedar cathedral ceiling. There are lots of books and a long plank table laden with breakfast goodies: assorted breads and pastries from Ventana's kitchens, fruit, juices, granola, and housemade yogurt. Breakfast is also served in

VENTANA INN

Highway 1,
Big Sur, California 93920

Telephone: (408) 667-2331,
in California (800) 628-6500

Accommodations: fifty-nine rooms with queen-size, double queens, or king-size beds; private baths with tub/showers; telephones; satellite television and VCRs.

Rates: very expensive, breakfast included.

Cards: AE, DC, MC, V

Open all year.

Ventana Inn

the main lobby of the inn or delivered to the guests' rooms. Across the meadow on another hilltop is the Ventana restaurant, which offers a diverse selection of lunch and dinner dishes, as well as fifty-mile vistas from its patio.

Ventana has two large swimming pools, as well as Japanese hot baths, a sauna, and a spa. Hiking trails meander through the mountains above. And down the road is Nepenthe, a restaurant and bar of intriguing design, built around a cabin that Orson Welles once bought for Rita Hayworth (although they never lived there).

Getting There: From San Francisco, follow directions to Monterey and take Highway 1 twenty-eight miles south. From Los Angeles, take Highway 101 to San Luis Obispo and Highway 1 north. The inn is south of the village of Big Sur.

When Interstate 5 first opened in the late 1960s, there was absolutely no place to eat in this sparsely populated section of the San Joaquin Valley. The highway did pass through the vast landholdings of the Harris Ranch, and in the early 1970s, owner J. A. Harris and his wife, Ann, built a beautiful restaurant by the side of the highway—midway between Los Angeles and San Francisco—offering grateful travelers produce from the ranch and the famed Harris beef. Now Harris' son John and his wife, Carole, have carried on the tradition of hospitality by creating the first luxury lodgings along the highway. But the big news is that these lovely rooms cost no more than a first-class motel.

The inn is constructed in the style of an early California hacienda with a tiled roof, curved archways, and many balconies. As you enter the lobby from a large loggia, you sense a serenity that's a welcome change from the fast lane of the freeway. Cowhide-covered couches are drawn up beside the carved stone fireplace, a bouquet of flowers sits on a marble table, and bookcases line the walls. Arched French doors lead to another loggia and patio overlooking an enormous swimming pool.

Each guest room is decorated in country style, with flowered draperies and quilted spreads, bleached pine furniture, rattan chairs, more fresh flowers, and a corner hutch that conceals the television. Some of the rooms have patios or balconies overlooking the courtyard and pool. An executive suite has its own private lanai, a living room with fireplace, a wet bar, a whirlpool tub, and antique furnishings. For an extra charge, a Continental breakfast is brought to the rooms at Harris Ranch, along with the morning papers. If you're still hungry, you need only stroll over to the Harris Ranch restaurant for eggs and a New York steak.

Getting There: The inn is located alongside Highway 5, midway between Los Angeles and San Francisco.

THE INN AT HARRIS RANCH
Interstate Highway 5 (Route 1, Box 777), Coalinga, California 93210

Telephone: (209) 935-0717, (800) 942-2333

Accommodations: eighty-eight rooms and suites with queen- or king-size beds; private baths with tubs and showers; some rooms fully equipped for the handicapped; telephones; television with HBO; air-conditioning.

Rates: moderate, no meals included; executive suite, very expensive. Nonsmoking rooms available. Children welcome.

Cards: AE, CB, DC, MC, V

Facilities for conferences and weddings. Open all year.

MONTEREY BAY

CARMEL
CARMEL VALLEY
MONTEREY
PACIFIC GROVE
SANTA CRUZ AREA

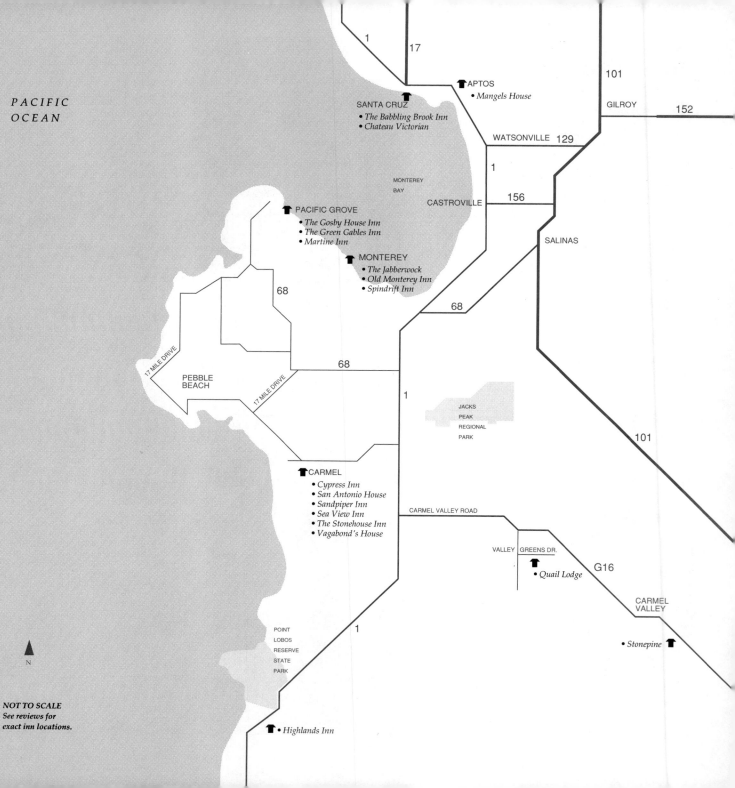

PACIFIC
OCEAN

APTOS
• *Mangels House*

SANTA CRUZ
• *The Babbling Brook Inn*
• *Chateau Victorian*

1

17

101

GILROY

152

WATSONVILLE   129

1

MONTEREY
BAY

CASTROVILLE   156

SALINAS

PACIFIC GROVE
• *The Gosby House Inn*
• *The Green Gables Inn*
• *Martine Inn*

MONTEREY
• *The Jabberwock*
• *Old Monterey Inn*
• *Spindrift Inn*

68

68

68

17 MILE DRIVE

PEBBLE
BEACH

17 MILE DRIVE

1

JACKS

PEAK

REGIONAL

PARK

101

CARMEL
• *Cypress Inn*
• *San Antonio House*
• *Sandpiper Inn*
• *Sea View Inn*
• *The Stonehouse Inn*
• *Vagabond's House*

CARMEL VALLEY ROAD

VALLEY GREENS DR.

• *Quail Lodge*

G16

CARMEL
VALLEY

POINT
LOBOS
RESERVE
STATE
PARK

1

• *Stonepine*

N

NOT TO SCALE
See reviews for
exact inn locations.

• *Highlands Inn*

MONTEREY PENINSULA

In 1770 Father Junípero Serra founded Mission San Carlos in Monterey, the second in California's chain of missions. The following year he moved the mission to Carmel, where he later returned to spend his last years. The Spanish military expedition that Serra accompanied had established a presidio in Monterey, which was designated capital of California by Spain in 1775. And so it remained through Mexican rule until the American flag was raised over the Customhouse in 1846.

Monterey had by this time become a cultivated town, where the Spanish families lived auspiciously in two-story adobes with roofs of red tile. Then the Yankees discovered the abundance of whales offshore and Monterey became a bustling whaling port. Sardine fishing brought added prosperity; Cannery Row was built west of town and later immortalized in the works of John Steinbeck. Today many of the old adobes are open to the public or house restaurants and shops. And after the sardines had all but disappeared, Cannery Row was converted into a complex of shops, hotels, and dining places.

Just over the hill from Monterey, the quiet village of Carmel was established at the century's turn and soon became a popular colony for artists and writers. Edward Weston, Maynard Dixon, Ambrose Bierce, Don Blanding, Lincoln Steffens, and Robinson Jeffers lived here over the years. Although Carmel was built in a potpourri of architectural styles, from quaint half-timbered cottage to neo-Spanish, new construction or remodeling is strictly controlled today to preserve the woodsy, villagelike quality of the picturesque streets.

Pacific Grove, west of Monterey, is vastly different from both Monterey and Carmel. Founded in the 1870s by the Methodist Church, the town became known as the Chautauqua of the West, famous for its summertime religious conferences, an educational tradition that's kept alive today at the Asilomar conference grounds. The city's streets and its rocky shores are lined with large Victorians that were built to house the conference attendees and, when Pacific Grove later gained favor as a summer resort, vacationers. Today many of these stately old mansions have been converted into inns.

Few places in the West offer such diverse recreational facilities as the Monterey Peninsula. There are eight public and four private golf courses. Sailboats may be chartered in Monterey Bay. Skin diving, scuba diving, fishing, tennis, polo matches—they're all here. One of the biggest draws is the spectacular shoreline, from the cypress-bordered white sand dunes of Carmel to the rocky coves and hidden beaches of Lovers Point. Carmel is a shopper's paradise with a plethora of crafts, antiques, jewelry, and clothing boutiques. The peninsula is a sightseer's mecca, too, with choices ranging from reliving history at the old mission to viewing the palatial mansions along Pebble Beach's famed Seventeen Mile Drive. The Monterey Peninsula probably has more restaurants per capita than any other area in California. And the latest attraction, visited by some two million people each year, is the Monterey Bay Aquarium.

Getting There: From San Francisco, take Highway 101 to the Monterey Peninsula cutoff north of Salinas; in Castroville this joins Highway 1, which goes through Monterey to Carmel. For a slightly longer and more scenic route from San Francisco, take Highway 280 to San Jose, Highway 17 through Los Gatos to Santa Cruz, and Highway 1 south to Monterey. From Los Angeles, take Highway 101 to Salinas and Highway 68 to Monterey.

D on Blanding lived here in the 1940s, but no one is certain whether his poem "Vagabond's House" was named for the inn, or the inn for the poem. Nevertheless Vagabond's House is a poetic half-timbered hideaway, with rooms looking through treetops into a stone courtyard filled with rhododendrons, camellias, azaleas, and roses. In the center, baskets of ferns, begonias, and fuchsias hang from the branches of an ancient oak.

Vagabond's House was originally built in 1941 as efficiency apartments, and later became an inn, presently owned by Dennis and Karen Levett. The rooms are large and charmingly furnished with Early American maple, wicker pieces, quilted bedspreads, antique pendulum clocks, books, and flowers. Most of the rooms have fireplaces, and all have refrigerators or kitchenettes, a holdover from apartment-house days.

A "European" breakfast is served, either in guests' rooms or on the patio—fresh fruit in season, hard-cooked eggs or casseroles on weekends, breads, muffins, coffee cake. No one goes hungry here, not even the squirrels; a big sack of peanuts is provided so you can feed the friendly little creatures that congregate in the gardens. Off the patio is a large common room with a fireplace, a collection of English hunting prints, and—you guessed it—bound copies of "Vagabond's House."

Getting There: From Highway 1, take Ocean Avenue westward, turn right on Dolores. Free pickup at Monterey airport.

VAGABOND'S HOUSE

Fourth and Dolores (Box 2747), Carmel, California 93921

Telephone: (408) 624-7738

Accommodations: twelve rooms with two doubles, queen-, or king-size beds; private baths with tub/showers or stall showers; telephones; color television.

Rates: moderate to expensive, breakfast included. Children over twelve welcome.

Cards: AE, MC, V

Open all year.

Vagabond's House

San Antonio House

This three-story shingled house was built in 1907 as a private residence, and during its early years served as a studio and weekend retreat for artists and writers from the San Francisco Bay Area. In the 1930s Lincoln Steffens lived next door and played host to a continuous flow of the literati of his day. In 1950 the handsome house, set back from the street by a spacious lawn, became a guest house. It is presently owned by Vagabond's House proprietors Dennis and Karen Levett.

The accommodations consist of two- and three-room suites, each with its own patio or garden. All of the units have fireplaces and refrigerators. In the morning the newspaper is at your door, and when you're ready for breakfast, just pick up the phone. Innkeeper Jewel Brown will send a tray laden with muffins, hard-cooked eggs, fresh fruit, or perhaps an apple crisp. San Antonio House is a place for people who seek complete privacy and the sound of the surf. It's only a block away from Carmel's beautiful beach.

Getting There: From Highway 1, take Ocean Avenue westward, then turn left on San Antonio.

SAN ANTONIO HOUSE

San Antonio between Seventh and Ocean (Box 3683), Carmel, California 93921

Telephone: (408) 624-4334

Accommodations: four units with queen-size beds; private baths with tub/showers; telephones; color television.

Rates: expensive, breakfast included. Children over twelve welcome.

Cards: AE, MC, V

Open all year.

Among those who nurtured Carmel as an artists' colony was an expatriate San Franciscan known as "Nana" Foster. In 1906 she built a house of hand-hewn stone on the sand dunes above the beach and invited the prominent writers of the era to be her guests. Today the inn's bedrooms bear the names of some of those visitors—Jack London, Mary Austin, Robinson Jeffers, and Sinclair Lewis. Even though the view of the ocean is now obscured by houses and trees, the feeling of early Carmel remains.

Literary ghosts, however, are not the only inhabitants of this charming retreat. Teddy bears and flocks of stuffed, ceramic, and wooden ducks occupy nearly every nook and cranny of the large living room and the cozy glassed-in sun porch. They even march up the stairs to the four guest rooms that nestle under the gabled and dormered roof. These and all other rooms in the house have the white-painted board-and-batten walls so typical of early Carmel architecture. The rooms are appointed with antiques, quilted bedspreads, ruffled curtains, a bevy of pillows, silk flowers, and bowls of fresh fruit. Downstairs are two other bedrooms, one with its own porch.

A sit-down breakfast is served in the tile-floored dining room, where multipaned windows on three sides look into gardens and foliage. Innkeeper Virginia Carey usually provides fruit, juices, a hot entrée, and homemade breads.

THE STONEHOUSE INN

Eighth Avenue below Monte Verde (Box 2517), Carmel, California 93921

Telephone: (408) 624-4569

Accommodations: six rooms with twin, double, queen-, or king-size beds; three shared baths with tub/showers or stall showers; no telephones; no television.

Rates: moderate to expensive, breakfast included. No smoking.

Cards: MC, V

Open all year.

Coffee, tea, and hot chocolate are offered all day. And in the late afternoon more refreshments and hors d'oeuvres are served beside the enormous stone fireplace in the living room, where the literati of yesteryear used to gather. If those stones could only talk.

Getting There: From Highway 1, take Ocean Avenue westward, turn left on Monte Verde and right on Eighth.

This cluster of shingled buildings clings to a pine-studded hillside that rises abruptly from the Pacific south of Carmel. The present Highlands Inn is a luxurious 1980s reincarnation of a rustic 1916 lodge surrounded by cabins. The lodge, constructed of locally quarried golden granite, houses an enormous common room graced by skylights and two huge stone fireplaces, as well as a restaurant and bar. Here a wall of glass provides awesome views of the Pacific framed by the craggy fingers of Point Lobos and Yankee Point. Downstairs, a more casual dining spot also has a stunning view of the coast from tables on an open deck overlooking the swimming pool.

A few refurbished cottages near the pool are the only other remnants of the past. Most of the 142 guest units are new suites and two-story townhouses, resplendent with wood-burning fireplaces, private decks, large whirlpool baths, and fully equipped kitchens with "honor bars" stocked with wine and cheese. The rooms are decorated with contemporary furnishings and Italian linen fabrics, and all have those dramatic views of the coast, punctuated by graceful Monterey pines.

Although Highlands Inn is only a short drive from Carmel or Monterey, the resort was conceived as a self-contained getaway spot. In addition to the large kidney-shaped swimming pool, three outdoor hot tubs are scattered around the grounds. You can hike or bike along trails in the hills above the inn, or you can walk along its private beach and muse on the truth of Robinson Jeffers' description of the Monterey area: "The greatest meeting of land and water in the world."

Getting There: The inn is located on Highway 1 about four miles south of Carmel.

HIGHLANDS INN

Highway 1 south (Box 1700), Carmel, California 93921

Telephone: (408) 624-3801, in California (800) 682-4811, nationwide (800) 538-9525

Accommodations: 142 units, mostly one- or two-bedroom suites with queen- or king-size beds; private baths with whirlpool tubs and stall showers; some rooms fully equipped for the handicapped; telephones; television.

Rates: very expensive, no meals included. Pacific's Edge restaurant open to the public for breakfast, lunch, and dinner; California Market open to the public for lunch and dinner. Children welcome.

Cards: AE, CB, DC, V

Conference facilities. Open all year.

This small hotel, with its red-tiled roofs, Moorish-Mediterranean facade, and ornate tower, looks as though it were built by the Spanish missionaries who settled Carmel. Actually, the inn was constructed in 1929 and recently restored. Off the ceramic-tiled vestibule is an enormous living room with a beamed cathedral ceiling, a large fireplace, and French doors opening to a flower-filled courtyard. Across the hall is a cozy library. In the morning, juice, coffee, teas, pastries, and croissants are served in the patio or in a sunny breakfast room.

A number of the second-floor guest rooms look out to this patio, and the deluxe rooms boast verandas or ocean views, as well as sitting areas and wet bars. But even the standard rooms are lovely, with quilted floral spreads and, in some rooms, canopies over king-size beds. You will find a decanter of sherry on a skirted table, and the morning paper delivered to your door.

Getting There: From Highway 1, take Ocean Avenue westward, then turn left on Lincoln.

CYPRESS INN

Lincoln and Seventh (Box Y), Carmel, California 93921

Telephone: (408) 624-3871, in California (800) 443-7443

Accommodations: thirty-three rooms with twin, double, queen-, or king-size beds; private baths with showers or tub/showers; telephones; color television.

Rates: moderate to expensive, breakfast included. Children welcome.

Cards: AE, MC, V

Open all year.

The Sea View has been operating as an inn since the mid-1920s, but Marshall and Diane Hydorn, the present owners, think the three-story shingled house was built just after the turn of the century. They also like to think it was designed by Bernard Maybeck, as one book on Carmel history suggests. Located three blocks from the ocean on a quiet residential street, the inn was obviously named for its view. Over the years large pines have grown up around the house, however, allowing only a peek at the sea from upstairs rooms today.

The inn retains the aura of Carmel in the twenties, even though the Hydorns recently redecorated the rooms in a sophisticated country style. Downstairs the dark, beamed ceilings of the parlor and library contrast with white board-and-batten walls and shuttered windows. Navy-blue love seats are pulled up in front of the fireplace in the parlor, and in the library a backgammon board is set by another fire. Breakfast is served here, by candlelight, and what a repast it is. On weekends the menu usually includes quiche and sausage, four cereals, freshly baked apple or date bread, croissants, seasonal fruits, and cheeses; on weekdays the fare is simpler.

Many of the second-floor bedrooms have sitting areas in alcoves or enclosed porches and shuttered window seats in bays. Canopies of floral fabrics adorn the beds, and handsome area rugs grace the polished oak floors. The cozy garret rooms on the top floor are done up in Victorian wicker, braided rugs, and flowery prints. All the rooms are filled with plants and the paintings of Marshall Hydorn.

SEA VIEW INN

Camino Real at Eleventh (Box 4138), Carmel, California 93921

Telephone: (408) 624-8778

Accommodations: eight rooms with queen- or king-size beds; private or shared baths with tub/showers or stall showers; no telephones; no television.

Rates: moderate, breakfast included. Children over twelve welcome. No smoking.

Cards: MC, V

Open all year.

Seaview is a romantic place with a loyal clientele. It is not uncommon these days for couples who honeymooned here to return for their fiftieth anniversaries.

Getting There: From Highway 1, take Ocean Avenue westward, then turn left on Camino Real.

Located at Carmel Point, just fifty yards from the beach, Sandpiper Inn is owned by Graeme and Irene Mackenzie, no starry-eyed novices to innkeeping. Born in Scotland, Graeme graduated from Lausanne Hotel School, did postgraduate work at Cornell University, and brings to Carmel over twenty years of experience in some of the world's finest hotels. Both the Mackenzies are multilingual (she was a United Nations interpreter), which makes their international clientele feel right at home. The inn's guest book now lists visitors from seventy-one countries.

Built in 1929, the inn was refurbished by the Mackenzies in 1975, though they keep improving it. Attending antiques auctions is their hobby, and they have furnished the place with American country, French, and English pieces; antique headboards for all of the beds are the latest acquisitions. Raising orchids and house plants is another avocation, and the inn is filled with the results of their efforts. Some of the guest rooms have wood-burning fireplaces and many have views of Carmel Bay and Pebble Beach.

In the evening guests gather around the stone fireplace in the living room; to one side is a cozy library with a writing desk and shelves stocked with books. At the end of the living room a long table is set for a breakfast that includes freshly squeezed orange juice and homemade muffins. Guests may help themselves to coffee in the kitchen at any time.

Flower gardens and brick patios for sunning surround the inn. Ten-speed bicycles are available for pedaling along the new walking and bicycling trail that fronts Carmel's glorious beach. Graeme is happy to introduce his guests to most of the golf and tennis clubs on the peninsula.

Getting There: From Highway 1, take Ocean Avenue westward and turn left on Scenic; proceed along Scenic, passing Santa Lucia Avenue, and turn left onto Martin.

SANDPIPER INN AT-THE-BEACH

2408 Bay View Avenue at Martin, Carmel, California 93923

Telephone: (408) 624-6433, in California (800) 633-6433

Accommodations: fifteen rooms with queen- or king-size beds, additional singles in some rooms; private baths with showers or tub/showers; no telephones; no television.

Rates: moderate to expensive, breakfast included. Smoking discouraged. Children over twelve welcome.

Cards: AE, MC, V

Open all year.

Sandpiper Inn At-the-Beach

Secluded in the upper Carmel Valley, amid 330 acres of wooded hills, is the ultimate inn. Stonepine was the estate of Henry Potter Russell, a noted racehorse breeder, and his wife, Helen, granddaughter of railroad tycoon Charles Crocker. In 1930 they constructed an exquisite French château, importing from Italy the rare stone pines that now tower above the mansion. Russell also built on the estate an elaborate equestrian center where his famous thoroughbreds were trained. In 1987 Stonepine became an inn.

In the living room, ever so gracious with its twenty-foot ceilings, eighteenth-century French tapestries hang above an Italian carved-limestone fireplace. The enormous hand-tied carpet was custom made for the inn in Tai 'Ping, as were the rugs in the rest of the château. Cognac is often poured by the fireside after dinner, and occasionally musicians are brought in to play the grand piano. By day the room is flooded with light from tall French windows that open on three sides to terraces, gardens, and a beautiful loggia with carved stone arches from ancient Rome; the loggia even has a fireplace.

The Crockers gave the nineteenth-century French oak paneling in the library and dining room to the Russells as a wedding present. Inn guests may elect to have dinner here; served precisely at seven-thirty, it's a formal five-course affair presented on Limoges and Royal Crown Derby china with wines in Baccarat crystal. A Continental breakfast of freshly squeezed orange juice, just-baked muffins, cold cereals, and a fruit platter is also offered.

A circular staircase with a filigreed iron railing leads to eight luxurious guest rooms in the château. Most have fireplaces, and each is individually decorated with handsome traditional furnishings. On arrival guests are welcomed with a basket of fruit and cheese and a bottle of Cabernet in the room, as well as bouquets of flowers from Stonepine's lovely gardens. Bathrooms are equipped with whirlpool tubs, designer soaps and shampoos, and his-and-hers bathrobes.

More informal but equally charming quarters are located near the equestrian center in the Paddock House, which also has its own living and dining rooms. The four guest units here are popular with families, the horsey set, and small groups, who take over the entire house. The stables are conveniently close.

Stonepine is still a working horse ranch that trains carriage horses and boards racehorses. The equestrian center also provides riding horses for the use of guests at the inn, and offers lessons in both English and Western riding as well as dressage. There's even a horse-drawn carriage and an old stagecoach to take guests

STONEPINE

150 East Carmel Valley Road, Carmel Valley, California 93924

Telephone: (408) 659-2245

Accommodations: twelve rooms with two queens or king-size beds; private baths with whirlpool tubs and showers; telephones; television.

Rates: very expensive, breakfast included; reservations for dinner required twenty-four hours in advance. Children welcome in Paddock House. Facilities for boarding pets and horses.

Cards: AE, DC, MC, V

Facilities for conferences and weddings. Open all year.

on tours of the inn's vast acreage, perhaps with a stop at the swimming hole on the Carmel River. If you don't care about horses or riding, you'll still find lots to do at Stonepine. Behind the château is a gorgeous swimming pool, as well as tennis and volleyball courts.

If you arrive in Monterey by air, Stonepine will send a Rolls Royce Phantom V to meet your plane. Obviously, everything is thoroughbred here.

Getting There: From Highway 1, take Carmel Valley Road east beyond Carmel Valley Village. The electronically operated gates to the inn are on the right. Pickup at Monterey airport with advance notice.

The Golf Club at Quail Lodge is spread over 245 exquisitely landscaped acres dotted with ten pretty lakes, lovely gardens, and an 18-hole, par-71 golf course. The jewel in its crown is Quail Lodge, a luxurious resort that offers its guests full privileges at the golf club facilities.

Some fifty years ago all this was but a dream of the club's developer, Ed Haber, who in the 1930s won San Francisco's amateur golf championship and aspired to build his own course one day. Four decades later he bought a dairy farm in Carmel Valley from Dwight Morrow, brother of Ann Morrow Lindbergh, and transformed it into the present club and resort.

The hub of Quail Lodge is a handsome contemporary building overlooking one of the lakes. In the main lobby a skylight in the high ceiling illuminates a fountain below. Coffee, tea, and sherry are set out here in the afternoons, to be enjoyed next to the fireplace in the adjoining library or in the sun room. The central lodge also houses The Covey, an elegant, award-winning restaurant.

One hundred guest units are located in sixteen smaller buildings scattered through the grounds. All have garden or lake views and private decks or balconies. The most desirable accommodations are the cottage suites, where the bedroom opens to a large, high-ceilinged living room with a fireplace and a wet bar completely stocked with just about everything you might want to drink. Four single rooms also occupy these cottages; when a group is traveling together, all may share the amenities of the living area.

Even if you're not a golfer, you'll find plenty to do at Quail Lodge: hot tubs, swimming pools, jogging and cycling trails, as well as steelhead fishing in season on the Carmel River, which winds through the grounds. You'll also find year-round

QUAIL LODGE

8205 Valley Greens Drive, Carmel, California 93923

Telephone: (408) 624-1581, for reservations only in California (800) 682-9303, nationwide (800) 538-9516

Accommodations: one hundred units with two queens or one king-size bed; private baths with tub/showers; telephones; television.

Rates: very expensive, no meals included. The Covey restaurant is open to the public for dinner; golf club open to lodge guests for breakfast and lunch, shuttle service provided. Children welcome.

Cards: AE, CB, DC, MC, V

Conference facilities. Open all year.

trout fishing and boating on a four-acre lake in a contiguous six-hundred-acre area that the resort recently acquired. And on most days throughout the year, you can be assured of sunny weather for these outdoor activities. Smart travelers know that the sun shines in Carmel Valley when the rest of the Monterey area is shrouded by a blanket of fog.

Getting There: From Highway 1, just south of the Ocean Avenue turnoff to Carmel, head east on Carmel Valley Road until you see the Quail Lodge sign on the right.

When Ann and Gene Swett decided to open their elegant Tudor-style home for bed and breakfast, they vowed they would make it the perfect inn. And they have succeeded, down to every detail. Built in 1929 by Carmel Martin, a former mayor of Monterey, the half-timbered house sits on an oak-capped hillside surrounded by an acre of beautiful gardens. Begonias, fuchsias, and hydrangeas abound, along with twenty-eight varieties of roses. The wooded banks of a creek are rampant with ivy, ferns, and rhododendrons.

The interior of the house is decorated with impeccable taste. Bedrooms are equipped with comfortable places to sit—wicker chairs or upholstered love seats or perhaps a chaise—and with books and magazines to read. Plants and well-chosen pieces of bric-a-brac make the house look homey but not cluttered.

Wood-burning fireplaces enhance most of the ten bedrooms. One of the loveliest is the Library, which has a fireplace, floor-to-ceiling bookshelves, a private balcony, and a king-size bed set in a niche with windows on all sides, screened on the outside by a massive, gnarled oak. On the third floor, tucked under the eaves, two enchanting rooms have fireplaces, half-timbered walls, and skylights in the slanted ceilings. And behind the inn is another unit with a fireplace and skylights: a two-room shuttered cottage dressed up with flowery patterns and antique linens.

In the evenings a fire also burns in the lovely high-ceilinged living room, where pre-dinner refreshments are served and a table is set up for backgammon or dominoes. Need some dining tips? Take a look at the book in which previous guests have written critiques of local restaurants. In the morning, you may have a breakfast tray brought to your room, or you may join the other guests in the formally appointed dining room, beside yet another fire. Breakfast starts with a glass of orange juice and a plate of fresh fruit, followed by the inn's now-famous cheese

OLD MONTEREY INN

500 Martin Street,
Monterey, California 93940

Telephone: (408) 375-8284

Accommodations: ten rooms with queen- or king-size beds; private baths with tub/showers or stall showers; no telephones; no television.

Rates: expensive to very expensive, breakfast included.

No credit cards.

Open all year.

Old Monterey Inn

puffs and popovers, plus a hot dish—perhaps Belgian waffles with sautéed pears or coddled eggs or orange-blossom french toast.

Although the Old Monterey Inn seemed quite perfect at its inception, the Swetts are continually adding improvements. Perfection, evidently, knows no end.

Getting There: Take Munras exit off Highway 1 and turn left on Soledad Drive. Turn right on Pacific and left on Martin.

Resorts once dotted the beaches west of Monterey, until the sardine industry claimed the area for its canneries. Now the pendulum has swung back again and Cannery Row—with its many shops, hotels, and restaurants—is once more a mecca for vacationers. Steinbeck would never recognize his old turf, but even he might think the Spindrift Inn, on the edge of the bay, was a survivor from the last century. From the outside it looks that way. The old-fashioned facade, however, conceals one of the newest and most luxurious small hotels in all of California.

When you enter the elegant lobby, you leave behind the hurly-burly of Cannery Row. If it's late afternoon, tea will be served next to the marble-faced fireplace flanked by gilded statues holding giant candelabras. Sun splashes in from a skylight atop the four-story atrium above the lobby. And an elevator will whisk you up to a lovely room with gleaming hardwood floors, Oriental rugs, European period furnishings, and window seats from which you can view the bay or the hills of Monterey through multipaned glass.

At night you will snuggle up in a sea of down pillows and comforters atop a feather bed. A wood fire burns in the hearth and, from the oceanside rooms, you can hear the surf breaking on the beach below. Romantic, yes. But if you're not in the mood, just press a bedside button to catch the latest HBO movies on the television, which is concealed in an armoire. In the morning, a silver tray bearing freshly squeezed orange juice, fruit, pastries, and a rose will be brought to your room.

The Spindrift Inn is but a short walk from the new aquarium and the many sights of Cannery Row. But you just might want to spend your day loafing on a chaise in the flower-bedecked roof garden with its 360-degree view of the ocean, bay, and Monterey.

Getting There: From the north, take Del Monte Avenue exit off Highway 1 into Monterey and follow signs to Cannery Row. From the south, take Munras Avenue exit off Highway 1, turn left on Soledad, right on Pacific, and follow signs to Cannery Row.

SPINDRIFT INN

652 Cannery Row,
Monterey, California 93940

Telephone: (408) 646-8900,
in California (800) 841-1879,
nationwide (800) 225-2901

Accommodations: forty-two rooms with two doubles or queen- or king-size beds; private baths with tub/showers, some with sauna; some rooms fully equipped for the handicapped; telephones; television.

Rates: expensive to very expensive, breakfast included. Children welcome.

Cards: AE, CB, DC, MC, V

Open all year.

Razzleberry flabjous might be on the morning menu, and you'll sleep in a room called Tulgey Wood or Borogrove with views of the garden or Monterey Bay. All this nonsense comes from the "Jabberwock" poem in *Alice in Wonderland.* But you won't need a looking glass to enjoy this place, though the binoculars and telescopes placed in the view rooms do help spot the seals and sea otters that bark in the bay. This towered and turreted house on the hillside, four blocks above Cannery Row, was built in 1911 and served as a Catholic convent for fifty years. When Jim and Barbara Allen bought it in 1982 to convert into an inn, they chose the name Jabberwock because Jim loved the sound of it. "When I was a kid, that's the only poem I ever learned," he admits.

The charming guest rooms are decorated with flowered papers, antique furniture, goosedown quilts, and ruffled pillows on which a handmade sachet of potpourri is placed; bathrobes are provided. The Toves, a downstairs bedroom, opens to a private brick patio, while Borogrove offers the best view, along with a fireplace and sitting area. Two garret rooms share a sitting area with a bay view that extends all the way to Santa Cruz.

Plenty of places for relaxation are provided: a homey living room with a brick fireplace, a glassed-in veranda with rattan chairs and tables for puzzles or games, and the garden, which is filled with ferns, roses, begonias, dahlias, and irises. A big Continental breakfast is served at fireside in the dining room, with Jabberwock-inspired names for the day's dish etched in reverse on glass. At five o'clock a bell bids you to gather with other guests for refreshments. At any time of the night or day you may help yourself to complimentary soft drinks from a refrigerator dubbed "The Tum Tum Tree." And when you retire with cookies, milk, and a Lewis Carroll volume on the bedside table, you'll truly think you're in Wonderland.

Getting There: From the north on Highway 1, take Del Monte Avenue exit into Monterey, following signs to Cannery Row through the tunnel to Lighthouse Avenue. Turn left on Hoffman to Laine, and turn left again. From the south, take Munras Avenue exit off Highway 1, turn left on Soledad and right on Pacific Street, which leads to Lighthouse Avenue. Pickup at Monterey airport by advance arrangement.

THE JABBERWOCK

598 Laine Street,
Monterey, California 93940

Telephone: (408) 372-4777

Accommodations: seven rooms with queen- or king-size beds; three rooms have private baths with showers, others share two baths with tub/shower or shower; no telephones; no television.

Rates: moderate to very expensive, breakfast included. No smoking.

No credit cards.

Open all year.

In the days when Pacific Grove was a major stopover on the Chautauqua circuit, many Victorian lodging houses were built around the town. In 1887 J. F. Gosby constructed one of these in a rather simple style. But as his guest register grew, so did the house—in both size and architectural complexity. He built the large Queen Anne tower that now distinguishes the house to spite a neighbor, who had built an intricately ornamented Queen Anne next door.

Gosby's traditions of hospitality, improvement, and growth have been carried on by the inn's present owners, Roger and Sally Post, who also own the Green Gables Inn. After an extensive renovation, they opened the Gosby House Inn in 1977 and have never stopped improving it, adding more units in rear buildings, which open to a pretty garden. Twelve of the guest rooms now have fireplaces, and all have flowered wallpapers and antique furniture. Bowls of fruit and fresh flowers are placed in the rooms.

A gracious innkeeper, dressed in old-fashioned attire, is always on duty to brew a cup of tea or chocolate at any time of the day or help you with restaurant reservations or sightseeing plans. Hot spiced cider and hors d'oeuvres are offered in the evening, and a full breakfast is served in the morning—either in the parlor or in an adjoining game room with a fireplace.

Getting There: From Highway 1, take Highway 68 west to Pacific Grove, turn left at Lighthouse Avenue, and proceed three blocks to the inn.

THE GOSBY HOUSE INN

643 Lighthouse Avenue,
Pacific Grove, California 93950

Telephone: (408) 375-1287,
(800) 342-4888

Accommodations: twenty-two rooms with double, two doubles, or queen-size beds; private baths with tub/showers or stall showers in all but two rooms, which share a bath; wheelchair access; telephones; no television.

Rates: moderate to expensive, breakfast included. Children welcome in some rooms. Smoking permitted only in certain rooms.

Cards: AE, MC, V

Facilities for small conferences. Open all year.

The advent of a railway to Pacific Grove brought affluent vacationers who erected elaborate homes along the craggy coast of Monterey Bay. One of these showplaces—a half-timbered Queen Anne mansion of many gables—was built in 1888 by William Lacy. Roger and Sally Post, who also own the Gosby House Inn, have transformed this handsome residence and an adjacent carriage house into one of the area's most exquisite inns.

The setting dazzles with breathtaking views of the water and mountains beyond, glimpsed from windows that are crafted in myriad sizes and shapes in a seemingly endless number of alcoves, dormers, and bays. From window seats in the bedrooms you can watch the sea otters at play and the seals sunning on the rocks in the bay, and occasionally spot a passing whale. But the most spectacular features of these rooms are the sloping, beamed ceilings that pitch every which way. One of the bedrooms, originally a chapel, has a quadruple set of carved doors and a stunning rib-vaulted ceiling. The Posts have appointed the guest rooms generously: soft quilts

THE GREEN GABLES INN

104 Fifth Street,
Pacific Grove, California 93950

Telephone: (408) 375-2095

Accommodations: eleven rooms with double and queen-size beds, some with trundle beds; four rooms in main house share two baths with tub or shower, others have private baths with showers; no telephones; television in some rooms.

Rates: expensive, breakfast included. Children welcome in carriage house. No smoking in main house.

Cards: AE, MC, V

Open all year.

The Carriage House at the Gosby House Inn

The Green Gables Inn

and a plethora of pillows on the beds, antique writing tables, bowls of fruit, plants, books, and magazines. Only two bedrooms in the main house have private baths, but a caddy of soap and towels, as well as robes, are provided. On the lower floor, a two-room suite has a fireplace edged with Delft tiles and a sofa that makes up into an extra bed.

More alcoves and bays embellish the living room, where a fireplace, rimmed with stained glass, rises to a twelve-foot ceiling. In the dining room, a crystal chandelier is suspended from a graceful medallion over a formal table. There's a fireplace here, too, and a dramatic view through windows framed with latticework. A sit-down breakfast combines a substantial main course—crêpes or Belgian waffles or a frittata—with fresh fruit, juices, granola, and muffins.

Behind the house is a patio planted with azaleas and impatiens; beyond that a carriage house contains five more rooms. These don't have the fairy-tale ambience of the main house, but they do provide more privacy, along with fireplaces, television, and modern baths.

Getting There: From Highway 1, take Highway 68 west to Pacific Grove, continue on Forest Avenue to Ocean View Boulevard, then turn right to Fifth Street.

In 1901 Laura and James Parke, of Parke-Davis Pharmaceuticals, bought one of the bayfront mansions in Pacific Grove, stripped away its Victorian gingerbread, and turned it into a Mediterranean-style villa with a stuccoed exterior and arched windows in front. The Parkes lived in the mansion for forty years. In 1972 Don Martine, former city councilman in Pacific Grove, purchased the house; now Don and his wife, Marion, have made it an inn.

Collecting and restoring antiques is one of their hobbies, and the furnishings of the inn's nineteen bedrooms have come from auctions all over the state: a mahogany suite that was exhibited in the 1893 Chicago World's Fair; a bedroom set that belonged to Hollywood designer Edith Head (and her portrait, as well); an Eastlake suite from the home of newspaper publisher C. K. McClatchy, to name a few. Many of the rooms have fireplaces, and some have partial or panoramic views of Monterey Bay. But even if you can't see the bay, you can hear the waves breaking on the rocks from every room in the house, and you can admire the view from sitting rooms on each floor or from the large breakfast room.

MARTINE INN

255 Oceanview Boulevard, Pacific Grove, California 93950

Telephone: (408) 373-3388

Accommodations: nineteen rooms with double, queen-, or king-size beds; private baths with tub/showers or stall showers; one room fully equipped for the handicapped; telephones; no television.

Rates: expensive to very expensive, breakfast included. Smoking permitted only in certain rooms.

Cards: MC, V

Facilities for weddings and small conferences. Open all year.

Each morning a buffet is set out here on Victorian and Sheffield silver: muffins or biscuits in a silver soup tureen, platters of fruit, a hot egg dish such as asparagus or avocado Benedict, and orange juice in crystal glasses. Silver coffee pots sit on the round tables, which are topped with lace cloths and roses. Hors d'oeuvres and wine are offered in the evening. Hospitality is important here. The Martines place a silver bridal basket of fruit in each guest room. And, if you want to go on a picnic, they'll pack a lunch for you for a modest fee.

Music plays an important role in the Martines' lives. The inn boasts a pump organ and three pianos: a baby grand in the parlor, an upright player piano in the library, and a Coinola in a game room off the rear patio; there's an 1870s pool table here, too.

Getting There: From Highway 1, take Highway 68 west to Pacific Grove, continue on Forest Avenue to Oceanview Boulevard and turn right.

SANTA CRUZ

In 1791 the Spanish padres erected the Santa Cruz Mission at the north end of Monterey Bay. By the 1890s the town had become the queen of the seaside resorts, noted for its boardwalk, casino, and fashionable homes on the hill above the beach. In this century, however, the town's status as a resort declined. The old Victorians near the beach became cheap rooming houses or were replaced by boxlike motels, and the boardwalk became best known for its giant amusement park, annual Miss California pageants, and shoddy clientele. Then in the 1960s the construction of a University of California campus on the hills behind the city infused new life into Santa Cruz. A gigantic downtown renovation was undertaken, and now the beach area is being reclaimed through the restoration of run-down Victorians as bed-and-breakfast inns.

If the boardwalk is too honky-tonk for your taste, many quieter beaches line the bay; deep-sea charters and facilities for pier fishing are also available. Stream fishing, hiking, and nature trails are found in the redwood-forested Santa Cruz Mountains, which rise behind the town. Just six miles north of town, a steam-powered narrow-gauge railroad provides a scenic ride through the big trees. A few miles south of Santa Cruz are the historic community of Aptos and the beach town of Capitola.

Getting There: From Monterey, take Highway 1 north. From San Francisco, take Highway 280 to San Jose and Highway 17 through Los Gatos to Santa Cruz.

A block from the Santa Cruz boardwalk, Chateau Victorian is one of the restored relics from the city's past. Today, with its exterior painted in burnt-orange with brown trim, the elegant house seems out of place among the nondescript motels around it. But once inside, you are treated to every luxury a Victorian inn can offer. Owner-innkeepers Franz and Alice-June Benjamin spent over a year on the renovation, adding modern tiled baths and plush mauve carpeting throughout. All of the seven bedrooms have wood-burning fireplaces, one with a marble facade. One room has a marvelous canopied four-poster; brass or iron bedsteads are found in other rooms. Springlike Laura Ashley prints adorn the walls, bedding, and curtains, and the rooms are appointed with comfortable wing or lounge chairs. One of these rooms opens to a flower-filled brick patio, which separates the main house from a small rear cottage containing two other units.

Franz Benjamin, a former engineer from Menlo Park, loves his new profession and his adopted city. He takes pride in serving local delicacies, such as croissants and muffins from nearby bakeries and fresh fruit from orchards in the area. Breakfast is served in the dining area at little tables covered with lace cloths or, on balmy days, out on a secluded deck.

Getting There: From Highway 1 or Highway 17, take Ocean into Santa Cruz. Turn right on Barson and left on Campbell, which becomes Riverside after it crosses the river. Turn right on Second, left on Cliff, and right on First.

CHATEAU VICTORIAN

118 First Street,
Santa Cruz, California 95060

Telephone: (408) 458-9458

Accommodations: seven rooms with queen-size beds; private baths with showers, one with tub/shower; no telephones; no television.

Rates: moderate to expensive, breakfast included. No smoking.

Cards: AE, MC, V

Open all year.

L ong before the Spaniards settled Santa Cruz, the brook that babbles through the hills above the town was offering hospitality of sorts. The Ohlone Indians lived on the wooded cliffs above the creek where they fished and bathed, and in 1796 the mission fathers built a grist mill on the stream. Early in this century a dozen silent movies were filmed by the side of the brook in a log cabin that is now the nucleus of the present three-story house. Early residents included a vice consul of the last Russian czar and, later, a European countess (allegedly self-proclaimed); both entertained lavishly. Then for some forty years the building housed the Babbling Brook restaurant. Finally, in 1981, it became Santa Cruz's first B&B.

Surrounded by redwoods, the main house has a wide deck overlooking a waterfall and the creek. In the common room, where wine and cheese are offered in the evening, comfortable chairs and sofas are clustered around a big fireplace. Breakfast is served at round tables for two—usually a hot dish accompanied by homemade muffins and breads, fresh croissants, orange juice, and platter of fruit.

THE BABBLING BROOK INN

1025 Laurel Street,
Santa Cruz, California 95060

Telephone: (408) 427-2437

Accommodations: twelve rooms with queen- or king-size beds; private baths with tub/showers; wheelchair access; telephones; television.

Rates: moderate to expensive, breakfast included. Children over twelve welcome. Smoking discouraged in guest rooms.

Cards: AE, MC, V

Open all year.

The Babbling Brook Inn

Four of the bedrooms are in the old house, while another eight are located in three recently built two-story shingled units amid the gardens. The beds are picture pretty with eyelet or floral print comforters, dust ruffles, and a plethora of pillows. All but two of the rooms have small Franklin-type fireplaces and most have private decks overlooking the brook or the lovely garden, which extends up a steep hillside to a stone wall built by the Ohlone Indians. Below is a stone patio, a barbecue pit (built by the countess), an old wishing well, and a six-step waterfall.

Tom and Helen King, the present owner-innkeepers, are no strangers to the hospitality business. He started Braniff's hotel division and developed hotels throughout the western hemisphere. Innkeeping also comes naturally to Helen. After raising six children and caring for a houseful of their friends, she says, "I'm just doing what I always did, except on a grander scale."

Getting There: From Highway 1 in Santa Cruz, turn toward the ocean on Laurel Street.

The sugar-rich Spreckels family built three look-alike summer houses in the late nineteenth century. Claus Spreckels constructed one for himself on his deer park near Aptos and prefabricated another for shipment to Hawaii. Spreckels' brother-in-law and business associate, Claus Mangels, built the third house in the 1880s, in the redwood-forested mountains above Aptos. The design of the houses, which are flanked by broad, columned verandas, had a distinctive southern look, most likely due to Spreckels' residency in Charleston after he immigrated from Germany. Descendants of the Mangels family owned the Aptos house until 1979, when Ron and Jacqueline Fisher bought it and later turned it into a bed-and-breakfast inn.

Today the Mangels House sits on four acres of lawn, orchards, and woodlands, bounded by the Forest of Nisene Marks State Park. The rooms, which still contain some of the original furnishings, combine rusticity with elegance. In the large living room, Oriental rugs adorn the polished redwood floors, and a grand piano contrasts with a rough-hewn stone fireplace. High windows offer views of the surrounding forests. The five upstairs bedrooms vary greatly in size and decor, ranging from a tiny room all frilly with eyelet to a spacious, masculine-looking room that contains African artifacts the Fishers collected on their travels. One room has a fireplace, another a private balcony, and all are festooned with bouquets of roses and other flowers grown in the garden.

MANGELS HOUSE

570 Aptos Creek Road (Box 302), Aptos, California 95001

Telephone: (408) 688-7982

Accommodations: five rooms with twin, double, queen-, or king-size beds; some shared and some private baths with showers or tub/showers; no telephones, no television.

Rates: moderate, breakfast included. No smoking in bedrooms. Children over twelve welcome.

Cards: MC, V

Open all year.

A full breakfast is served in the Mangels House's formal dining room: fresh fruit and juice, muffins and croissants, and a hot egg dish such as an apple soufflé. After breakfast you might want to engage in a game of darts or table tennis on the veranda. For other diversions, the beach at Capitola is only minutes away, and behind the inn, Nisene Marks Park maintains trails through its ten thousand acres of redwood forests.

Getting There: From Highway 1, south of Santa Cruz, take Seacliff-Aptos exit east to Soquel Drive. Turn right and just after the underpass turn left into the Forest of Nisene Marks State Park. You will be on Aptos Creek Road; continue into the redwoods until you see the Mangels House sign on the right.

SAN FRANCISCO BAY AREA

THE PENINSULA

SAN FRANCISCO

SAUSALITO

POINT REYES AREA

BERKELEY

BENICIA

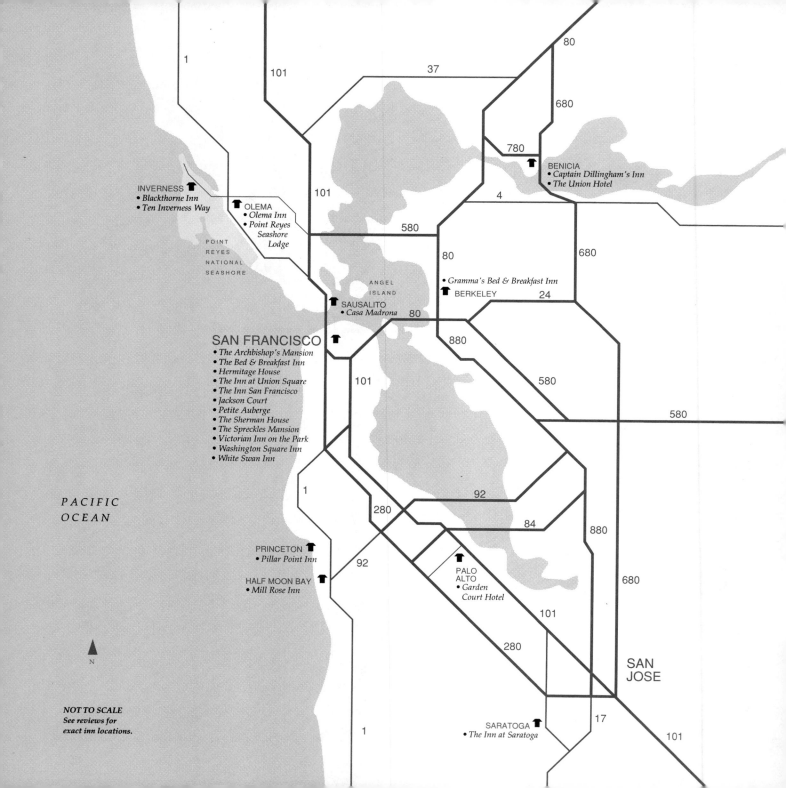

1

101

37

80

680

101

780

BENICIA
• Captain Dillingham's Inn
• The Union Hotel

INVERNESS
• Blackthorne Inn
• Ten Inverness Way

OLEMA
• Olema Inn
• Point Reyes
  Seashore
  Lodge

101

4

580

POINT
REYES
NATIONAL
SEASHORE

ANGEL
ISLAND

80

680

• Gramma's Bed & Breakfast Inn

BERKELEY

24

SAUSALITO
• Casa Madrona

80

880

SAN FRANCISCO
• The Archbishop's Mansion
• The Bed & Breakfast Inn
• Hermitage House
• The Inn at Union Square
• The Inn San Francisco
• Jackson Court
• Petite Auberge
• The Sherman House
• The Spreckles Mansion
• Victorian Inn on the Park
• Washington Square Inn
• White Swan Inn

101

580

580

PACIFIC
OCEAN

1

92

280

84

880

PRINCETON
• Pillar Point Inn

92

PALO
ALTO
• Garden
  Court Hotel

680

HALF MOON BAY
• Mill Rose Inn

101

280

N

SAN
JOSE

NOT TO SCALE
See reviews for
exact inn locations.

1

SARATOGA
• The Inn at Saratoga

17

101

THE SOUTH BAY

Most Californians think of Napa and Sonoma as the wine country, but the San Francisco Bay Area has another premium wine region: the Santa Cruz Mountains. In the eastern foothills of the mountains that rise above Silicon Valley, you'll find such prestigious winemaking names as Ridge, Mount Eden, Martin Ray, and David Bruce. Also nestled in the foothills are the picturesque villages of Los Gatos and Saratoga, where smart shops and chic restaurants serve those who have cashed in their silicon chips for splendid mansions in the hills.

In the flatlands of Silicon Valley sprawls metropolitan San Jose. Founded in 1777, San Jose was the first California town to be settled as a pueblo, rather than as a fort or mission. It served as capital of California from 1849 to 1851 and for the next century was primarily an agricultural area. Though its suburbs have now displaced the orchards, the most famous farm of all still thrives in nearby Palo Alto—Stanford University.

Now Saratoga can boast an inn of a class equal to the clientele of the local restaurants and shops. The Inn at Saratoga is a small luxury hotel, built in 1987 primarily as a hostelry where the computer kings could lodge their visiting VIPs in style. Apple Computer's headquarters are only ten minutes away. Though the hotel is located just half a block off Saratoga's main street, its setting is restful and sylvan; all the rooms and suites, each with private balcony, overlook a creek and a pretty park filled with eucalyptus, sycamore, and maple trees.

The rooms are tastefully decorated with contemporary furnishings and contain all the amenities world-class travelers expect: oversized beds, remote-control color television, hair dryers and double vanities in the bathrooms, wet bars and whirlpool baths in the top-of-the-line suites. They also contain a feature unique to Silicon Valley: telephone outlets for computer modems!

Continental breakfast and tea are served in a lovely little lobby or on a terrace overlooking the park. Full meals are not served since the many fine restaurants of Saratoga are only a stroll away.

Getting There: From San Jose or Santa Cruz, take Highway 17 to Los Gatos and head north on Highway 9 to Saratoga. Once in town, turn left on Big Basin Way and right on Fourth Street. To reach Saratoga from San Francisco, take Highway 280 to Sunnyvale and head west on Saratoga-Sunnyvale Road.

THE INN AT SARATOGA

20645 Fourth Street,
Saratoga, California 95070

Telephone: (408) 867-5020,
in California (800) 543-5020,
outside California (800) 338-5020

Accommodations: forty-seven rooms or suites with two doubles or king-size beds; private baths with tubs and showers; telephones; color television; air-conditioning.

Rates: expensive to very expensive, breakfast included. Children welcome.

Cards: AE, MC, V

Open all year.

This gracious mission-style structure, with wrought-iron balconies and a central courtyard filled with flowers and fountains, conjures visions of a long and colorful history—but in fact it was built in 1986, a project of interior designer Nan Rosenblatt. And if you have stayed at her hostelries in San Francisco—The Inn at Union Square and the Washington Square Inn—you'll recognize some of her touches in the decor.

Most of the rooms have canopy-draped four-posters in king and queen sizes, with down comforters and pillows; some have fireplaces, whirlpool tubs, and balconies or terraces overlooking the courtyard. All are decorated in restful pastel hues of green, peach, and mauve, and all have comfortable sitting areas. In the luxurious tiled bathrooms, you'll find a rose on the marble counter and fluffy terry cloth robes. Little touches are important here, such as *The Wall Street Journal* as well as the local paper delivered to your door each morning, along with your shoes, freshly shined.

Each of the hotel's three upper floors has a sitting room where a Continental breakfast and high tea are served. But you would be just as happy sitting in the beautiful first-floor parlor/lobby, which also has a fireplace. Entering the hotel from the street, you see first a giant bowl of fruit, which says something about the kind of hospitality dispensed at the Garden Court.

Getting There: From Highway 101, take University Avenue exit and head west to Cowper Street; turn left.

GARDEN COURT HOTEL

520 Cowper Street,
Palo Alto, California 94301

Telephone: (415) 322-9000,
in California (800) 556-9595,
nationwide (800) 824-9028

Accommodations: sixty-one rooms or suites with two doubles, queen-, or king-size beds; private baths with tub/showers; some rooms fully equipped for the handicapped; telephones; remote-control television.

Rates: very expensive, breakfast included. Children welcome.

Cards: AE, MC, V

Facilities for conferences and weddings. Open all year.

The coastal town of Half Moon Bay, some thirty miles south of downtown San Francisco, is becoming a popular getaway spot for Bay Area residents. The town's Main Street is lined with turn-of-the-century streetlights and buildings, and the surrounding area is dotted with nurseries and fields of artichokes and pumpkins, which create a blaze of orange in the autumn. Beaches and the fishing village of Princeton are nearby.

On a quiet side street in Half Moon Bay, the Mill Rose Inn is tucked behind a rose-covered picket fence and an English garden bursting with hundreds of petunias, daisies, bougainvillea, and the like. This romantic spot is the creation of landscape designer Terry Baldwin and his wife, Eve, an interior decorator. The main house is an old-fashioned cottage with a cozy parlor and sitting room where afternoon refreshments are served. Adjoining is a charming two-story inn where all the antique-filled rooms have wood-burning fireplaces, private entrances, and pretty

MILL ROSE INN

615 Mill Street,
Half Moon Bay, California 94019

Telephone: (415) 726-9794

Accommodations: six rooms with double, queen-, or king-size beds; private baths with showers or tub/showers; telephones; television.

Rates: expensive to very expensive, breakfast included. Children over twelve welcome. No smoking.

Cards: AE, MC, V

Facilities for small conferences. Open all year.

Mill Rose Inn

baths with claw-foot tubs for two; a refrigerator in each room is stocked with complimentary goodies.

Downstairs a fire burns in the tile-faced hearth of a lovely breakfast room; French doors lead to the gardens on either side. In the mornings, Eve serves a full champagne breakfast here or in your room, if you choose. In addition to fruit, juices, pastries, and homemade jams, she offers a hot dish, such as quiche or eggs, along with bacon or sausages.

But the pride of the inn is a seven-foot octagonal spa and cascading fountain, surrounded by fragrant blooms, in a large gazebo behind the house. And in your room you'll find fluffy robes for your walk to the spa.

Getting There: From San Francisco, take Highway 280 south to Highway 92 and head west; when you reach Half Moon Bay, turn left on Main Street, then turn right on Mill Street. From Monterey, take Highway 1 to Kelly Avenue exit, turn right, then turn left on Church to Mill Street.

This pretty harbor north of Half Moon Bay has a shady history of smuggling, gambling, and prostitution. But today the tiny village is a commercial and sportfishing center and the site of several good seafood restaurants. And very recently, with the construction of the Cape Cod–style Pillar Point Inn, it's become a place for an overnight getaway.

The inn is located across the street from the harbor, and all eleven guest rooms have views of the boats bobbing in the water. For the most part the rooms are look-alikes, but it's a terrific look: navy-blue carpeting, fireplaces on raised hearths of blue and white tiles, window seats with café curtains and pillows in good-looking blue and white prints. You sleep on a feather bed covered with sheets and down quilts in the same print, and no less than six ruffled pillows. Each room has a modern refrigerator encased in a replica of an old-fashioned wooden ice box. But one feature distinguishes each room: a collection of historical photographs of the area based on various themes.

Downstairs a parlor and breakfast room, with a see-through tiled fireplace between them, are decorated in the same style as the guest bedrooms. Guests are offered tea in the evening, and in the morning innkeeper Mary Lococo prepares a full breakfast, which includes juice, homemade muffins, and a hot dish such as Italian quiche or eggs Benedict.

Getting There: From San Francisco, take Highway 1 south to Princeton. Turn right and follow Capistrano Road past Pillar Point Harbor.

PILLAR POINT INN

380 Capistrano Road,
Princeton, California
(Mailing address: Box 388,
El Granada, California 94018)

Telephone: (415) 728-7377

Accommodations: eleven rooms with queen- or king-size beds; private baths with tub/showers; one room fully equipped for the handicapped; telephones; television.

Rates: moderate to expensive, breakfast included. Smoking and nonsmoking rooms.

Cards: AE, MC, V

Open all year.

SAN FRANCISCO

San Francisco is the needle's eye through which the threads of California history have converged. Spanish missionaries first introduced European culture to the area when they arrived in 1776. But it was the fortunes in gold from the Mother Lode in the 1850s, and later the silver from the Comstock Lode, that built the city by the Golden Gate. To her teeming port came the European immigrants who planted California's fertile valleys with grapes and returned their wines to San Francisco's splendid tables. And from the redwood forests to the north came the lumber for the ornate houses that soon covered her hills and valleys. The earthquake and fire of 1906 obliterated most of the Victorian houses east of Van Ness Avenue, but many thousands of "the painted ladies" still impart a nineteenth-century aura to the outlying neighborhoods.

Indeed, San Francisco is a city of intimate neighborhoods. North Beach, for example, is as far removed in spirit from Pacific Heights as Genoa is from Boston. Now a number of B&Bs have opened in these neighborhoods, many in Victorians only ten or fifteen minutes from the heart of the city. But if you must be downtown, you'll find a number of small hotels that offer the charm of a country inn.

Getting There: For the sake of simplicity, directions to each establishment are given from Van Ness Avenue. If you are entering the city from the Bay Bridge or on Highway 101 from the south, follow the freeway signs to the Golden Gate Bridge until you come to the Van Ness exit. If you are entering via the Golden Gate Bridge, follow the signs to downtown and Lombard. Go east on Lombard to Van Ness.

This extraordinary hostelry is in a class by itself, and class it does have. The magnificent Pacific Heights mansion, with only fourteen rooms and suites, is closer to the size of a bed-and-breakfast inn, but it operates in the style of a grand hotel. The house was once the home of Leander Sherman, who started his career in San Francisco sweeping streets, but in his twenties became the owner of the city's major music store, later known as Sherman-Clay.

Sherman moved into this exquisite Italianate-baroque villa in 1876, and several decades later built an adjoining three-story, colonnaded music salon where he entertained the prominent musicians of the day—and very often they entertained his other guests. Caruso sang here, and Paderewski played the grand piano. Victor Herbert, Lillian Russell, Lotta Crabtree, and Lola Montez were among other distinguished visitors to the Sherman House.

THE SHERMAN HOUSE

2160 Green Street,
San Francisco, California 94123

Telephone: (415) 563-3600

Accommodations: fourteen rooms and suites with twin or queen-size beds; private baths with tub/showers, some with whirlpool tubs; telephones; color television.

Rates: very expensive, no meals included. Children welcome.

Cards: AE, DC, MC, V

Facilities for weddings and small conferences. Open all year.

The Sherman House

In the early 1980s Manouchehr Mobedshahi, an Iranian-born San Francisco economist, bought and restored the mansion, a rear carriage house, and the formal English gardens, which were originally designed by Thomas Church. The late Billy Gaylord created the interiors—the last project of this noted designer. Most of the suites are done in the style of the Second Empire and some in Biedermeier, with authentic furnishings that Gaylord tracked down at auctions all over the world.

Carrara-marble fireplaces were installed in the guest rooms, which have beds with feather mattresses, down quilts, and brocaded canopies. In many rooms you can enjoy spectacular views of the bay from window seats extravagantly strewn with a dozen or more down pillows. In most rooms the walls are not papered, but upholstered with padded fabric. Even the paint on the walls is a work of art: In the Beidermeier suites, for example, the wainscoting and cornice are hand painted in the *faux bois* technique to emulate natural wood. The baths have walls and fixtures of South American black granite and tiny television sets, so you won't miss the morning news.

The Sherman Suite is the place to stay if you plan to entertain. It opens to a private brick terrace, big enough to accommodate thirty people, with a panoramic view of the bay. The large executive suites in the carriage house lend themselves to parties, too—particularly the lower unit, which has its own private terrace, garden, and gazebo. For even more grandiose entertaining, guests may take over the impressive music hall, which of course has a Sherman-Clay grand piano. But not to worry if you have no pianist. Classical music is piped through the house; in the music room it's accompanied by the soft serenade of a colony of finches that inhabit a bird cage built to look like a French château. Up a grand staircase is a more intimate salon with a fireplace and a bar.

Sherman House employs a Swiss chef who, with the help of two sous chefs, turns out elegant breakfasts, lunches, and dinners for hotel guests and their guests only—the restaurant is not open to the general public. Meals are served on Royal Doulton china in the dining room or in the adjoining solarium and deck. You can order anything you like for breakfast; for dinner the chef prepares an eight- or nine-course *menu dégustation*. Twenty-four-hour room service is available, too. As in most grand hotels, meals are not included in the room rate, but if you have to ask, you shouldn't come here.

If you arrive in San Francisco by air, Sherman House will send a chauffeured limousine to meet your plane. During your stay here, the concierge will arrange for almost anything you need, from word-processing services to personalized shopping, from the translation of foreign documents to obtaining temporary privileges in local clubs. Want to charter a yacht? That's no problem, either.

Getting There: From Van Ness Avenue, turn west on Green Street. From the Golden Gate Bridge, take Lombard to Fillmore, turn right, and turn left on Green Street. The hotel has valet parking.

HERMITAGE HOUSE

2224 Sacramento Street,
San Francisco, California 94115

Telephone: (415) 921-5515

Accommodations: five rooms with twin, double, queen-, or king-size beds, studio couches in some rooms as well; private baths with tubs or showers; private-line telephones on request; television on request.

Rates: moderate to expensive, breakfast included. Children over five welcome. Smoking permitted only in living room.

Cards: MC, V

Open all year.

This seventeen-room, four-story Greek Revival mansion, a block away from Lafayette Park, was built at the turn of the century for Judge Charles Slack. The house was maintained as a single-family residence until the 1970s, when it served as a drug-rehabilitation center. In 1978 Ted and Marian Binkley bought the place to turn into an inn.

On entering, one is impressed by the exceptionally fine carved details in the redwood beams, pillars, and stairway scrolls. A carved mantel, inlaid floors, and a graceful curved bay distinguish the large living room. Marian has decorated a cozy breakfast room with mauve-and-white chintz wallpaper and matching cloths on little round tables. Magnificent leaded-glass cabinets line the walls of this room and of the formal dining room, where a buffet of juices, fruit, freshly baked breads, and cold cereals is laid out each morning.

Most of the bedrooms have working fireplaces, and sitting areas and desks are provided wherever possible. Walls are papered with chintz or floral patterns, beds are brass or four-postered or canopied, and each is stacked with about a dozen pillows of various patterns, sizes, and shapes. Comfort is the byword here. The most unusual room is Judge Slack's former study, under the gabled eaves on the top floor. Paneled in redwood, the room is lined with bookshelves and has a large stone fireplace and a southern view of the city.

With private-line telephones and direct bus service to Nob Hill and downtown San Francisco, Hermitage House is an ideal headquarters for people on the go. But it's also a place to relax. An upstairs refrigerator is filled with ice and cold drinks that can be taken outside and enjoyed on a small sun deck. Or you may laze in a chaise in the sunny western garden.

Getting There: From Van Ness Avenue, head west on Sacramento.

You enter this lovely old mansion through a plant-filled courtyard shared by an adjacent twin house. In the gracious wood-beamed and paneled living room, a fire bids welcome under a monumental mantelpiece of carved Italian marble flanked by love seats upholstered in cinnamon velvet. The hospitable feeling is emphasized by a "welcome home" sign on the wall of the staircase that leads to the upstairs bedrooms. These are light and spacious, painted in bright colors with contrasting trims, and furnished with a blend of antiques and contemporary pieces: Oriental rugs on the hardwood floors, custom-made quilts on the beds. Several of the rooms have fireplaces, and all have comfortable sitting areas, desks, color cable television, and telephones with private lines; the rooms were designed with business travelers in mind. Plants, flowers, and books are scattered about.

Each of Jackson Court's three floors has a kitchen; one has a small brick fireplace. Juices, coffee or tea, croissants, muffins, and jams are set out here each morning, and if you wish to cook yourself something more substantial, you are free to do so if you provide the groceries. A concierge will be happy to make restaurant reservations, obtain theater tickets, and arrange transportation for you.

Getting There: From Van Ness Avenue, head west on Jackson.

JACKSON COURT

**2198 Jackson Street,
San Francisco, California 94115**

Telephone: (415) 929-7670

Accommodations: ten rooms with double, queen-, or king-size beds; private baths with showers; private-line telephones; color cable television.

Rates: moderate to expensive, breakfast included.

Cards: AE, MC, V

Facilities for small conferences. Open all year.

The area around Alamo Square contains an inordinate number of picture-postcard Victorians because it was spared from the great fire of 1906. On the north side of the square, in contrast to the neighboring houses, stands a stately three-story mansion with a slate mansard roof that looks like a manor house in the French countryside. This château was built in 1904 as a residence for Archbishop Patrick Riordan; for four decades he and his successors entertained Catholic dignitaries from all over the world in the imposing first-floor reception rooms. Pope Pius XII stayed here in the 1930s when he was still a cardinal.

In the 1980s the talented team of Jonathan Shannon and Jeffrey Ross (owners of the Spreckels Mansion) restored this spectacular building to create one of the city's most exquisite inns. In keeping with the Second Empire style of the house, they have decorated it with museum-quality furnishings from France. In the grand hall, a splendid brass chandelier hangs from the coffered mahogany ceiling. Fourteen-foot-high redwood columns with intricately carved capitals flank the base of a three-story stairway crowned with an oval dome of stained glass. In the formal parlor, the triple-vaulted ceiling is painted with a motif derived from a Louis XIV

THE ARCHBISHOP'S MANSION

**1000 Fulton Street,
San Francisco, California 94117**

Telephone: (415) 563-7872

Accommodations: eighteen rooms with queen- or king-size beds; private baths with tubs and/or showers; direct-dial telephones; television available on request.

Rates: expensive to very expensive, breakfast included. No smoking in most public rooms.

Cards: AE, MC, V

Facilities for small conferences. Open all year.

The Archbishop's Mansion

carpet. Wood-burning fireplaces, most with mirrored and carved mantels, enhance almost every room of the house, including all but two of the guest units.

Since the Archbishop's Mansion is only six blocks from San Francisco's opera house, Shannon and Ross named the rooms and suites after romantic nineteenth-century operas. A bedstead with ivory inlays of Japanese flowers and birds sets the theme for Madame Butterfly's room. A chaise upholstered in silver velvet reclines on a base formed by a gilded silver swan in Der Rosenkavalier's enormous bath-and sitting room. There's also a chaise—as well as a fireplace and freestanding tub—in Carmen's bathroom. In the third-floor rooms, the mansard dormers are fitted with window seats for a peek at the square or the city's hills and skyscrapers rising above the neighboring rooftops. Also on the third floor is the pièce de résistance of this inn: the Gypsy Baron suite, which was once the archbishop's chapel.

The amenities of the Archbishop's Mansion match the decor: embroidered linens, fresh flowers in the rooms, and French milled soaps. A friendly staff is on hand to make dinner reservations, hire a limousine, and offer any other assistance you might need. And of course your Continental breakfast is delivered to your room on a silver tray.

Getting There: From Van Ness Avenue, head west on Fell Street to Steiner and turn right to Fulton; the inn is on the corner. Off-street parking available for eight cars.

San Francisco's first urban inn occupies two brightly painted Italianate houses in a cul-de-sac off Union Street. Marily and Robert Kavanaugh pioneered the B&B movement in this city in 1976 when they remodeled a former boardinghouse. Decorated with extraordinary flair, the inn contains several family heirlooms from England combined with vividly colored contemporary accents. Two years later the Kavanaughs purchased the house next door and added three deluxe units.

The Bed and Breakfast Inn is a place for romance, and its pièce de résistance is a room called Celebration, where a queen-size bed reposes in an alcove papered and curtained with a dainty blue-and-white flowered print. A love seat upholstered in blue velvet occupies a little sitting area, and beyond a divider containing pots of blooming flowers is a sunken bathtub for two.

Each room has its own theme. Mandalay, for example, is decorated with grasscloth, rattan furniture, a Burmese-style ceiling fan, and sheer draperies emulating mosquito netting around the queen-size bed. Green Park and Kensington Garden

THE BED AND BREAKFAST INN

4 Charlton Court,
San Francisco, California 94123

Telephone: (415) 921-9784

Accommodations: ten rooms with twin, double, queen-, or king-size beds; some rooms share half-baths with showers or tub/showers; some have private baths with showers or double tubs; telephones and television in suites.

Rates: moderate to very expensive, breakfast included. Smoking permitted in public rooms only.

No credit cards.

Open all year.

The Bed and Breakfast Inn

open to a flower-filled deck behind the inn. And for those who travel in style, a penthouse suite provides a living room, a dining area, a full kitchen, and a latticed terrace filled with plants; a spiral staircase leads up to a bedroom loft that, like Celebration, is outfitted with a double tub. All the rooms have special touches: a bouquet of fresh flowers on the nightstand, a bowl of fruit and selection of current magazines on a table, beds turned down to reveal the pretty printed sheets and pillowcases, and on each pillow a fortune cookie.

Breakfast is as important as the beds here. Juice, freshly ground coffee, and hot croissants (or occasionally "sticky buns") are served on antique flowered Copeland china. Some guests prefer to enjoy this meal in the breakfast room or outdoors on umbrella-covered tables in the garden, but Marily likes to pamper you with a breakfast tray in bed.

The Bed and Breakfast Inn is located in San Francisco's Cow Hollow district, named for the dairy farms that once covered the area. The neighborhood is a treasure trove of Victorian architecture, notably along Union Street, where the colorfully painted old houses have been turned into chic shops, bars, and restaurants. But if you prefer to while away a day in the inn, a cozy library contains a game table for backgammon, cards, or puzzles, a color television, and a leatherbound collection of the works of Dickens.

Getting There: From Van Ness Avenue, turn west on Union Street to Charlton Court (between Buchanan and Laguna) and turn left.

San Francisco's ethnic mix is mirrored in Washington Square, a small park at the base of Telegraph Hill. This square started out ignobly in the 1840s as the potato patch of Juana Briones, the hill's first settler, and was later dubbed the "Spanish Lot." During the gold rush, when an influx of Chilean forty-niners settled here, the area around the park became known as Little Chile. Later came the Italians, who moored their fishing boats at nearby wharves, and then the Chinese, who have overflowed into North Beach from neighboring Chinatown.

Today, in the early mornings the buttoned-down-collar types walk their dogs in Washington Square while runners jog and middle-aged Chinese faithfully perform their t'ai chi exercises. Later in the day, elderly Italian gentlemen take over the park benches, reading *Italo-Americana.* On the square's western perimeter, once the site of a Russian Orthodox church, the Washington Square Bar & Grill attracts the city's literati, among others. And on the east side, with a view of the park and Russian Hill beyond, is the Washington Square Inn.

WASHINGTON SQUARE INN

1660 Stockton Street,
San Francisco, California 94133

Telephone: (415) 981-4220

Accommodations: fifteen rooms with twin, double, queen-, or king-size beds; private and shared baths with tubs, showers, or tub/showers; telephones; television on request.

Rates: moderate to very expensive, breakfast included. Children welcome. Smoking not permitted in lobby.

Cards: AE, MC, V

Open all year.

In 1978 this two-story corner building was totally refurbished by interior designer Nan Rosenblatt. The fifteen bedrooms are individually decorated with bright French florals and chinoiserie, European antique armoires and dressers. Most of the beds are draped with canopies. Three of the rooms are large bedroom–sitting room combinations with sofa beds, suitable for families of four. The others vary from small to spacious.

Breakfast, which may be taken in your room or in the lobby, is a spread of orange juice, fresh fruit, and an assortment of breads—muffins, croissants, scones, cheese brioche, *pain au chocolat.* Afternoon tea is served beside an intricately carved fireplace in the lobby: cucumber sandwiches, imported cheeses, and a variety of cookies; guests may also purchase a bottle of wine from the inn's cellar.

Washington Square is midway between downtown San Francisco and Fisherman's Wharf, and there is much to see and do in the immediate vicinity. A block away is upper Grant Avenue, the center of the Beat movement in the 1950s and now the site of a conglomeration of crafts shops, antiques stores, coffeehouses, and so forth; a few blocks south, Grant leads into Chinatown. Many of the city's finest restaurants are within walking distance of the inn. If you wish to wander farther afield, the innkeeper will arrange a car rental or just about anything else to enhance your visit—from theater tickets to a stenographer to a picnic.

Getting There: From Van Ness Avenue, take Union Street east to Stockton and turn left.

In the 1890s many wealthy San Franciscans built their mansions along the Panhandle, a wooded, grassy plot one block wide and eight blocks long leading to Golden Gate Park. One of these houses—an ornate four-story Victorian with an open Belvedere tower—was built in 1897 for United States congressman Thomas Clunie. In more recent years, the place was occupied by a cult group that believed in rebirthing, a rite that took place in a hot tub in the basement. Now the house itself has been reborn as an inn under the aegis of Lisa and William Benau and Lisa's parents, Shirley and Paul Weber.

The woodwork is spectacular: The parquet floors are inlaid with oak, mahogany, and redwood; the entry hall is intricately paneled in mahogany; and the dining room is distinguished by oak wainscoting and an unusual spooled plate rack. Lisa and her mother furnished the inn with authentic period pieces: a velvet-upholstered Queen Anne set in the parlor, brass and carved-wood headboards in the bedrooms, marble-topped sinks in the baths.

**VICTORIAN INN
ON THE PARK**

301 Lyon Street,
San Francisco, California 94117

Telephone: (415) 931-1830

Accommodations: twelve rooms with twin or queen-size beds; private baths with showers or tub/showers; telephones and television on request.

Rates: moderate to expensive, breakfast included. Smoking not permitted in dining room.

Cards: AE, MC, V

Open all year.

Victorian Inn on the Park

Six guest rooms occupy the second floor. The largest has a fireplace and view of the Panhandle from the curved bay of the tower. The smallest is a light-splashed, glassed-in porch with a sunken tub in the bathroom. And the most unusual is decorated with Art-Deco stained glass and posters. Four rooms share the top floor; one claims the open tower as its private deck.

Breakfast, served in the dining room, consists of fresh fruit, cheeses, orange juice, flaky croissants, and homemade breads. If guests wish, the Benaus will arrange catered dinners or allow the use of a small library for private meetings.

With the Panhandle parkway at its front door, this inn is also popular with walkers, joggers, and cyclists. Golden Gate Park, containing museums and the Japanese Tea Garden, is only seven blocks away; at its entrance bicycles can be rented for exploring a thousand acres of flower-filled meadows, woods, and lakes.

Getting There: From Van Ness Avenue, take Fell Street west to Lyon. The inn is on the corner.

After enduring a turbulent notoriety in the 1960s as the blossoming place for San Francisco's flower children, the Haight Ashbury district has become again a quiet residential neighborhood. This area on the northern slopes of Twin Peaks was countryside until the 1890s, when a flurry of building activity made it a popular suburb. Today some twelve hundred relics of Victorian architecture line the area's streets. One of these houses, a splendid example of the Colonial Revival style, was built in 1898 for Richard Spreckels, superintendent of the Western Sugar Refinery owned by his uncle, sugar baron Claus Spreckels. The stately mansion, facing the heavily wooded Buena Vista Park, has had a way of attracting artistic people. Jack London reportedly worked in the top-floor ballroom at one time, as did Ambrose Bierce. And during the 1960s, the Grateful Dead's producers owned the house and used the old ballroom as a rock recording studio.

In 1979 architect Jeffrey Ross and designer Jonathan Shannon bought the house and converted it into an inn. An amazing number of the original embellishments were still intact: seven fireplaces, some with rare detailing such as a tortoiseshell tile hearth in the master bedroom; hand-painted Meissen chandeliers; museum-quality windows of leaded stained glass (many with Art Nouveau overtones); embossed wall coverings with gilt friezes; and Corinthian columns in the hall and parlor. Ross and Shannon blended French and English *fin de siècle* furnishings. All of the rooms have sitting areas with wing chairs, and fanciful touches are found throughout. The bed in one room, for example, is set in a columned alcove

THE SPRECKELS MANSION
737 Buena Vista West,
San Francisco, California 94117

Telephone: (415) 861-3008

Accommodations: ten rooms with queen-size beds; some shared baths, mostly private baths with tubs and/or showers; telephones; television on request.

Rates: expensive to very expensive, breakfast included.

Cards: AE, MC, V

Open all year.

with a canopy swooping up to Corinthian capitals. Many of the bedrooms—and even the master bathroom—have fireplaces, and most have views of Buena Vista Park or look out over Golden Gate Park to the ocean.

The third-floor ballroom is now a stunning two-bedroom suite suitable for small conferences. A gabled redwood ceiling soars some thirty feet over the living room, which also boasts a huge fireplace and raised sitting areas with spectacular views as far as the Marin headlands.

Next door to the mansion is a handsome Edwardian building that is now part of the inn. The bedrooms here are designed to inspire fantasies. Entering the very Edwardian English Rose, one would not be surprised to find Sherlock Holmes sitting in the black wing chair in front of the brick fireplace. Gypsy Hideaway also has a fireplace, as well as a view and a paisley-engulfed bed that will make you think you've been abducted by a gypsy caravan. And the many skylights in Stargazers' Suite encourage flights of fancy to outer space.

In the morning trays of juice, croissants, just-baked breads, and coffee are brought to the rooms. In the evening refreshments are served in the library of the main house. From here it's a pleasant stroll to Haight Street, where the former hippie hangouts have been transformed into upscale shops and restaurants.

Getting There: From Van Ness Avenue, go west on Market Street to Haight and head west to Buena Vista West.

In 1776 the Spanish chose the flattest and warmest part of San Francisco as a site for Mission Dolores and its surrounding farmlands. The area was ignored by later settlers until the 1860s, when a streetcar line connected the boomtown of San Francisco with the sunny fields to the south. Amusement parks, a racetrack, and fashionable homes soon lured the gold-rich San Franciscans to the Mission District. In this century, however, the affluent moved to the hills on the north side of the city and abandoned the area "South of the Slot" to working-class residents and a growing number of Latin American immigrants. But the pendulum again swung to the Mission in the 1960s, when a new generation of San Franciscans discovered the bargain-priced Victorians and the blue skies that bless the district when most of the city is shrouded by fog.

Among the newcomers was Joel Daily, who restored an 1872 three-story Italianate mansion that had been converted into a hotel. The inn opened in 1980, but the improvements never end. Downstairs, the double parlor is resplendent with fourteen-foot ceilings, redwood paneling and wainscoting, and carved fireplaces.

THE INN SAN FRANCISCO

943 South Van Ness Avenue, San Francisco, California 94110

Telephone: (415) 641-0188

Accommodations: fifteen rooms and one suite with double, queen-size, or two queen-size beds, rollaways available; most rooms have private baths with showers, tubs, or tub/showers; direct-dial telephones; color television.

Rates: moderate to expensive, breakfast included. Children welcome.

Cards: AE, MC, V

Facilities for small garden weddings. Open all year.

The Inn San Francisco

Here (starting at six o'clock in the morning for the convenience of business travelers) Joel lays out a buffet of tropical fruits, hard-cooked eggs, and home-baked breads and muffins.

Most of the inn's fifteen bedrooms have private baths, a few have hot-tubs-for-two with views, and a first-floor room has its own outdoor spa. These pools are somewhat redundant, however, because Joel has built, for all the guests' use, a lovely spa in a gazebo amid English gardens on the side of the house. He also owns the house next door, which has a large garden suite with a parlor and a Victorian kitchen; this unit sleeps six. In addition to the gardens, a favorite place to relax is a rooftop deck that commands a panoramic view of San Francisco and the mountains of Marin beyond.

Despite all the renovation that is going on, the Mission District today is still an economically and ethnically mixed neighborhood. The brightly painted restored Victorians along South Van Ness are interspersed with run-down buildings and commercial properties, and a block away on Mission Street you are likely to hear more Spanish than English. But the area is only minutes from downtown by bus or BART, and it has the best weather in the city.

Getting There: Take Van Ness Avenue south across Market, where it becomes South Van Ness. Parking garage across the street from the inn.

For those who want to stay in the heart of San Francisco, the Inn at Union Square offers a personalized alternative to the commercial hotels. One-half block from the square and its elegant shops, the inn had been a sixty-room hotel for transients before it was renovated in 1980 by interior designer Nan Rosenblatt, owner of the Washington Square Inn. She cut the number of guest units to thirty, creating some two-room suites from the smaller rooms and a luxurious sixth-floor suite with a fireplace, wet bar, whirlpool bath, and sauna.

The decor and service at the Inn at Union Square are very similar to those at the Washington Square Inn. The bedrooms are furnished with English antiques, bright fabrics drape the beds and cover the goosedown pillows, and fresh flowers are set in the rooms. Each floor has a small lobby with a fireplace, where an English tea and hors d'oeuvres are offered in the afternoons. Bottles of wine may be purchased from the inn. A Continental breakfast—croissants, juice, fruit, and coffee—is served by the fireside in each lobby or in the rooms.

THE INN AT UNION SQUARE

440 Post Street,
San Francisco, California 94102

Telephone: (415) 397-3510

Accommodations: thirty rooms with twin, queen-, or king-size beds; private baths with tub/showers; telephones; color television.

Rates: expensive to very expensive, breakfast included. Children welcome.

Cards: AE, MC, V

Open all year.

As at Washington Square, the Inn at Union Square has a concierge to take care of restaurant reservations, theater tickets, and the like. Valet parking is available at the door.

Getting There: From Van Ness Avenue, go east on Post Street.

Halfway up Nob Hill from Union Square, these small sister hotels offer the charm of a French or English country inn and every personalized service you can imagine. An attendant will park your car and a houseman will escort you to your room, where the scent of potpourri fills the air and the flick of a switch starts a gas flame in the fireplace. Each room is richly appointed with flowered wallpapers, antique writing desks, comfortable chairs or sofas, plants, bowls of fresh fruit, and armoires that conceal color television sets.

Although the amenities are the same at both hotels, their decors are different. Petite Auberge is frilly French with its baroque facade, ruffled muslin curtains, and quilted spreads. The newer White Swan is done up in a cooler English style with white shuttered windows, white spreads, Laura Ashley prints, and tones of aquamarine, mauve, and burgundy throughout. Both are older hotels that have been renovated by Roger and Sally Post, who also own the Gosby House and Green Gables inns in Pacific Grove.

Petite Auberge and White Swan both have lovely parlors with fireplaces where afternoon tea is served; the White Swan also has a handsome, very British-looking library with another fireplace and a fine selection of books. Adjacent to the parlor in each inn is a breakfast room where a substantial morning buffet is offered—fruit, juices, breads, pastries, muffins, cereals, granola, cheese, and a main dish that changes daily, sometimes a soufflé, frittata, or quiche. For fine weather there are outdoor eating areas, too.

At each inn a concierge will help with your dinner reservations. When you return to your room, your bed will be turned down, with a Swiss chocolate and a rose placed on the pillow. Both inns are romantic places to share with someone special. But if you happen to be traveling alone, you'll find a teddy bear on the bed to cuddle with. If you like, you can even take your furry friend home, for a price.

Getting There: From Van Ness Avenue, head east on Bush.

PETITE AUBERGE

863 Bush Street,
San Francisco, California 94108

Telephone: (415) 928-6000

Accommodations: twenty-six rooms with queen-size beds; private baths with showers or tub/showers; direct-dial telephones; color television.

Rates: expensive to very expensive, breakfast included. Children welcome.

Cards: AE, MC, V

Open all year.

WHITE SWAN INN

845 Bush Street,
San Francisco, California 94108

Telephone: (415) 775-1755

Accommodations: twenty-seven rooms with queen- or king-size beds; private baths with tub/showers; wet bars; direct-dial telephones; television.

Rates: expensive to very expensive, breakfast included. Children welcome.

Cards: AE, MC, V

Facilities for small conferences. Open all year.

J ust across the Golden Gate Bridge from San Francisco is the colorful town of Sausalito, once a Portuguese fishing village and now a chic residential community where houses cling to the steep, wooded hills that rise from the bay. On one of these hillsides overlooking the harbor stands a stately mansion, which since its construction in 1885 has metamorphosed into a hotel, bordello, beatnik boardinghouse, and European-style pension. Finally, under the present ownership of John Mays, Casa Madrona is one of the state's most elegant inns.

After buying the property in 1978, Mays restored the rooms in the mansion, decorating them in turn-of-the-century style with different themes—one reminiscent of a bordello, another with a nautical touch, and so forth. Next, he renovated three adjoining cabins as guest rooms. Then in 1983 he took the plunge—literally—and constructed a cluster of cottages down the bank from the mansion to the waterfront. Each is different, but all are built in a style characterized by peaked roofs, dormers, bays, skylights, balconies, and decks. And each of the sixteen units was decorated by a different designer, resulting in a mix of styles ranging from Oriental to Victorian to Art Nouveau. One room emulates the look of a French château, another an Italian villa, another a New England summer retreat. Perhaps the most unusual is a Parisian artist's loft with skylights and a raised platform equipped with an easel, canvas, and paints; paintings by former occupants of this room are hung on the walls. Most of the rooms have working fireplaces, and all have dazzling views of the bay.

Another magnificent view of the yacht harbor and Belvedere Island is glimpsed from the dining room of the old mansion, where a buffet breakfast is served. Along with juice, fruit, yogurt, and croissants, copies of the *Los Angeles Times, New York Times,* and *San Francisco Chronicle* are provided. Later in the day, the dining room becomes a romantic restaurant, serving creative adaptations of American fare for lunch, dinner, and Sunday brunch.

Many of Casa Madrona's guests are actually visitors to San Francisco who want to get away from the city milieu. Sausalito itself offers much to do with its quaint shops, crafts galleries, coffeehouses, and restaurants. Commuting to the big city can be a pleasant event via a thirty-minute ferryboat ride across the bay.

Getting There: From San Francisco, take Highway 101 north across the Golden Gate Bridge. Take the Alexander Avenue exit, which becomes Bridgeway, and follow it into the center of town. Marin Airporter offers service from San Francisco International Airport to Sausalito, where the hotel will pick up guests. Daily ferryboat service from Sausalito to Fisherman's Wharf or the Ferry Building in San Francisco.

CASA MADRONA

801 Bridgeway,
Sausalito, California 94965

Telephone: (415) 332-0502

Accommodations: thirty-two rooms or suites with twin, double, queen-, or king-size beds, rollaway beds and Japanese futon mats available; private baths with showers and/or tubs; some rooms with wheelchair access and one room fully equipped for the handicapped; telephones; color television on request.

Rates: moderate to very expensive, breakfast included. Children welcome.

Cards: AE, CB, DC, MC, V

Facilities for small conferences and weddings. Open all year.

Casa Madrona

POINT REYES AREA

The San Andreas Fault runs down the center of Tomales Bay, a long, fingerlike inlet separating the Point Reyes peninsula from the mainland. A railroad once ran down the east shore of the bay, bearing lumber from the northern timberlands. Today Highway 1 follows its tracks, carrying carloads of Sunday drivers to the town of Marshall to feast on the bay's gastronomic gift to California: oysters. The west side of the bay shelters the village of Inverness, a popular resort. Beyond this is the Point Reyes National Seashore: seventy thousand acres of coastal wilderness, beaches, and trails for hiking, biking, and horseback riding. In the park a model village has been built, typical of those inhabited by the Miwok Indians, who once dwelled on these shores. And here is the harbor that purportedly sheltered Sir Francis Drake's *Golden Hinde* during his expedition to the Pacific in 1579. Point Reyes is one of the best spots for birdwatching in the country; over four hundred species have been observed in the park. In the winter months whale watching draws enormous crowds. On weekends park rangers conduct nature walks along the beaches and lectures in the visitors' centers at Bear Valley and Drakes Beach.

Getting There: From San Francisco, take Highway 101 north to the San Anselmo exit. Continue westward on Sir Francis Drake Boulevard (Highway 17) over the mountains to the intersection with Highway 1 at Olema. To reach Inverness, turn north on Highway 1, and just before Point Reyes Station, turn left on Sir Francis Drake.

In the mid-nineteenth century, Olema was a lively vacation spot and commercial center for the surrounding ranches and dairy farms. The town boasted three hotels and a racetrack, and was even a candidate for the county seat. One of these hotels, now the Olema Inn, started as a saloon in 1876, and was later called Nelson's Hotel after its owner, John Nelson, who operated the stagecoach from San Rafael to Olema. In its heyday the hotel attracted visitors from throughout the state, including celebrities like Jack London and John Steinbeck; Teddy Roosevelt reportedly visited here, too. After serving as an army barracks during World War II, the hotel was boarded up for some three decades.

In the mid-1970s Sausalito architect Gene Wedell spearheaded a project to restore the Colonial American–style hotel as a historic landmark. The Olema Inn reopened in 1980, but shut down again some six years later. Now new owners, working with Wedell, have spruced it up, gutting the top floor to create six cozy bedrooms.

OLEMA INN

10,000 Sir Francis Drake Boulevard, Olema, California 94950

Telephone: (415) 663-9559

Accommodations: six rooms with twin or queen-size beds; private baths with showers or tubs with hand-showers; no telephones; no television.

Rates: moderate, breakfast included. Children welcome.

Cards: AE, MC, V

Open all year.

These are decorated with furnishings from the early 1900s (mirrored armoires and the like) and bright prints ranging from Early American to contemporary Marimekko. The rooms are small, but they have private baths dressed up with brass fixtures and blue-and-white French tiles.

The Olema Inn restaurant occupies most of the first floor area. Its three high-ceilinged dining rooms look out to the woodsy surroundings and are filled with works by local artists depicting the Point Reyes area. A little bar-library serves as a sitting room for inn guests by day, a gathering spot for locals at night. In the rear, an open deck provides tables for relaxing and dining, and a seafood bar dispenses oysters just plucked out of Tomales Bay. The restaurant is open to the public for dinner and weekend lunch, but in the morning a full breakfast is served here to inn guests only. House-baked breads and muffins are offered, along with fresh fruit, juices, and a choice of hot entrées.

Getting There: The inn is at the intersection of Sir Francis Drake Boulevard and Highway 1.

Until recently about the only visitor attraction in Olema was the Olema Inn. But in 1988 a spectacularly designed three-story lodge of knotty cedar was constructed there. It fronts the highway, but its rear lawns and gardens slope down to a creek, where a bridge leads to the Point Reyes Wilderness. All the guest rooms are oriented to the rear, with views of the wooded mountains beyond.

Running the lodge is a family affair. Brothers Tom and Jeff Harriman own the inn; their sister, Judy Burkes, and her husband, John, manage it. John actually built most of the ash furnishings because the Burkes' couldn't find what they wanted ready-made. The guest rooms have a contemporary look, with beds covered with down quilts, and paintings by local artists on the walls. Many rooms boast single or double whirlpool tubs that share the view from the room or, if you wish, they may be screened off with sliding shoji panels for privacy. Many units also have decks or balconies, and some have fireplaces set in hearths of vibrantly colored tiles. Three suites have two-story-high sitting rooms and loft bedrooms.

A breakfast room with a stone fireplace in the corner opens to the terrace and lawns. A buffet of fresh fruit and pastries is set out here. And if the weather isn't right for a stroll in the woods, you'll find indoor recreation: A billiards room holds a magnificent antique Brunswick pool table. High tea is served in the afternoons.

Getting There: When Sir Francis Drake Boulevard intersects Highway 1, turn right.

POINT REYES SEASHORE LODGE

10021 Coastal Highway 1 (Box 39), Olema, California 94950

Telephone: (415) 663-9000

Accommodations: twenty-one rooms and suites with twin, double, or queen-size beds; private baths with showers or whirlpool tub/ showers; telephones; no television.

Rates: moderate to expensive, breakfast included. Children welcome.

Cards: AE, MC, V

Open all year.

Here is an inn for young-at-heart romantics. The nucleus of Blackthorne is a 1930s cabin on a steep forested hillside. In 1975 patent attorney Bill Wigert designed an amazing structure around it using salvaged pier beams. An eight-sided tower with a spiral staircase rises from the cabin through two floors flanked with decks to an octagonal eagle's nest room, topped by a platform that peeks out of the treetops. Bridges connect tower rooms to hillside walkways and a deck with a hot tub, cold tub, and bathhouse.

The two bedrooms in the main cabin have private entrances and sitting areas; one has its own deck. Above are a glass-walled solarium and the living room with its dramatic, skylighted A-frame ceiling of rough-hewn wood. A walk-in stone fireplace shelters a cast-iron stove and pillows, often occupied by the inn's cats. Oriental rugs on burnished wood floors, along with comfortable sofas and chairs, create a gracious aura. Bill's wife, Susan, manages the inn, and serves a breakfast of juice, cakes or muffins, quiche, fruit salad, granola, and yogurt.

A climb up the spiral staircase brings you to two other bedrooms with arched windows and pitched ceilings. Balconies off of one of these rooms overlook both the deck and the living room. At the top of Blackthorne is the eagle's nest. This eight-sided room is enclosed by multipaned floor-to-ceiling windows that look out onto oak, Douglas fir, and bay trees. A skylight offers a view of the stars, and a ladder leads up to the rooftop deck. This is not exactly your conventional inn.

Getting There: Take Sir Francis Drake Boulevard through Olema towards Inverness. Turn left on Vallejo Avenue at the Inverness Park Grocery, two miles south of Inverness.

BLACKTHORNE INN

266 Vallejo Avenue (Box 712), Inverness, California 94937

Telephone: (415) 663-8621

Accommodations: five rooms with double or queen-size beds; one private and two shared baths within the inn, one in outside bathhouse, all with showers; no telephones; no television.

Rates: expensive, breakfast included. No smoking in guest rooms.

Cards: MC, V

Open all year.

This lovely redwood-shingled house, surrounded by gardens, is typical of the summer residences built in Inverness early in this century. The inn's owners, writer Mary Davies and her husband, Jon Langdon, provide a peaceful, homelike environment for those who want to escape the pressures of city life. One guest summed it up: "Coming here is like going home, when you don't live there any more." That's exactly how you feel when you enter the restful, fir-paneled living room, furnished with antiques and Oriental rugs—a quiet spot for reading or playing Scrabble during the day, but livelier in the evening when guests congregate around the big stone fireplace for some music from the player piano.

Upstairs the cozy bedrooms, paneled with white-painted beaded tongue-and-groove siding, are simply furnished with patchwork quilts, many made by Mary, and rag rugs. The nicest room is in front, with windows along one side offering a

TEN INVERNESS WAY

10 Inverness Way, Inverness, California 94937

Telephone: (415) 669-1648

Accommodations: four rooms with twin, double, or queen-size beds; private baths with showers or tub/showers (some across hall); no telephones; no television.

Rates: moderate, breakfast included. "Well-behaved people of all ages" welcome.

Cards: MC, V

Open all year.

Ten Inverness Way

peek at Tomales Bay. Next door is a tiny room, made romantic by skylights. Some of the baths have skylights, too. But the ultimate bath—a hot tub for two—is located in its own tiny outbuilding in the rear gardens.

In the morning, you'll awake to the aroma of bread baking. Mary not only bakes all the breads for the inn, she makes the preserves, too. Blackberry-buttermilk pancakes are a favorite breakfast standby, but sometimes she whips up something exotic like curried scrambled eggs served with homemade chutney. Food is not the only diversion in the sunny breakfast room. A set of binoculars permits a close look at the acorn woodpeckers that inhabit the trees and the ospreys that sometimes swoop by. Mary will also give you expert advice on where to hike, bike, ride horses, and swim.

Getting There: Take Sir Francis Drake Boulevard into Inverness village, and turn left at the Inverness Inn Restaurant.

No real gramma actually lives here, but a large portrait of the owner's grandmother, Elizabeth Taber, hangs in the stairwell. She was an Irish immigrant who ran a boardinghouse in Boston. Kathy Kuhner has dedicated this inn to her and instigated some grandmotherly practices, such as keeping a cookie jar stocked at all times.

Gramma's is located in a complex of turn-of-the-century buildings, a five-minute walk from the University of California's Berkeley campus. The main house is a Tudor-style mansion with most of the original detailing intact, such as the intricately inlaid hardwood floors and foliated plaster friezes. In the living room, a graceful bay of leaded-glass windows looks out to the big trees that screen the inn from busy Telegraph Avenue. In the rear, the enormous windows of the breakfast area open to a broad deck and gardens, where a fountain bubbles away.

Rooms in the main house range from small to quite large, with sitting areas and window seats; one has a private deck. In the rear of the garden, the former servants' quarters have been reconstructed into elegant accommodations with tiled fireplaces and windows on two sides. Recently Kathy acquired a Queen Anne Victorian next door with a carriage house in the rear, adding another ten guest rooms to the inn. The Queen Anne is a showplace with inlaid floors, hand-painted ceilings, marble fireplaces, and stained-glass windows.

GRAMMA'S BED AND BREAKFAST INN

2740 Telegraph Avenue, Berkeley, California 94705

Telephone: (415) 549-2145

Accommodations: thirty rooms with twin, double, queen-, or king-size beds; all but two rooms have private baths with tubs and/or showers; some rooms fully equipped for the handicapped; telephones; television.

Rates: moderate to expensive, breakfast included. Children by special arrangement.

Cards: AE, MC, V

Facilities for weddings. Open all year.

For breakfast, Gramma's serves some of the best granola in town, along with fresh fruit, croissants, cereal, and French-roast coffee. On Sundays, the public is invited in for an elaborate champagne brunch, which includes buffets of cold dishes, hot dishes, and desserts. For inn guests, complimentary coffee and tea are available all day; wine and cheese are served in the evening Monday through Friday. And if you want to entertain at Gramma's, a greenhouse room will seat up to twenty-five for dinner.

Getting There: From San Francisco, cross the Bay Bridge and follow signs to Berkeley via Highway 80. Take Ashby Avenue exit east to Telegraph Avenue and turn left.

BENICIA

Benicia was founded in 1846 on the Carquinez Straits, where the Sacramento and San Joaquin rivers flow into San Francisco Bay. During the gold rush, Benicia's strategic location brought such prosperity that the town rivaled San Francisco as a commercial center, and for a year in the 1850s Benicia was the capital of California. It was also the site of a major United States Army arsenal, and so noted for its educational institutions that it was dubbed the Athens of California. Then history and commerce bypassed Benicia, resulting in a rare phenomenon—an entire nineteenth-century town largely intact, possessing some of the most significant buildings of California's early history.

Today Benicia is enjoying a renaissance as both a growing suburban community and a mecca for antiques hunters and history lovers. Along First Street, the center of Benicia's Old Town, you'll find numerous antiques shops, crafts studios, and art galleries. And almost every weekend there's some sort of celebration—parades, handicraft fairs, and a peddlers fair in August that brings some three hundred antiques dealers to the town. Year-round attractions include fishing, cycling, birdwatching, and strolling around the historic buildings of this nineteenth-century town.

Getting There: From San Francisco, take Highway 80 northeast to Vallejo and Highway 780 east to the downtown Benicia exit. Turn left on Second Street, turn right on Military, and then turn left on First Street, which leads to Old Town.

One of Benicia's restored buildings is the Union Hotel, built in 1882 not far from the water's edge. The interior of the three-story structure was rebuilt to provide comforts like modern tiled bathrooms, all with whirlpool tubs. Each of the twelve guest rooms is decorated around a different theme: Louis le Mad with tufted, gilded pseudo-French furnishings; Four Poster with a Queen Anne canopy bed; Mei Ling with Chinese Chippendale; 1932 with metallic Art Deco pieces, and so forth. Many of the rooms have lovely views of Carquinez Bay and the bridge that arches over the straits. All are scented with potpourri.

A bar and restaurant occupy the first floor, separated from the street by floor-to-ceiling windows of stained and leaded glass. A hand-carved 1886 bar lines one wall of the saloon, which is furnished with armchairs and love seats around low marble-topped tables. The hotel has no common room, so this saloon also serves as a salon for a complimentary breakfast of orange juice, cereals, and freshly baked muffins and breads.

Getting There: Continue on First Street to Old Town; the hotel is on the right.

THE UNION HOTEL

401 First Street,
Benicia, California 94510

Telephone: (707) 746-0100

Accommodations: twelve rooms with queen- or king-size beds; private baths with whirlpool tub/showers; telephones; color television.

Rates: moderate to expensive, breakfast included; lower rates on weeknights. Children welcome.

Cards: AE, CB, DC, MC, V

Open all year.

Shipping and shipbuilding were major industries in Benicia's heyday, and many sea captains made the town their home. One of these was William W. Dillingham, who booked lodgings with the widow Jane Paladini. He eventually married his landlady and enlarged her home, which was originally built in the 1850s. Their residence became a center for the town's social life and was owned by the Dillingham heirs until 1981.

Benicia booster Roger Steck and some partners bought the house, built a two-story addition in the rear, and opened Captain Dillingham's Inn in 1985. Steck had owned an antiques business, and furnished the inn with authentic and unusual pieces from ports of call around the world. In fact, each bedroom is decorated in a different theme—Arabic, French, Spanish, Chinese, and suchlike—as if a roving sea captain had collected these treasures during his journeys.

In one room you will find a gaudy wall hanging that was once the interior of a Bedouin tent. A rare collection of framed navigational charts from the 1800s distinguishes another room. And in another there's a headboard from Brittany with a curtained opening; originally this was the entrance to an enclosed bed. One of the nicest bedrooms is the former parlor of the old house, which boasts a beautiful onyx

CAPTAIN DILLINGHAM'S INN

145 East D Street,
Benicia, California 94510

Telephone: (707) 746-7164

Accommodations: ten rooms with twin, double, queen-, or king-size beds; private baths, most with whirlpool tubs; wheelchair access; telephones; television.

Rates: moderate to expensive, breakfast included.

Cards: AE, CB, DC, MC, V

Facilities for weddings and small conferences. Open all year.

fireplace and a large whirlpool tub. In the new wing, French doors open from the rooms to either a deck or a brick patio, both of which face a large garden abloom with marigolds and zinnias in summertime, mums in the fall. The upstairs rooms have cathedral ceilings, one with a skylight, and all are equipped with standard-size whirlpool tubs.

Hand-pegged plank floors of cherrywood gleam in the handsome breakfast room, where a buffet (once the end piece of an English hunt table) holds a selection of fresh fruit, breads, pastries, cereals, granola, and marinated veggies, such as artichokes, cauliflower, and pickled beets. Guests may eat here at a twelve-foot-long refectory table from France, or outside at umbrella-topped tables on the multitiered decks, brick patio, and adjacent gazebo. This area, which will comfortably accommodate over a hundred people, is popular for weddings.

Behind the house, a small grove of gnarled eucalyptus trees recalls a little-known chapter of Benicia's history. No trees grew in the town until a local priest encouraged the sea captains to bring back saplings from their travels. Thus the exotic greening of Benicia.

Getting There: Proceed down First Street and turn left on East D.

THE GOLD COUNTRY

SACRAMENTO

THE MOTHER LODE

FROM JAMESTOWN TO NEVADA CITY

LAKE TAHOE

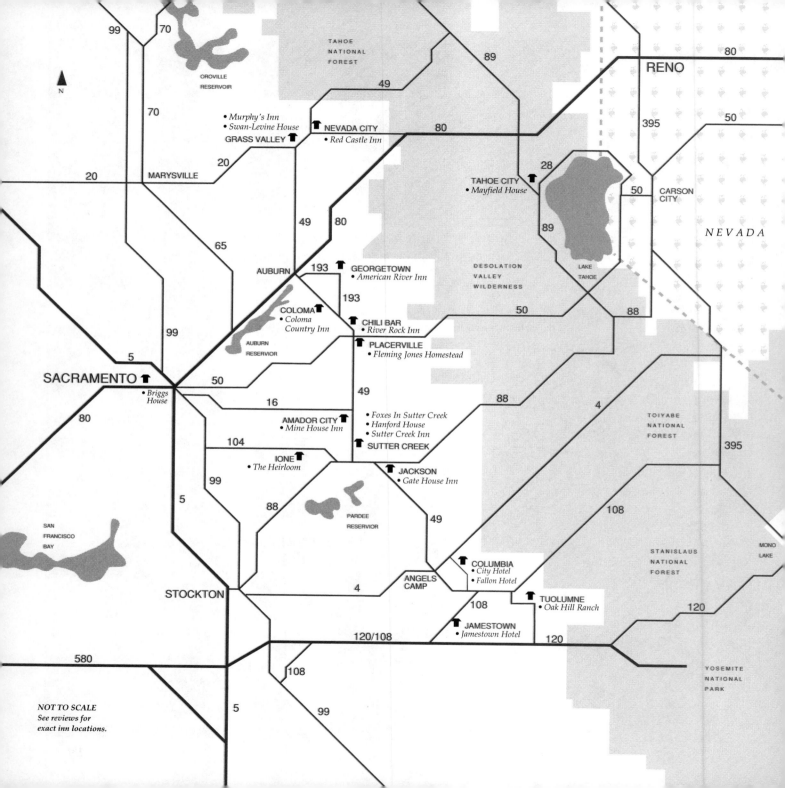

SACRAMENTO

In 1839, when California was still part of Mexico, a Swiss adventurer named John Sutter obtained a Mexican land grant to establish the colony of Nuevo Helvetia at the spot where the American River, coming down from the Sierras, flows into the Sacramento River. Here, on the site of present-day Sacramento, he built Sutter's Fort with timber extracted from the nearby mountains. Then on January 24, 1848, at one of Sutter's sawmills in Coloma, up in the Sierra foothills, James W. Marshall found some glittering specks in the mill tailrace. These turned out to be gold, and the destiny of California was forever changed. Marshall rushed back to Sacramento to share his discovery with Sutter, who agreed to keep the strike a secret. But the news leaked out and within the next decade some hundred thousand prospectors came to the Mother Lode, taking $550 million in ore from her rich veins.

Neither Sutter, who lost his holdings and was bankrupt by 1852, nor Marshall, who died a pauper, ever prospered from the Sierra mines. Among those who really struck it rich during the gold rush were the merchants of Sacramento, where the miners came to spend their diggings. Four of the wealthiest shopkeepers—Charles Crocker, C. P. Huntington, Mark Hopkins, and Leland Stanford—later turned their profits into gigantic fortunes by starting the Central Pacific and Southern Pacific railroads. In 1854 Sacramento became the capital of California and later the western terminus of the Pony Express.

Today the colorful early history of this city has been recaptured in Old Sacramento, a restoration and reconstruction of the old town along the riverfront. Here wooden sidewalks pass by the Huntington Hopkins Hardware Store, Pony Express terminus, an old Wells Fargo office, and a bevy of restaurants and shops. Other tourist attractions in Sacramento include the Crocker Art Gallery, the Railroad Museum, the reconstruction of Sutter's Fort, riverboat cruises, and, of course, the capitol itself and the many Victorian mansions that were built nearby. In a quiet area just east of the capitol, several of these older homes have been turned into inns.

Getting There: From San Francisco, Highway 80 leads to Sacramento; from Los Angeles, take Highway 5. Sacramento is serviced by Amtrak.

S ue Garmston and a group of dedicated women brought the bed-and-breakfast concept to Sacramento in 1981, when they transformed a lovely 1901 Colonial Revival home near the capitol into an inn. They furnished the place with family antiques: Oriental rugs on the hardwood floors, lace curtains, crocheted, patchwork, or quilted bedspreads, and pretty printed sheets. A downstairs bedroom has a wood-burning fireplace, one of the upstairs units has a private sun deck, and out back a rustic garden cottage contains two suites. The rooms are filled with fresh flowers and touches that make this a very special place: engraved stationery, bathrobes for the guests' use, and in each room hardbound diaries where tenants record their impressions of the inn or their adventures in Sacramento.

The day begins with a full breakfast served on old-fashioned china either in your room, in the parlor, or in the pretty rear garden, which is planted with camellias, firs, and orange trees. In season, oranges from these trees provide the freshly squeezed juice for the morning meal. Homemade breads, muffins, and jams are also served, along with the cook's daily creation—things like frittatas and baked apples with cinnamon sauce. In the early evening, beverages, fruit, and nuts are served before the fire. An unusual sauna set in a wine cask and a big hammock offer relaxation in the garden. And if you want to take a spin on a bicycle, the inn will provide that, too. As one guest wrote in his diary: "The house is exquisite! I plan to tell only very special people about it."

Getting There: Take 15th Street exit from Highway 80, turn right to 16th Street, turn left, and stay on 16th until you reach Capitol Avenue. Turn right on Capitol.

BRIGGS HOUSE

2209 Capitol Avenue, Sacramento, California 95816

Telephone: (916) 441-3214

Accommodations: five rooms and two suites with twin, double, or queen-size beds; some private and some shared baths, tub/showers and stall showers; telephones in some rooms; no television; air-conditioning.

Rates: moderate, breakfast included. Younger children welcome in garden cottage. No smoking.

Cards: AE, MC, V

Facilities for small conferences. Open all year.

TUOLUMNE COUNTY

Sonora is the seat of government and commerce for this southern Mother Lode county. But two nearby gold rush towns—Jamestown and Columbia—are the central tourist attractions of the Sonora area. They look as though they were sets for wild-west movies, and indeed, many westerns have been shot on their streets. The gold rush came to Tuolumne County in 1848, when a seventy-five-pound nugget was discovered in Woods Creek, which once flowed down the present main street of Jamestown. Hordes of prospectors swarmed to the area, among them Colonel George

James. A Philadelphia lawyer and veteran of the Mexican War, James founded the town but later skipped, deeply in debt to suppliers and employees. So embittered were the local folk that they renamed the town American Camp, but the original name of Jamestown was soon revived, and later it became a bustling railroad center. Today "Jimtown" is one of the most picturesque sights in the Mother Lode, with the balconied facades of the old buildings overhanging raised wooden sidewalks. Movie fans will recognize the typical Old West town as the site of *High Noon, Duel in the Sun,* and *Butch Cassidy and the Sundance Kid.* Another hundred feature films were shot on the line of the Sierra Railway, whose steam-powered locomotives now pull trainloads of vacationers through the oak-studded Sierra foothills. The railway depot is in Jamestown's Railtown 1897, now a state historic park with a twenty-six-acre roundhouse and shop complex where vintage rolling stock is exhibited. You can even pan for gold near Jamestown today; prospecting expeditions are conducted daily from the old livery stable on Main Street.

In 1850 gold was discovered at Columbia (then called Hildreth's Diggings), to the northeast of Jamestown. Within three years the town's population grew to some twenty thousand, and the city ranked as second largest in California. In its heyday, this boomtown boasted forty saloons, one hundred and fifty gambling houses, eight hotels, four banks, and two volunteer fire companies. Despite the efforts of the latter, most of the original frame structures were destroyed in two early fires, and the town was almost completely rebuilt in brick. The Columbians' paranoia about fire has benefitted posterity. The durability of these brick buildings prompted the state of California to purchase the town in 1945 and restore it as the Columbia Historic State Park. Today, except for an onslaught of sightseers, the tree-shaded Main Street with its boardwalks and balconied buildings looks much the way it did in the 1860s. No automobiles are allowed in the town itself, but a stagecoach does lumber through, offering visitors a ride. The old blacksmith shop, harness and saddle shop, carpenter shop, and a Chinese herb store are in working condition.

If you tire of sightseeing, other recreational activities in the area include tennis, fishing, hunting, swimming and waterskiing in nearby lakes, horseback riding, golf, and river trips down the Stanislaus. Yosemite National Park is close by, as are several ski areas in the Sierras. Sonora and Jamestown offer a number of good restaurants, but two of the best places to eat in the area happen to be at the historic hotels described on the following pages.

Getting There: From San Francisco, take Highway 580 east to Tracy; then go east on Highway 205 to Manteca and east on Highway 120 to Highway 108, which leads east to Sonora.

Among the historic buildings in Columbia that were restored by the state are the City and Fallon hotels. Both are operated by the Hospitality Management Program at Columbia Junior College as on-the-job training sites. The first to be restored (for some $800,000) was the City Hotel, with its wrought-iron balconies overhanging the sidewalk of Main Street. Built in 1856, the hotel was ravaged by fire in 1867 and rebuilt four years later. The bedrooms have been impeccably furnished with massive Victorian burled-wood bedsteads (framing comfortable mattresses), brass coat racks, and marble-topped bureaus. An upstairs parlor, reserved for guests' use, is stocked with books and games.

Downstairs are the What Cheer Saloon and a high-ceilinged dining room, which is a serene setting for the magnificently appointed tables set with cut-glass goblets, graceful wine glasses of varying sizes, flowered service plates, small brass hurricane lamps, and even silver napkin rings on the sparkling white napery. The food here is far removed from the mountain-country cooking you might expect to find in the Mother Lode. The sophisticated, classical French menu would come as no surprise in New York or Paris. Now it's really no surprise in Columbia, either, because the restaurant has become well established as one of northern California's finer dining places.

In 1986 the state completed a $3.5 million restoration of Columbia's Fallon Hotel. The rooms were decorated in an ornate high-Victorian style that is more gay nineties than gold rush; many of the furnishings are original to the hotel. Downstairs is an old-fashioned ice-cream parlor where breakfast is served to hotel guests. Next door is the Fallon House Theatre, which is now the year-round home of the Columbia Actors Repertory.

At both hotels, the staff and their student helpers are attired in nineteenth-century dress. Both places serve a light breakfast of orange juice and freshly baked breads, muffins, and rolls. Rooms have only half baths, but the trip down the hall to the showers is made as pleasant as possible; the management thoughtfully provides each guest with a "bathroom caddy," a basket containing soap, washcloth, shower cap, and even terry cloth shower shoes.

The City and Fallon hotels cosponsor "An Evening on the Town in Columbia," a package that includes dinner at the City Hotel, dessert at the Fallon Ice Cream Saloon, and a ticket for a Fallon Theatre production.

Getting There: From Sonora, head north on Highway 49 until you come to the sign for the road to Columbia.

CITY HOTEL

Box 1870,
Columbia, California 95310

Telephone: (209) 532-1479

Accommodations: **nine rooms with twin, double, or two double beds; private half baths, community showers; no telephones; no television.**

Rates: **moderate, breakfast included. Children welcome.**

Cards: **AE, MC, V**

Facilities for small conferences. Open all year except Christmas and Christmas Eve.

FALLON HOTEL

Box 1870,
Columbia, California 95310

Telephone: (209) 532-1470

Accommodations: **thirteen rooms with twin, double, or two double beds; private half baths, community showers; one room fully equipped for the handicapped; no telephones; no television.**

Rates: **inexpensive to moderate, breakfast included. Children welcome. No smoking in guest rooms.**

Cards: **AE, MC, V**

Facilities for conferences and weddings. Open all year.

City Hotel

Oak Hill Ranch

On an oak-studded knoll, surrounded by the pine forests of the lower Sierra, stands a replica of a Victorian that few could distinguish from the real thing. Sanford Grover and his wife, Jane, built the four-bedroom house in 1979 as a family home and then turned it into an inn. Although the structure is new, designed by their architect son, the details—a mahogany fireplace, redwood doors, and an intricate staircase—are period pieces collected by the Grovers.

Furnishings include a pump organ and a dining room table that seats twenty. Here the Grovers, dressed in turn-of-the-century attire, serve a hearty full breakfast, typically melon, an omelet with bacon, and biscuits with homemade jelly.

There are four guest rooms in the main house, two with private baths and Eastlake furniture. Of the two rooms that share baths, one has a canopied bed and a private balcony. Down the hill from the main house is a small cottage that was once a milking barn for this fifty-acre dairy ranch. The "cow palace," as it's known, has its own living room with a large slate fireplace, a bedroom, and complete kitchen; the cottage will accommodate up to six persons.

A Victorian gazebo and dance patio in the gardens have made Oak Hill a popular spot for weddings; the inn is also used as a site for small conferences. Although Oak Hill Ranch is but fifteen minutes from Sonora, this is peaceful countryside with the quiet broken only by the sounds of cows, roosters, crickets, and bullfrogs.

Getting There: From Sonora, take Highway 108 to Tuolumne Road (E-17), which leads into Tuolumne. There turn right on Carter Street, left on Elm Street, and right on Apple Colony Road, which leads out of town; turn left on Connally Lane.

OAK HILL RANCH

18550 Connally Lane (Box 307), Tuolumne, California 95379

Telephone: (209) 928-4717

Accommodations: four rooms in the main house with double or queen-size beds; two with private baths, two that share a bath, all with tub/showers; cottage has private bath and kitchen and is fully equipped for the handicapped; no telephones; no television; air-conditioning.

Rates: inexpensive to moderate, breakfast included. No smoking.

No credit cards.

Facilities for weddings and small conferences. Open all year.

Jamestown's colorful Main Street boasts several hotels that look as though they housed the forty-niners. You'd expect to see Black Bart shooting his way out of the saloon or Lola Montez dancing on the balcony. You might guess that the Jamestown Hotel, with its brick walls and ornate wood-balconied facade, is the most authentic hostelry in town, but actually it's the new kid on the block. The building was constructed as a hospital in the 1920s, but in the 1970s a massive renovation project was started, and continued under a number of owners, to transform the place into a gold-rush hotel.

Eight guest rooms and suites occupy the second floor, up a steep flight of stairs, and have been named for colorful characters of the Old West: Black Bart, Lotta Crabtree, Buffalo Bill, Calamity Jane, and the like. Walls are gaily papered and antiques abound: brass bedsteads, wicker settees, patchwork and flowered quilts

JAMESTOWN HOTEL

Main Street (Box 539), Jamestown, California 95327

Telephone: (209) 984-3902

Accommodations: eight rooms and suites with double, queen-, or king-size beds; private baths with showers or tub/showers; no telephones; no television.

Rates: moderate, breakfast included. Children welcome.

Cards: AE, MC, V

Open all year.

Jamestown Hotel

But comforts that Black Bart never would have imagined have been added: queen- or king-size beds and private baths, many with claw-foot tubs. The two front rooms open to the front balcony, and all rooms have access to a large rear deck festooned with planter boxes and umbrella-topped tables.

The first-floor public rooms are quite opulent. Etched-glass doors swing into a handsome, comfortably furnished saloon. And the dining room is lovely, with floral wallpaper in restful hues of mauve, blue, and green; balloon curtains match the print. But Black Bart surely wouldn't recognize the food, which is quite contemporary (grilled seafood, pastas, some Cajun fare, appetizers such as brie encased in phyllo) and consistently good. In the morning a Continental breakfast is served to hotel guests in the dining room or on an adjoining patio.

Getting There: Jamestown is on Highway 108, west of Sonora, shortly after the cutoff to Yosemite. As you turn into Jamestown, you will be on Main Street.

AMADOR COUNTY

Located in the heart of the Mother Lode, this is one of California's smallest counties, yet its mines yielded more than half the gold that came out of the entire Sierra foothills. Gold may still be panned in the streams, and many of the old mines are open to the public. But today the commercial interests of the Amadoreans have turned from the mines to the vines. Amador County's Shenandoah Valley produces some of the state's most distinctive Zinfandel, and many wineries are open for touring.

In Amador County, Highway 49 winds through oak-covered hillsides and the old mining towns of Jackson, Sutter Creek, and Amador City. The brick and clapboard buildings, with their second-story balconies covering raised wooden sidewalks, now house antiques shops, art and craft galleries, and saloons. A visit to the mining town of Volcano is a worthwhile side trip.

Besides mine and wine touring, visiting museums, shopping, and sightseeing, there is fishing and boating at nearby Amador, Pardee, and Camanche lakes; rafting on the Mokelumne River; hunting, tennis, and golfing on a nine-hole course; and even skiing at nearby Kirkwood Meadows. You can also eat well in Amador County. Jackson is particularly noted for its family-style Italian restaurants.

Getting There: From San Francisco, take Highway 580 east through Tracy to Manteca, Highway 99 north to Stockton, and Highway 88 northeast to Jackson. From here Highway 49 leads north through Sutter Creek and Amador City. This area may also be reached by taking Highway 50 to Placerville and proceeding south on Highway 49.

The miners were not the only forty-niners to reap the riches of the Mother Lode. Workers at the mines outside of Jackson toted their ore to the Chichizola General Store to exchange it for food, clothing, and supplies. With this fortune, the Chichizola family built a handsome two-story home next to the store at the turn of the century. Frank and Ursel Walker bought the house and opened its doors for bed and breakfast in 1981.

The original floral wallpaper (in mint condition) and a white tile fireplace distinguish the master bedroom. All the light fixtures were imported from Italy when the house was built, as was the marble fireplace in the living room. Fin de siècle furnishings decorate the rooms, along with fresh flowers and the Walkers' collection of over one hundred priceless old clocks. The choice quarters in the house are a suite with one room overlooking the inn's pretty garden and orchards, and a private staircase to the kitchen—a convenient exit to the lovely swimming pool.

In the garden, a grape arbor leads to a guest cottage where the Walkers have installed a wood-burning stove in the combination bedroom–sitting room, and stained-glass windows in an immense cedar-paneled bathroom. Across the lawn, a screened-in barbecue area is for guests' use. The Walkers, who own a restaurant in Sutter Creek, feed their guests well. Promptly at nine o'clock, a repast of juice, fresh fruit, pastries, muffins, and coddled eggs is served. The large table in the formal dining room is set with bone china, lace and linens, and a rose on each napkin.

Getting There: From Highway 49, head east on Jackson Gate Road, just north of the intersection with Highway 88.

GATE HOUSE INN

1330 Jackson Gate Road, Jackson, California 95642

Telephone: (209) 223-3500

Accommodations: three bedrooms and two suites with queen-size beds; private baths with tub/showers or stall showers; no telephones; no television.

Rates: moderate, breakfast included. No smoking.

No credit cards.

Open all year.

In the 1800s some Virginians settled in the Ione Valley, in the lower foothills west of Highway 49. One of these settlers left a legacy of the Old South: a brick antebellum mansion faced with classical columned porticos. In 1980 Patricia Cross and Melisande Hubbs, two women whose children were grown, bought this architectural heirloom and turned it into an inn.

Indeed, it is a surprise to find this treasure in the small agricultural town of Ione. A long driveway bordered by acacias, eucalyptuses, and fruit trees leads to the house and its secret garden from another era. A giant gnarled wisteria, graceful magnolias, a lush lawn with a gazebo, and a brick terrace nestle up to the lovely old house. A croquet course and hammocks are set up for guests.

The hospitality is as southern as the house. Melisande, who was born in Nashville, and Pat greet their guests warmly and pamper them well. The living room

THE HEIRLOOM

214 Shakely Lane (Box 322), Ione, California 95640

Telephone: (209) 274-4468

Accommodations: six rooms with twin, double, queen-, or king-size beds; two rooms share a bath, four have private baths with showers, tub/showers, or tubs and showers; no telephones; no television.

Rates: inexpensive to moderate, breakfast included.

No credit cards.

Open all year.

Gate House Inn

bids an inviting welcome, too: Comfortable couches are placed by the fireside, and scattered about are Oriental rugs, antiques, tables set with dominoes and jigsaw puzzles, and a square piano once owned by dancer Lola Montez. Adjoining is a cozy breakfast room and the big country kitchen where the innkeepers prepare a morning meal consisting of fresh fruit, dark-roast coffee, and an entrée such as crêpes, quiche, or a soufflé. Many guests prefer to have their breakfast in the gardens or on the balconies that adjoin the upstairs rooms.

The bedrooms are decorated with irresistible charm, using family antiques from the innkeepers' former homes, brass bedsteads with flowered or patchwork quilts, and fresh flowers. One of these rooms has a fireplace, along with its own private entrance, bath, and balcony. Next to the old house, Melisande and Pat built a woodsy cottage with two additional bedrooms. In addition to privacy, these offer skylights, cast-iron wood-burning stoves, and wood-paneled private baths.

Getting There: From Highway 49, take Highway 124 or Highway 88 west to Ione. Turn left on Main Street, right on Preston, and left on Shakely Lane.

California's first bed-and-breakfast inn opened over two decades ago in a century-old, two-story house in the heart of Sutter Creek. In 1966, Jane Way fell in love with the house, once the biggest in town, and soon her B&B shingle was inviting travelers to spend the night. Word spread and later many of the visitors included would-be innkeepers who borrowed her ideas and incorporated them into their own places. Sutter Creek is truly the prototype of a California country inn.

Jane has dressed up every inch of the inn with a riot of color and charm. The living room contains large, comfortable sofas, a hutch filled with antique china, a small piano, and a grandfather clock. A chess set by the fireplace and a tray of homemade cookies and lemonade or coffee await your enjoyment.

But the highlight of a stay at Sutter Creek Inn is breakfast in the combination country-kitchen–dining room, where two long, polished plank tables are gaily set with orange mats, gold-rimmed china, and a pewter pitcher filled with dried flora. Shuttered windows look out to the lawn and gardens. Jane's menu is ambitious: fresh fruit—berries or perhaps peaches just picked from the inn's own trees—along with pancakes full of chopped nuts and apples, cornbread, or a soufflé.

Several bedrooms are located upstairs in the main house, but the most desirable rooms are in the rear outbuildings—the woodshed, carriage house, storage shed, and old laundry house—that Jane has extensively remodeled and furnished

SUTTER CREEK INN

75 Main Street (Box 385),
Sutter Creek, California 95685

Telephone: (209) 267-5606

Accommodations: seventeen rooms with twin, double, or queen-size beds; private baths with showers and/or tubs; no telephones; no television.

Rates: inexpensive to moderate, breakfast included; lower rates on weeknights.

No credit cards.

Open all year except Thanksgiving and Christmas Eve and Day.

Sutter Creek Inn

with flair. Nine of these have fireplaces and four have "swinging beds" suspended by chains from the ceiling. But if you suffer from motion sickness, you won't need Dramamine; the beds can be stabilized easily.

No two of the rooms are alike, except that they are perfectly appointed down to the tiniest details: books, magazines, a deck of cards, and the like. In one you might find a fireplace, in another a Franklin stove, in yet another a sunken bathtub. Some open out to private patios or porches, others into the lovely back garden. Some are furnished in solid Early American maple, others have canopied four-posters, still others contain brightly painted wickerware. Jane transforms whatever she finds around the countryside: an old drum topped with a wicker tray for a table, a miner's scale for a planter, a milk can for a lamp base, two water barrels for the base of a bathroom sink. All is visual joy.

Though there is much to see and do in the Sutter Creek area, one diversion is unique to this particular inn: a session of Jane's handwriting analysis, performed with the warning: "This might change your life completely." So might a visit to Sutter Creek Inn.

Getting There: Highway 49 becomes Main Street in Sutter Creek.

A two-story brick building on the northern edge of Sutter Creek looks like a restored relic from the gold rush days. Actually, it's only a few years old, but behind it is an old Spanish adobe that serves as the nucleus of the Hanford House. The builder of the inn aspired to mix the old with the new. Retired stockbroker Jim Jacobus and his wife, Lucille, acquired the inn in 1983. "But we feel as though we have been innkeepers forever," says Lucille.

The ambience is warm and homey. The old adobe with its whitewashed walls and high, beamed ceiling houses the parlor, where books and magazines are spread out on the coffee table. But creatures other than guests inhabit this room: A gigantic teddy bear sits in a chair by the door and all around are stuffed bears of various sizes and shapes. "We never really collected teddy bears," Jim recalls, "but our son's girlfriend brought one to the inn as a gift. Then all our guests thought we collected bears and sent them to us." The menagerie of teddys now spreads throughout the premises.

In the rear another new brick wing houses the guest rooms. These contain queen-size beds (most with headboards fashioned from antique doors), luxurious modern baths, and European or American furnishings that in some cases date back to the eighteenth century. All the rooms are air-conditioned and carpeted. And each

HANFORD HOUSE

61 Hanford Street (Box 1450),
Sutter Creek, California 95685

Telephone: (209) 267-0747

Accommodations: nine rooms with queen-size beds; private baths with tub/showers; one room completely equipped for the handicapped; no telephones; no television.

Rates: inexpensive to moderate, breakfast included; discounts on weeknights. No smoking.

Cards: MC, V

Facilities for small conferences. Open all year.

offers those often-neglected touches that ensure a relaxing stay: four pillows on each bed, bedside reading lamps, ample seating, plants, and fresh flowers. On the top floor of the bedroom wing, a large deck commands a panoramic view of Sutter Creek and the surrounding hills. Sharing the view upstairs is a deluxe unit with a gas-burning fireplace.

Back in the old adobe, breakfast is served at small tables in the dining area; juice, fruit, cheese, and muffins or sweet rolls are usually offered. You might want to read the morning paper, but you will be distracted by the writing on the walls. From floor to ceiling are inscriptions to the Jacobuses from grateful guests. In fact, this three-dimensional guest book has overflowed onto the ceiling. Ask for a ladder at checkout time.

Getting There: The inn is on the west side of Highway 49 at the north end of town.

Pete and Min Fox had absolutely no intention of becoming innkeepers when they bought this 130-year-old house on Sutter Creek's Main Street in 1979. Pete moved his real estate office there, and Min operated her antiques business downstairs. Then, one room at a time, they started lavishly redecorating the house with Min's antiques and taking in guests. Finally, they built a carriage house in the back, with three more high-ceilinged rooms that, although new, recapture the aura of the nineteenth century. Lo and behold, the Foxes now have a full-fledged inn. "One advantage of turning an antiques store into an inn," Min laughs, "is that you don't have to buy a lot of furniture." Only four pieces were purchased for the new annex.

The furnishings are exquisite and mostly authentic, such as an 1807 French armoire and a gilt Louis XV daybed in the Blue Room, and a nineteenth-century carved Austrian bedroom set in the Anniversary Suite. Some of the rooms have fireplaces, and even the bathrooms are romantic here, many with claw-foot tubs and pedestal sinks, but with modern stall showers as well. Min has strewn the inn with dramatic bouquets of silk flowers and a collection of "foxy" artifacts. You might even find a pair of furry foxes cuddled up on your bed.

In each room a table is set, and breakfast is delivered on silver service. You may also be served on a little side patio that's especially pretty when the garden is ablaze with pink dogwood. There's a formal parlor at the front of the inn and a big dining room, but most guests prefer to congregate in a seating area in the huge kitchen while Pete and Min cook up a storm. They give their guests a number of choices of juices, hot beverages, and four kinds of muffins, and they often serve

FOXES IN SUTTER CREEK

77 Main Street,
Sutter Creek, California 95685

Telephone: (209) 267-5882

Accommodations: six rooms with queen-size beds; private baths with stall showers or tub/showers; no telephone; remote-control cable television in carriage house.

Rates: moderate to expensive, breakfast included; lower rates on weeknights. No smoking.

Cards: MC, V

Open all year.

Foxes in Sutter Creek

coddled eggs. "But we've done just about everything—sourdough french toast, eggs Benedict, even biscuits and pan gravy at a customer's request," Min recollects. She also likes to know when guests are celebrating a special occasion—honeymoon, anniversary, or birthday—so she can plan a surprise for them. Though nowadays she often knows without being told, as more and more of the honeymooners return for their anniversaries.

Getting There: Highway 49 becomes Main Street in Sutter Creek.

Over $23 million in gold was removed from the Keystone Consolidated Mines in Amador City before they were closed in 1942. The mining company's offices and grinding and assay rooms were located in a two-story brick building on a hillside across the highway from the mines. In 1954 Marguerite and Peter Daubenspeck purchased this building, at that time abandoned, and opened an inn. It's now run by their son Peter and his wife, Ann Marie.

The senior Daubenspecks furnished the entire building with authentic period furniture found within a hundred miles of Amador City—treasures that would be impossible to find in the area today. The handsome rooms contain burled-walnut pieces, Empire dressers, commodes topped with Italian marble, platform rockers, armoires, and carved bedsteads. Under each bed is an old-fashioned bed warmer, and in many of the rooms old wash basins and pitchers are set on commodes. But these are for show only; you will find modern wood-paneled bathrooms throughout.

Each of the inn's rooms is named for the activity that originally took place there. Downstairs is the Mill Grinding Room, where the supports that held the shafts for the ore-grinding machinery are still on the ceiling. Next door are the Assay Room and the Stores Room. All the interiors are of painted brick. The upstairs rooms are the most attractive, with thirteen-foot-high ceilings paneled in redwood. On one side these rooms open to a wide balcony overlooking the highway, on the other to a covered patio dug out of the grassy hillside. The second-floor rooms once housed the Keystone's offices, and one still contains the safe in which the bullion was stored until the stagecoach transported it to San Francisco.

Back on the first floor, the former retort room, where the gold was smelted into bullion, now serves as a parlor for guests and also as a gallery for the paintings of Ann Marie and other local artists. In warm weather you can also relax by the swimming pool behind the inn. And in the morning you'll find a tray of orange juice, sweet rolls, and hot beverages by your door.

Getting There: The Mine House is on the west side of Highway 49 in Amador City.

MINE HOUSE INN

Highway 49 (Box 245), Amador City, California 95601

Telephone: (209) 267-5900

Accommodations: seven rooms with one or two double beds; private baths with showers; no telephones; no television.

Rates: inexpensive, breakfast included. Children welcome.

No credit cards.

Open all year.

EL DORADO COUNTY

Within months of James Marshall's discovery of gold at Coloma in 1848, thousands of fortune hunters were roaming the nearby mountains and rivers seeking *el dorado* (the gilt). One of the most popular camps, about seven miles south of Coloma, was named Dry Diggings because the miners had to tote the gravel that contained the ore to water for washing. But many of the rough and tough adventurers who inhabited the camp found an easier way to get their gold: Murder and robbery became so rampant that a vigilante committee was formed to hang the culprits. And as the number of hangings increased, the camp was known as Hangtown until a more respectable group of citizens changed its name to Placerville.

In the early years of the gold rush, both Coloma and Placerville thrived, and they became engaged in a heated rivalry for the county seat. Coloma, which had grown to a city of over ten thousand inhabitants within a few years of the gold strike, won at first, but in 1857 the county government was moved to Placerville, which was then the third largest city in California. Meanwhile, the gold in El Dorado County was being depleted and the fickle prospectors had moved on to the vast mines located to the south and north. Placerville managed to prosper as a government and commercial center, but by 1868 the population of Coloma had dwindled to two hundred, among them a bitter and impoverished James Marshall, who survived by occasionally working as a gardener.

Today Coloma, barely a speck on the map, is best known for its historic park that contains the reconstruction of Sutter's Mill where gold was first discovered. Placerville, still a thriving town, contains a number of historic buildings and the old Gold Bug mine, which is open to the public. Nearby attractions include white-water river rafting and a number of prize-winning wineries. Higher in the mountains are ski resorts.

Getting There: From Sacramento, Highway 50 leads to Placerville; Highway 49 heads north from there to Coloma.

The mining camp of Growlersburg, in the mountains above Coloma, once had a population of three thousand and yielded some $2 million in gold. Now called Georgetown, it is a sleepy village whose principal treasure is the American River Inn. Originally built in 1853 as a miner's boardinghouse, the inn is now one of the loveliest hostelries in the Mother Lode. Will and Maria Collins purchased and renovated the old hotel in 1984, and then annexed two adjacent buildings.

Today the inn complex occupies an entire block, centered around exquisite gardens. A century-old fig tree spreads over a broad wooden deck where breakfast is often served. In season, this meal includes figs, cherries, peaches, or persimmons from the gardens. The Collinses encourage guests to pick fruit and take it home with them. "You'd be surprised how many people have never picked a fig," Will says. The gardens also seclude a large lawn studded with chaises; a kidney-shaped swimming pool and spa; courts for croquet and badminton; and table tennis. But the pièce de résistance of the gardens is a large aviary where Will raises doves and golden pheasants.

Pheasant eggs often appear as hors d'oeuvres at the evening social hour in the hotel's attractive parlor, where on chilly nights a fire burns in the cast-iron stove. Taped classical music is played here by day, but in the evening livelier tunes emanate from the player piano. The rooms house some stunning antiques, such as a ten-foot-high leaded-glass breakfront from a Belgian castle, which stands in the dining room. Breakfast is served here, too, and you do receive a full morning meal: A typical menu includes juice, baked apples, and quiche, as well as that fruit from the garden.

Bedrooms on the hotel's second floor are equipped with revolving ceiling fans and beds dressed up with quilted spreads and dust ruffles of pastel-colored floral prints. Some of the brass bedsteads are museum pieces, inlaid with mother-of-pearl or hand-painted porcelain. Across the gardens from the hotel, a two-story Queen Anne provides more guest quarters and a large living room with a fireplace—a popular setting for small conferences. "The Woodside Mines Suites," in a third unit, are actually apartments that the Collinses converted into one- and two-bedroom suites with wet bars, countryish wicker furnishings, and balconies overlooking the gardens. But the ultimate lodgings at the American River Inn are the two honeymoon suites. Both feature wood-burning fireplaces or stoves, outlandish bathtubs for two, and oversized beds; one has a canopied four-poster with a mirrored ceiling and a bathtub big enough for an entire family.

AMERICAN RIVER INN

**Main at Orleans Street,
Georgetown, California 95634**

Telephone: (916) 333-4499

Accommodations: eighteen rooms and seven suites, with two doubles, queen-, or king-size beds; private and shared baths, most with clawfoot tub/showers or hand showers in older buildings, and tubs and showers in suites; one room with wheelchair access; no telephones; color television on request.

Rates: inexpensive to moderate, breakfast included. Children over eight welcome.

Cards: MC, V

Open all year.

Obviously there's no lack of activity at this inn. You can even have a massage, if you like; innkeeper Carol La Morte is a licensed therapeutic masseuse. If you want to venture out into the world, the inn provides bicycles. The surrounding area offers hiking, fishing, and golf. And white-water rafting is found at Coloma and Chili Bar, each nine miles away. That's as close as you'll get to the American River at the American River Inn.

Getting There: From Placerville, take Highway 49 (Coloma Road) north to Highway 193, which leads east to Georgetown. From Coloma, Marshall Road leads to Georgetown. From Auburn, take Highway 49 south and follow the signs to Georgetown. Once in town, you can't miss the inn.

Among the hordes who rushed to the gold country in 1851 were Fleming Jones' parents, dairy farmers from Wisconsin. But instead of panning for gold, they staked their claim on a homestead of ninety-seven wooded acres just east of Placerville. Fleming liked to gamble and also acquired an interest in a saloon. After one particularly good night at the tables, he arrived home with twelve hundred dollars and told his wife to go build herself a house. She did, and descendants of the Jones family lived there until the late 1970s. In 1980 the old farmhouse and eleven acres of the land were acquired by Janice Condit, who ever since then has devoted her considerable energies to re-creating an old-fashioned farm—the kind of place most people dreamed of visiting when they were kids.

You enter through the farmhouse kitchen, filled with the aroma of freshly baked bread or simmering preserves of fruit from the pear, apple, and fig trees in the surrounding orchards. A well-used Steinway grand and an old church pump organ sit in the homey parlor. In the adjoining dining room, a massive oak table is set for breakfast with gold-rimmed Haviland and Limoges china. And a hearty farm breakfast it is: homemade hot muffins, baked apples, Janice's preserves and breads (frequent blue-ribbon winners at the county fair), and eggs from the chickenhouse.

Four of the guest rooms are located in the 1883 farmhouse and two in the recently restored bunkhouse. Furnishings include cast-iron or carved-oak bedsteads (equipped with *new* mattresses, flowered quilts and matching sheets). Children's school desks, with vases of fresh flowers, serve as nightstands.

A favorite pastime of Homestead guests is helping with the farm chores: feeding the chickens and ducks, collecting eggs, helping to tend the vegetable gardens or harvest the fruit from the trees, or petting Janice's Welsh and miniature

FLEMING JONES HOMESTEAD

3170 Newtown Road, Placerville, California 95667

Telephone: (916) 626-5840

Accommodations: six rooms with double beds (two of these also have singles at an extra charge); four rooms have private baths with tubs or tub/showers, two rooms share a bath with shower; some rooms with wheelchair access; no telephones; no television.

Rates: inexpensive to moderate, breakfast included. Children over twelve welcome.

No credit cards.

Facilities for weddings and small conferences. Open all year.

Fleming Jones Homestead

Shetland ponies. Other guests prefer just to loaf on the porch swing, throw the ball for Rocky (the tireless fetching dog), and admire the view of the rolling, wooded countryside.

Getting There: From Placerville, take Highway 50 east to the Newtown Road/Point View Drive exit. At the base of the off ramp, jog to the right to another stop sign and turn left onto Broadway, which runs parallel to the freeway and becomes Newtown Road. The Homestead is on the right just past a pond.

D uring the 1850s the South Fork of the American River between Coloma and Placerville was heavily populated with miners. Today it swarms with the rafts and kayaks of white-water aficionados who come from all over to enjoy the thrills of the very fast river and to see the relics of old mining camps en route. Chili Bar (a gold rush camp founded by Chilean miners) is headquarters for the river raft expeditions, and just downstream is River Rock Inn. This contemporary stone-and-brick house furnished with antiques was the country home of Dorothy Irvin, who has turned it into an inn.

All the rooms front on a wide deck with spectacular views of the river, which is illuminated by floodlight at night. Chaises, tables, a hot tub, and potted flowers grace the deck, where breakfast is served on sunny mornings. On chilly days the morning repast is taken before a fire in the stone-walled dining room, and a bounteous meal it is. On a typical day Dorothy might serve an orange-banana frappé, eggs Benedict, apple crêpes, freshly baked rolls and baking powder biscuits, homemade jams, and fresh fruit. In fact, one might say she is a compulsive cook. The big country kitchen is the hub of this house and usually cookies, pies, or cakes—for the guests' enjoyment—are baking in the oven while bread rises on an ancient wood-burning cookstove. By special arrangement Dorothy will prepare dinners or picnic lunches for her guests.

Dorothy will also arrange for one- or two-day raft trips down the river, conducted by qualified guides. For the less adventurous, excellent trout and white-salmon fishing awaits on the banks near the inn. And if you're truly lazy, you can just lie on the deck and watch the white water rush by.

Getting There: From Placerville, take Highway 49 (Coloma Road) north to the intersection of Highway 193 (Georgetown Road), which leads to Chili Bar. After crossing the American River, turn left immediately on the first road, which leads to the inn.

RIVER ROCK INN

1756 Georgetown Drive, Placerville, California 95667

Telephone: (916) 622-7640

Accommodations: one two-room suite with private bath and queen-size bed; three rooms with double beds; one with private bath with tub/shower, others with half baths and shared shower; no telephones; color television; air-conditioning.

Rates: moderate, breakfast included. Children welcome.

No credit cards.

Open all year.

The few gold rush buildings left in Coloma are secluded in a country-like area off Highway 49. One is a fine old 1852 farmhouse built by Hugh Miller, one of the town's early saloonkeepers, just down the road from two 1850s churches that have also survived. The old Miller house is now the Coloma Country Inn, owned and operated by Cindi and Alan Ehrgott, nostalgia buffs who came here from southern California for a holiday—and stayed.

The house is furnished with Early Americana, which Cindi has been collecting since she was fifteen (and she doesn't look a whole lot older today). "When I was in high school," she confesses, "I worked and saved all my money to buy antiques, while my girlfriends were buying clothes." She is particularly proud of her collection of patchwork quilts, some of which are over a hundred years old. One of these hangs on the wall of the living room, originally the summer kitchen, where a stunning assortment of old crocks, sugar buckets, and other Early American crafts are also displayed. But the room is by no means cluttered; in fact, its pitched roof and the long raised hearth under the fireplace impart a feeling that is more contemporary than quaint.

The five bedrooms are done up in the same tasteful style. Most popular is the Cottage Room, splashed by sun from windows on three sides, and containing a rare eight-piece set of hand-painted cottage furniture from the East Coast. "It's poorman's Victoriana," Cindi explains. "People who couldn't afford walnut or oak just painted the pine."

The Ehrgotts serve late-afternoon refreshments by the fire or, on warm days, out in the gazebo, surrounded by pretty gardens. Breakfast (homemade baked goods, fruit, and coffee) is brought to your room, if you like, or served in the formal dining room. Here, over lace café curtains, you can glimpse apple and persimmon trees and a small pond, where a canoe might lure you for a little morning fishing. But if you're truly adventurous, you will have already had your morning recreation. Alan Ehrgott is a licensed hot-air balloon pilot and the inn offers special packages that feature a pre-breakfast flight. If that's too daring for you and the pond is too tame, packages that include white-water rafting down the American River are also offered.

Getting There: From Placerville, take Highway 49 north. On the south edge of Coloma, the highway makes a sharp turn to the right. Continue straight ahead on Church Street and turn right on High Street.

COLOMA COUNTRY INN

High Street (Box 502), Coloma, California 95613

Telephone: (916) 622-6919

Accommodations: five rooms with double beds; one private bath with tub/shower and two shared baths with tub or shower; no telephones; no television.

Rates: moderate, breakfast included. Children over ten welcome. No smoking.

No credit cards.

Open all year.

NEVADA COUNTY

In Grass Valley, California's richest mines produced a fortune in gold; a mining display with a thirty-one-foot waterwheel may still be viewed. Also open to the public are the homes of the infamous dancer Lola Montez and actress Lotta Crabtree. Four miles from Grass Valley is the semiabandoned town of Rough and Ready, which once tried to secede from the Union in protest of mining taxes.

Just north of Grass Valley, Nevada City was the third largest town in California during the peak of the gold rush, with a population of twelve thousand. Today, with only two thousand residents, it's a much quieter place, except for a freeway that unfortunately cuts through its hilly streets. Despite a few misbegotten modern buildings, the town retains much of its 1850s character, with picturesque gas lamps along the main street and many of the old buildings restored.

This area is dotted with good restaurants. Nearby lakes in the mountains around the towns offer swimming and fishing. Cross-country skiing is only twenty-five minutes away, and it's less than an hour's drive to the Sugar Bowl ski area.

Getting There: From San Francisco, take Highway 80 through Sacramento to Auburn. From here Highway 49 leads north to Grass Valley and Nevada City. From Reno or Lake Tahoe, take Highway 80 west to Highway 20, which leads to Nevada City.

T his three-story, double-towered Queen Anne will not suit everyone. But if you have an interest in the arts; if you like dogs, cats, teenagers, and the music of the sixties; and if you enjoy a casual lifestyle, you'll love staying at the Swan-Levine House.

Howard Levine and his wife, Margaret Warner Swan, are award-winning professional artists, graduates of the printmaking program at San Francisco State University. In 1975 they bought this 1880-vintage, twenty-room, 8,000-square-foot mansion on a hill overlooking Grass Valley because they needed space: space to raise a family (now grown to three kids, four cats, and a dog); space for a studio (a litho press and two etching presses are housed in an outbuilding); and space to hang hundreds of prints, drawings, and paintings (their own work and that of others).

They also needed space for guests. The Swan-Levine House was one of the Mother Lode's first B&Bs, popular with their actor and musician friends and fellow artists—a sort of gold-country salon. Guests are welcome to use the printmaking facilities, for a fee, and the Levines also conduct art classes. They use muted colors

SWAN-LEVINE HOUSE

328 South Church Street,
Grass Valley, California 95945

Telephone: (916) 272-1873

Accommodations: four rooms with twin, double, queen-, or king-size beds; private and shared baths with showers, tubs, or tub/showers; no telephones; no television.

Rates: inexpensive to moderate, breakfast included; printmaking classes twenty dollars per day, plus materials. Children welcome. Pets accepted by special arrangement. No smoking.

Cards: MC, V

Open all year.

154

in their own work. Peggy's etchings are black and white, and Howard is now working with pastels. But they painted the rooms with the most vibrant colors in an artist's palette: shocking pink in a corner room where white-tile wainscoting and floors are splashed with light from a wall of glass and more windows in a bay; periwinkle blue in a cozy garret room with a skylight in the eaves; cardamom yellow in a kid's room that contains bunk beds and a bevy of toys. The only muted colors are in a suite in the other tower bay where old-fashioned printed wallpaper and furniture are found. An adjoining parlor with fireplace has a couch that folds out to a bed—a perfect spot for families. And kids are indeed welcome here.

On the first floor two high-ceilinged parlors are filled with antique furnishings and, as elsewhere, contemporary works of art. An old jukebox blasts out the rock classics of the sixties—Elvis, The Beatles, The Safaris. Fireplaces grace both parlors and the formal dining room, where breakfast is officially served. But if there's not a full house, guests usually wander into the big country kitchen and join the family. The fare is good and hearty—perhaps huevos rancheros or pecan waffles or asparagus omelets with homemade breads.

The Levines found space in the gardens, too, for a small swimming pool set in a deck, for a much-used badminton court, and for a small orchard that bears apples, nectarines, plums, apricots, and almonds.

Getting There: From Highway 49, take Colfax exit (Highway 174) into Grass Valley. Turn left on South Auburn, left on Neal, and then left on Church Street.

Edward Coleman, owner of the famous North Star and Idaho mines, constructed this Grass Valley house in 1866. "He built it to last forever," comments the present owner, innkeeper Marc Murphy. The house was in excellent shape when Murphy bought it in 1982, with the original chandeliers, wainscoting, and fireplaces in mint condition. Nevertheless, Marc began by lavishing improvements on the house, and has never stopped.

He installed private baths in most of the bedrooms, some with double-spigoted showers. Next he built an addition to house a big, cheerful kitchen that opens into a dining area so he can chat with his guests while cooking breakfast. A typical feast might include fresh fruit and hand-squeezed juices, Belgian waffles, Polish sausage or coddled eggs, cottage fries, and freshly ground coffee. Hospitality comes naturally to Marc: His family has owned Murphy's Resort on the Russian River since 1902.

Marc and his wife, Rose, usher their guests into two first-floor parlors where they can relax by the fireside. Or if the weather is warm guests can opt for a dip in

MURPHY'S INN

318-319 Neal Street,
Grass Valley, California 95945

Telephone: (916) 273-6873

Accommodations: nine rooms or suites with double, queen-, or king-size beds, rollaway cots available; private and shared baths with tubs and/or showers; wheelchair access to some rooms; no telephones; no television; air-conditioning.

Rates: moderate to expensive, breakfast included. Older children welcome. No smoking.

Cards: AE, MC, V

Facilities for weddings. Open all year.

Murphy's Inn

the sixteen-foot swim-spa on a large deck that Marc has recently built in the rear of the house under an ancient sequoia. Three of the bedrooms have fireplaces and all are decorated with antiques, lace curtains, and floral wallpapers. Marc's latest addition to the inn is the house across the street, which contains two suites decorated in a country style with king-size beds and double-shower baths; the lower unit has a kitchen, too.

Murphy's Inn offers a number of midweek packages, such as a winter ski special whereby inn guests receive a discount on lift tickets at Sugar Bowl, as well as a discount on their room rate. Marc also arranges golf and white-water rafting specials in the summer and fall.

Getting There: From Highway 49, take Colfax exit (Highway 174) into Grass Valley. Turn left on South Auburn, then left on Neal.

This heavily ornamented, four-story brick structure has been cited as one of the best examples of Gothic Revival architecture in the West. Judge John Williams, a prominent mine owner in Nevada City, built the imposing house between 1857 and 1860. The judge's son and his family also occupied the house, and, according to local lore, young Williams used to serenade the townsfolk every Sunday afternoon from the top veranda of the Red Castle with impromptu recitals on the trumpet or cornet.

Since 1963 several owners have operated the Red Castle Inn. The latest are architect Conley Weaver and his wife, Mary Louise, who took over in 1986. They have kept much of the former decor, but are slowly adding their own touches such as a pump organ in the living room, huge ficus trees here and there, and a croquet court in the woodsy garden. Mary Louise serves afternoon tea in the parlor with homebaked goodies like Scotch shortbread. And she sets out, buffet style, a generous morning spread of orange juice, muffins and breads, fruit compote, and a hot casserole dish. Guests may eat where they please—in their rooms, at a table in the garden, or on the wide veranda.

Guest rooms occupy all four floors of the building. The furnishings are old-fashioned eclectic: You'll find lace curtains, four-posters, wing chairs, love seats, Oriental rugs, and the like. All but two of the rooms have private baths, in which old-fashioned wash basins remain but new stall showers have been added. From the

RED CASTLE INN

109 Prospect,
Nevada City, California 95959

Telephone: (916) 265-5135

Accommodations: eight rooms with double or queen-size beds; six rooms with private baths with showers or tub/showers, two rooms share a bath; telephones available; no television.

Rates: moderate, breakfast included. No smoking.

Cards: MC, V

Open all year.

spacious, high-ceilinged rooms on the lower floor, French doors open out to the veranda. The middle floor contains "parlor suites," each composed of a sitting room with a tiny iron wood-burning stove, and a bedroom almost entirely filled by a double bed. Two garret rooms on the top floor have Gothic windows and share a parlor, a bath, and the balcony where Judge Williams' son conducted his concerts a century ago. From here and from the lower verandas that surround the house, you look down on terraced, wooded gardens and across to the picturesque town of Nevada City on the opposite hillside.

Getting There: From Highway 49, take Broad Street exit in Nevada City; turn right to Sacramento Street, turn right again, and proceed up the hill to the first road on the left; make a hard left turn onto Prospect Street.

High above the Mother Lode, cradled among the peaks of the Sierra Nevada, lies Lake Tahoe, one of California's most popular year-round playgrounds. This two-hundred-square-mile body of blue water is ringed by sandy beaches and lush forests of pine, cedar, dogwood, and aspen trees. Swimming, boating, and waterskiing lure the summer visitors, while excellent skiing—at Squaw Valley and Heavenly Valley, for example—attract the winter trade. The lake is bisected by the California-Nevada border, and all year hordes of gamblers flock to the Nevada casinos, which also offer big-name entertainment acts on a par with those of Las Vegas.

Far from the neon glitter of the casinos is the Mayfield House, on the edge of Tahoe City. This sturdy house was built of wood and stones among the pines in 1932 by contractor Norman Mayfield, and in 1980 was converted into an elegant little inn. Signs of impeccable taste pervade the place, from the taped classical music in the living room to the restful rosy-beige–and–blue color scheme throughout. The living room, with its dark-stained pine paneling, beamed ceiling, and large stone fireplace, is furnished with Early American pine tables, chairs, and love seats upholstered in blue, kerosene-filled hurricane lamps, an assortment of books and games, and some of the African violet specimens that flourish throughout the house.

All the bedrooms have flowers, a selection of books, down pillows and comforters, bathrobes for the guests, and watercolors by Margaret Carpenter—yet

MAYFIELD HOUSE

236 Grove Street (Box 5999), Tahoe City, California 95730

Telephone: (916) 583-1001

Accommodations: six rooms with twin, queen-, or king-size beds; three shared baths with tub/showers or stall shower; no telephones; no television.

Rates: moderate, breakfast included. Children over ten welcome.

Cards: MC, V

Open all year.

Red Castle Inn

each has its own distinctive decor. Mullioned windows offer views of the mountains, woods, or the golf course across the road. You may opt for breakfast in bed or in the small dining area. It's a full meal, too, served on pretty blue-and-white-flowered English china, featuring goodies such as Finnish pancakes, Portuguese toast with fruit sauce, or cheese blintzes with berry sauce.

From Mayfield House it's only a short walk to the beach for summer guests. In winter, skiing at Squaw Valley is about fifteen minutes away, but several smaller ski resorts are closer. The casinos of Tahoe's north shore can be reached in about fifteen minutes, as well. And good restaurants are plentiful in the area.

Getting There: From San Francisco or Reno, take Highway 80 to Truckee, turn south on Highway 89 to Tahoe City, turn north on Highway 28 to Grove Street, turn left.

THE
WINE COUNTRY

SONOMA

NAPA VALLEY

RUSSIAN RIVER VALLEY

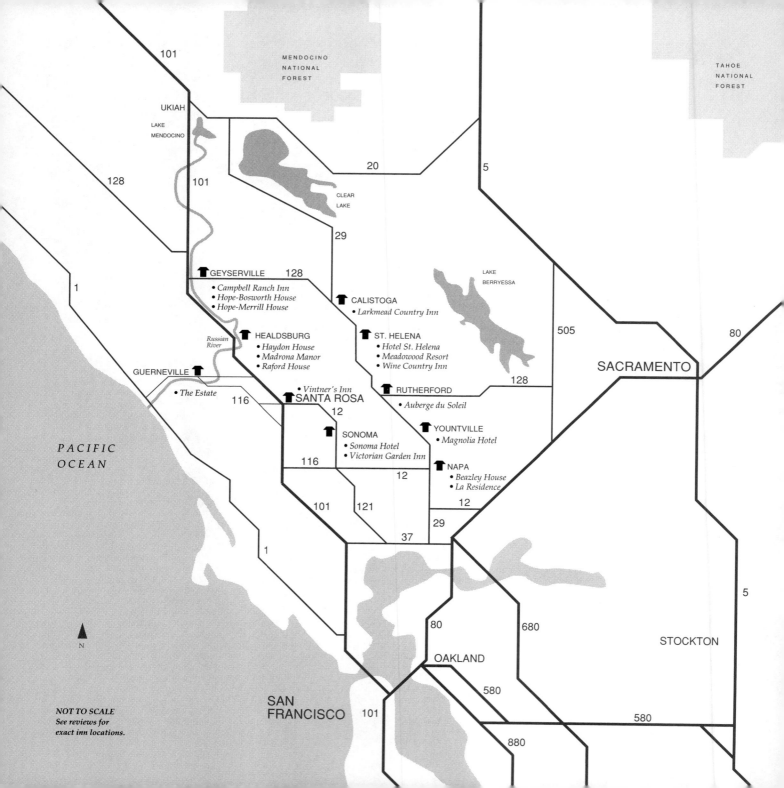

MENDOCINO
NATIONAL
FOREST

TAHOE
NATIONAL
FOREST

101

UKIAH

LAKE
MENDOCINO

20

5

128

101

CLEAR
LAKE

29

128

1

128

GEYSERVILLE

• Campbell Ranch Inn
• Hope-Bosworth House
• Hope-Merrill House

CALISTOGA
• Larkmead Country Inn

LAKE
BERRYESSA

Russian
River

HEALDSBURG

• Haydon House
• Madrona Manor
• Raford House

ST. HELENA
• Hotel St. Helena
• Meadowood Resort
• Wine Country Inn

505

SACRAMENTO

80

GUERNEVILLE

• The Estate

116

• Vintner's Inn
SANTA ROSA

12

RUTHERFORD

• Auberge du Soleil

128

PACIFIC
OCEAN

SONOMA
• Sonoma Hotel
• Victorian Garden Inn

YOUNTVILLE
• Magnolia Hotel

116

12

NAPA
• Beazley House
• La Residence

101

121

12

37

29

5

80

680

STOCKTON

N

OAKLAND

580

580

SAN
FRANCISCO

101

580

880

NOT TO SCALE
See reviews for
exact inn locations.

SONOMA

General Mariano Guadalupe Vallejo laid out Sonoma's large tree-shaded plaza in 1835 when he founded Pueblo de Sonoma as Mexico's most northerly outpost against hostile Indians. Twelve years earlier, Mission San Francisco Solano de Sonoma had been built there, the northern tip of California's chain of missions. Vallejo built himself a two-story adobe *palacio* on the plaza where his regiment of Mexican soldiers marched daily. The peace of the settlement was shattered on June 14, 1846, however, when a band of three dozen armed Americans, acting on their own authority, captured the town, imprisoned Vallejo, and proclaimed Sonoma capital of the Bear Flag Republic. The Bear Flag flew over the Sonoma plaza until the following month, when California became part of the United States.

Sonoma's second important settler after General Vallejo was Agoston Haraszthy, a Hungarian nobleman who planted his Buena Vista vineyards here in the 1850s and started northern California's winemaking industry. Sonoma has ever since been an important viticultural center. The Buena Vista's old stone cellars are open to the public, and tours are also conducted at the Sebastiani Winery, Hacienda Cellars, and dozens of other wineries in the area.

Rich in Californiana, Sonoma still possesses the aura of an early Spanish settlement. The Sonoma State Historic Park maintains the mission, General Vallejo's home, and the Toscano Hotel, all of which are open to visitors. The old barracks, which have headquartered three armies—the Mexicans, the Bear Flag rebels, and the Americans—have also been restored. Near Sonoma at Glen Ellen is the last home of Jack London, now also preserved as a state park.

Getting There: From San Francisco, take Highway 101 north through San Rafael to Ignacio; there take Highway 37 east to Highway 21; turn north and continue to Sonoma's plaza.

In the 1860s Sonoma was a tranquil town surrounded by prosperous farms and proud houses that relied on enclosed two-story towers topped by windmills for their water supply. In 1983, interior designer Donna Lewis transformed one of these farmhouses into a most romantic and sophisticated inn. The farmlands are long gone and subdivided, but nearly an acre of lush gardens and fruit trees remains on the property, as does the old water tower (now sans windmill). In the tower Donna has created three charming, high-ceilinged guest rooms decorated with a riot of colorful Marimekko and Laura Ashley prints. The rooms have comfortable seating areas, and one boasts a wood-burning brick fireplace.

Just a few steps away from the water tower, separated from it by a deck and grape arbor, is the old farmhouse with one guest room upstairs. Downstairs are the large living room, decorated in restful tones of beige, and the sunny, plant-filled dining area. Here Donna serves a "California breakfast" resplendent with fruits and unusual breads. Wicker trays are also available if you prefer to carry your goodies to one of the many tables on the deck and in the gardens.

The Victorian Garden Inn offers nineteenth-century pastimes, such as strolling in the gardens and playing lawn croquet, but it also offers a twentieth-century treat: a dip in the lovely swimming pool behind the house.

Getting There: From the south, when you reach the plaza turn right on East Napa.

VICTORIAN GARDEN INN

316 East Napa Street,
Sonoma, California 95476

Telephone: (707) 996-5339

Accommodations: four rooms with double or queen-size beds and electric blankets; water-tower rooms have private baths with showers or tub/showers, room in main house has shared bath with tub/shower; no telephones; no television.

Rates: moderate to expensive, breakfast included.

Cards: AE, MC, V

Open all year.

At the northwest corner of Sonoma's plaza is a three-story hotel. No one knows for certain when the hotel was built, but the lower two stories, made of adobe, are at least a century old. The third floor with its high gables was added circa 1880, when the building housed a dry goods store and a two-story meeting hall above. About 1920, the winemaking Sebastiani family converted the building to the Plaza Hotel. In 1974, John and Dorene Musilli bought the hotel and decorated the seventeen guest rooms with antiques. "There's not one reproduction in the place," Dorene points out.

Most of the rooms are furnished with French or English bedroom sets of matching pieces—dresser, armoire, headboard, even chairs. Quilted floral bedspreads, ruffled organdy curtains, and a watering can full of dried flowers and grasses add a homey note to each room. One room is named after General Vallejo because it contains an Italianate hand-carved burled-walnut bedstead that belonged to his sister. The bed looks fit for the general himself, with an eleven-foot-high

SONOMA HOTEL

110 West Spain Street,
Sonoma, California 95476

Telephone: (707) 996-2996

Accommodations: seventeen rooms with twin or double beds; some private baths with tubs, community baths with showers; no telephones; no television.

Rates: moderate, breakfast included. Children welcome.

Cards: AE, MC, V

Open all year.

Victorian Garden Inn

Sonoma Hotel

backboard and a bedspread of scarlet velvet. The Musillis stripped eight coats of paint off the wainscoting in the hotel lobby to reveal the natural dark fir. Here, in front of a large stone fireplace, guests are served a morning repast of freshly squeezed orange juice, house-baked croissants, and a choice of teas, coffee, or hot chocolate. The hotel also has a bar and restaurant that are open to the public.

Getting There: From the south, turn left when you arrive at Sonoma's plaza, turn right on the west side of the plaza and continue to West Spain Street on the north side.

NAPA VALLEY

This lovely long valley, rimmed by gentle mountains, is one of the world's most important winemaking regions. Although the Franciscan fathers from nearby Sonoma Mission started making wine here in the 1820s, it was an inferior wine made from their Mission grapes. But after Agoston Haraszthy proved that the European *vinifera* grapes would thrive north of San Francisco Bay in his Sonoma-based Buena Vista vineyards, French, Italian, and German immigrants flocked to the Napa Valley, planting cuttings from Haraszthy's stock. In 1858 Charles Krug produced the first European-style wine for which the valley is now known.

This viniferous valley stretches north from the city of Napa, an early timber-shipping center and once even a mining town during a silver rush in 1858. The valley ends at the town of Calistoga, whose mineral spas have attracted the weary since Mormon settler Sam Brannan discovered underground hot springs here in 1859. Towering above Calistoga is the 4,500-foot peak of Mount St. Helena, which Robert Louis Stevenson described as the "Mont Blanc of the Coastal Range" after spending his honeymoon in a bunkhouse at the mountain's base in 1880.

One of the most colorful settlements in the valley is Yountville, named after Napa's first white settler, George Yount. (In exchange for a favor to his friend General Vallejo, the Mexican government granted Yount an eleven-thousand-acre tract of land comprising most of the Napa Valley.) The old Groezinger Winery in Yountville has been converted to a complex of shops, galleries, and restaurants called Vintage 1870. Next door, the train depot and railroad cars house more shops, and the town's picturesque streets are lined with antiques stores, restaurants, and a growing number of country inns.

North of Yountville is Rutherford Square, where outdoor musical productions are presented in the summer months. Just north of Rutherford is St. Helena, where a museum containing Robert Louis Stevenson memorabilia is housed in the town's library. Beyond the town is an old gristmill with a waterwheel forty feet in diameter. Scattered throughout the valley and nestled in the surrounding hillsides are over 150 wineries, most of which offer conducted tours of their cellars and tastings of their bottlings.

Wine touring is unquestionably the most popular pastime in the area. Other forms of recreation include aerial gliding and ballooning around Calistoga and swimming, fishing, and boating at nearby Lake Berryessa. The valley also offers some of the finest dining in California. The cuisine is most often French nouvelle or Californian, but other ethnic styles are represented, too.

Getting There: From San Francisco, take Highway 101 north through San Rafael to Ignacio; there take Highway 37 east to Highway 21; turn north on Highway 21 and continue to the intersection of Highway 12, which leads east to Napa. From Napa, Highway 29 extends north through Yountville, Rutherford, and St. Helena to Calistoga.

In a residential area near downtown Napa, a handsome brown-shingled house with blue and white awnings sits on a half acre of lawns and gardens. Built in 1902, the house was well maintained as a Napa showplace throughout the years, but it's likely that no other owners have bestowed as much love and care on the place as Carol and Jim Beazley. They bought the house in 1981 with the intention of making it both their home and Napa's first B&B.

Guests arriving in the late afternoon are greeted by the Beazleys. Classical music flows through the house, and stained-glass windows cast rainbows on the floor of polished oak inlaid with mahogany. A fire burns in the hearth of the spacious living room and a tea cart bears cookies fresh from the oven. In the rear of the room, a window seat offers views of the garden through multipaned windows. The garden is Jim's domain and he has surrounded the lawns with beds of azaleas, rhododendrons, roses, irises, and primroses. There is fountain encircled with impatiens, and a swing hangs from a huge old oak.

Carol's domain is the kitchen. She has developed a number of original breakfast recipes such as a crustless chili quiche and a potato torta. These are served with a platter of fruit, yogurt sauce, and freshly baked muffins—perhaps pumpkin or blueberry or cinnamon crunch. The freshly ground coffee is the Beazley's own custom blend. Breakfast is served in the wood-paneled dining room, where the Beazley family collections of antique silver and cut glass are displayed.

BEAZLEY HOUSE
1910 First Street,
Napa, California 94559

Telephone: (707) 257-1649

Accommodations: nine rooms with queen- or king-size beds; private baths with showers, some with whirlpool tubs also; one room completely equipped for the handicapped; no telephones; no television.

Rates: moderate to expensive, breakfast included. No smoking.

Cards: AE, MC, V

Open all year.

A notable feature of Beazley House is the striking stained-glass window, complete with window seat, on the landing of the broad staircase that leads to the second floor. Upstairs are four cozy bedrooms furnished with antiques, queen-size beds, and wing chairs in which you might find one of the Beazley's oversized teddy bears. But the prize accommodations are in the carriage house beyond the garden. These rooms all boast fireplaces, wood-beamed ceilings, and double whirlpool tubs set out in the rooms. Two of the lower units have private gardens; the two upstairs rooms have peaked ceilings soaring to fifteen feet at the ridge.

Getting There: From Highway 29, take First Street exit, which brings you into central Napa via Second Street. Proceed to Warren Street, turn left to First Street. The house is on the northwest corner of Warren and First.

Midway between Napa and Yountville, alongside the highway, La Residence developed in only seven years from a quaint B&B in a historic house to one of the valley's loveliest country inns. Focal point of the complex is The Mansion, a splendid example of Gothic Revival architecture. It was built in 1870 by Harry C. Parker, a New Orleans river pilot who was lured to California by the gold rush and wound up farming in the Napa Valley. In 1987, David Jackson and Craig Claussen, present owners of the inn, extensively restored the house, equipping it with air-conditioning, soundproofing, and modern baths, while leaving intact the marble fireplaces that grace many of the rooms. Upstairs, French doors lead to a balcony over the columned veranda. Rooms are furnished with period American antiques.

Behind The Mansion is a brick patio with a whirlpool spa and plenty of chaises for sunning. Next to the house, Jackson and Claussen have built a swimming pool surrounded by brick paving, boxwood hedges, and beds of azaleas and rhododendrons. A wisteria-covered arbor leads to a second structure on the property: a French-style barn topped with cupolas. Though recently built, the barn looks as if it has been there forever, and its rustic shingled exterior belies the luxury within: The rooms (also soundproofed and air-conditioned) all have fireplaces, sitting areas, private baths, and French doors leading to patios or balconies. French and English antique pine furniture and Laura Ashley floral prints lend an aura of country elegance.

On the lower floor of the barn, a spacious dining room is warmed by a fire in nippy weather. An ample breakfast is served in here or on an outside deck; an egg dish—omelet, quiche, or soft-cooked eggs—is offered, along with mixed fresh fruit

LA RESIDENCE

4066 St. Helena Highway North, Napa, California 94558

Telephone: (707) 253-0337

Accommodations: twenty rooms with queen-size beds; private baths with showers or tub/showers in all but two rooms, which share a bath; no telephones; no television; air-conditioning.

Rates: moderate to very expensive, breakfast included. Smoking permitted in some areas.

Cards: MC, V

Facilities for small conferences. Open all year.

and sweet and savory pastries. In the evening the dining room is the center for socializing and a sip of wine, and on weekends the innkeepers hire a professional pianist to play their Steinway grand.

Getting There: Take Highway 29 north from the town of Napa. Just past Salvador Road, you will see the inn's sign on the right of the highway. Turn right at the next road and right again to head back to the inn along a frontage road.

Built in 1873 with large stones from the Silverado Trail, this small three-story hotel has had a checkered history. Originally a traveler paid a dollar a night for a room, including a stall and feed for his horse; those who could afford the luxury of rail travel were met at the Yountville depot by a surrey. At one time the Magnolia was reputedly a brothel, and it is a fact that the cellar was a center for bootlegging activities during Prohibition. After that the hotel was boarded up until 1968, when it was restored as an inn of eminent charm and respectability. Present owners Bruce Locken, former general manager of the Clift Hotel in San Francisco, and his wife, Bonnie, have continued the improvement process. They've added four luxurious new rooms with decks and fireplaces in an adjoining building and refurbished an old carriage house.

Furnishings are from the Victorian era: marble-topped tables with crystal decanters of port in the bedrooms, antique brass or wooden bedsteads with crocheted or quilted spreads, and everywhere dozens of handmade dolls and pillows that Bonnie has collected over the years. Concessions to twentieth-century living have been made, however, with private tiled baths throughout. Many of the rooms have splendid views of the vineyards across the road.

Breakfast, announced by the sounding of a gong at precisely nine o'clock, is an important event here. Guests gather in the little building adjoining the hotel, introduce themselves, and share wine-touring tips. The Lockens' system of devising the menu is unique: First-nighters are served french toast with port-wine syrup, second-nighters get shirred eggs, third-nighters enjoy a sherry-mushroom omelet, and so on, so that no one has the same breakfast two mornings in a row.

After a day of winery touring, you can relax in the large swimming pool surrounded by lawns. Here or in your room, Bruce will serve you a bottle of wine purchased from his fine collection of Napa Valley offerings. And behind the hotel, set in an enclosed redwood deck, is a commodious spa with underwater lighting.

Getting There: From Napa, take Highway 29 to first Yountville exit and head into town on Washington Street until it veers to the left; continue straight ahead on Yount.

MAGNOLIA HOTEL

6529 Yount Street,
Yountville, California 94599

Telephone: (707) 944-2056

Accommodations: twelve rooms with double, queen-, or king-size beds; private baths with showers; no telephones; no television.

Rates: moderate to very expensive, breakfast included. No smoking.

No credit cards.

Open all year.

Magnolia Hotel

The original concept was to create a French country inn amid the olive groves on a hillside above the Napa Valley. Somewhere along the way a southwestern motif was introduced. The result is a wine-country retreat that is uniquely Californian with stunning panoramic views of the lush vineyards below.

And *every* room does have a view and a deck outfitted with chaises from which to admire the vista. In fact, you might just want to spend the whole day here, starting with a breakfast tray of orange juice, coffee, croissants, bran muffins, and the morning paper. Later, help yourself to some fruit from the well-stocked wet bar, where you will also find pâté, cheese, wine, champagne, beer, and liquors for toasting the sunset. (The fruit and breakfast are complimentary; there's an "honor-bar" charge for the other goodies.) And on those rare days when the sun doesn't shine at the "Inn of the Sun," you can build a cheery fire in the handsome hearth faced with Spanish tile. Even taking a bath here is special; tubs for two are positioned under a skylight. Some of the newer rooms have whirlpool baths.

The guest accommodations are located in nine buildings on the terraced hillside, with pool and tennis courts nearby. And sited above all is the inn itself and its renowned restaurant, which made international culinary headlines when the late, great Masa Kobayashi was the chef here.

Getting There: From Napa, take the Silverado Trail north to Rutherford Hill Road. From Rutherford, take Highway 128 east to the Silverado Trail and turn left.

AUBERGE DU SOLEIL
180 Rutherford Hill Road, Rutherford, California 94573

Telephone: (707) 963-1211

Accommodations: forty-eight rooms and suites with twin or king-size beds; private baths with tubs and showers; one room fully equipped for the handicapped; telephones; color television.

Rates: extremely expensive, breakfast included. Restaurant open for lunch and dinner. Children welcome. Pets permitted with deposit.

Cards: MC, V

Open all year.

In 1881, while the Beringers and Krugs were busy expanding their wineries, an elegant two-story hotel opened on St. Helena's Main Street. But as the wineries flourished the hotel deteriorated until eventually its rooms were little better than those in a flophouse. Almost a century later, the hotel was restored to a degree of luxury it had probably never known.

Entering the hotel through a flower-filled arcade, you'll reach the lobby and a cozy wine bar. Here and in an adjoining patio a complimentary breakfast of juice, fruit, croissants, and muffins is served. Upstairs, a lounge and eighteen guest rooms have been skillfully decorated by combining antiques with modern comforts. The hall is papered with a striped and floral pattern of burgundy, tan, and brown, setting the color scheme for all the rooms. In the sitting room at the top of the stairs, love seats upholstered in burgundy velvet flank a fireplace.

The bedrooms are painted in burgundy, mauve, chocolate brown, dark tan, or pale gold; patterned, quilted bedspreads and dust ruffles echo these hues. Four rooms

HOTEL ST. HELENA
1309 Main Street, St. Helena, California 94574

Telephone: (707) 963-4388

Accommodations: eighteen rooms with twin or queen-size beds; fourteen rooms have private baths with stall showers or tub/showers, four rooms share two baths; no telephones; no television.

Rates: moderate to expensive, breakfast included. No smoking.

Cards: AE, MC, V

Open all year.

Hotel St. Helena

without private baths have bent-willow headboards and marble-topped commodes with baskets of fresh towels and soap. There's also a suite with a sitting room. All the rooms are richly carpeted and all the windows are shuttered in white. At the rear of the hotel, overlooking the arcade, is a wide deck with chaises and tables—a restful spot to relax after a day of winery touring.

Getting There: Highway 29 becomes Main Street in St. Helena. The hotel is in the center of town on the west side of the street.

Though constructed in 1975, the Wine Country Inn is one of the oldest continuously operated wine-country hostelries in this book. That shows how recent is the inn boom in Napa Valley. Owners Ned and Marge Smith had long dreamed of opening an inn, and for several years they spent vacations touring the inns of New England to get ideas and advice. One warning they heeded: "Don't restore an old building, build a new one. There will be fewer headaches and more comforts." Nevertheless, the Wine Country Inn looks as though it has been sitting on its hillock surrounded by vineyards forever. That's the way the owners wanted it to look. The three-story stone-and-wood structure, with its dormered windows and gabled tower, represents a composite of ideas borrowed from historic buildings in the valley. Several years after the initial construction, the Smiths added two smaller buildings nearby, and recently put in a pool and spa.

Comfort is the key word here. All rooms are carpeted and have modern baths. The furnishings are antique, from a potpourri of periods, but the old four-posters have been widened to queen size and the brass-framed double beds elongated. The rooms are papered with a floral motif; each is different and romantic in its own way. Fifteen of the rooms have freestanding fireplaces, seven have patios landscaped for privacy, and twelve have intimate balconies. Some rooms have window seats in alcoves with views of the surrounding countryside.

On the ground floor of the main building is a large, homey common room, equipped with card tables and books on wine. Here, at a long refectory table, a Continental breakfast of fresh fruits and juices, assorted hot breads, and beverages is offered. On warmer days this repast is served outside on a deck.

Getting There: From Napa, take Highway 29 two miles past St. Helena and turn right on Lodi Lane.

WINE COUNTRY INN
1152 Lodi Lane,
St. Helena, California 94574
Telephone: (707) 963-7077

Accommodations: twenty-five rooms with twin, double, or queen-size beds; private baths, some with tub/showers, some with stall showers; seven rooms with wheelchair access; no telephones; no television.

Rates: expensive, breakfast included.

Cards: MC, V

Open all year.

174

Wine Country Inn

The mountains east of St. Helena rise from the vineyards to embrace a small, secluded canyon studded with pines and oaks. This sylvan vale shelters the Meadowood Resort, a complex of lodges and cottages scattered over a 256-acre reserve, secluded on the wooded hillsides or overlooking the golf course, pool, or tennis and croquet courts.

From the outside, the fourplex lodges that house the guest accommodations look quaint and old-fashioned. Inside, the suites and bedrooms are luxurious and modern—many with skylights set in pitched ceilings, comfortable sitting areas, fireplaces of Silverado stone, and wet bars abundantly stocked with wine, beer, soft drinks, and fruit. (The bar is replenished daily; whatever you use is charged to your bill.) Meadowood pampers. No less than six pillows are heaped on the king-size beds, which are covered with quilts by day, down comforters at night. Terry cloth robes hang in the closets. If you want a massage in your room, just lift the phone.

The clubhouse contains two restaurants, both with views of the golf course and hills from outside decks. The Starmont Restaurant is for formal dining, the Fairway Grill for casual meals. The resort also serves as headquarters for the Napa Valley Vintners Association and the Napa Valley Wine Auction, so it's no surprise that it has one of the best selections of California bottlings in the state.

Getting There: From Napa, take Silverado Trail north to Howell Mountain Road, turn right and follow signs to Meadowood. From St. Helena, go east on Pope Street, which becomes Howell Mountain Road.

MEADOWOOD RESORT

900 Meadowood Lane,
St. Helena, California 94574

Telephone: (707) 963-3646,
in California (800) 458-8080

Accommodations: sixty studios and suites with king-size beds, some also with sofa beds; private baths with tub/showers or stall showers; some rooms with wheelchair access; telephones; television.

Rates: very expensive, no meals included. Restaurants open for breakfast, lunch, and dinner. Children welcome.

Cards: AE, MC, V

Open all year.

Lillie Coit is best known for the tower that she built on Telegraph Hill in San Francisco honoring the city's firemen. Few people connect her with wine history, but in the 1880s she owned the Larkmead Vineyards south of Calistoga. This land is now the site of the Hanns Kornell winery and, smack in the middle of the vineyards, Larkmead Country Inn. The inn, a sprawling clapboard Victorian, was built in 1918 by a former owner of the vineyards. Some time ago Gene and Joan Garbarino bought the lovely old house as a second residence, and in 1979 decided to make it a country inn.

Through fieldstone gates the driveway leads to a wisteria-covered loggia in the rear of the house. Up some stairs is the gracious living room appointed with a Persian carpet, antiques that the Garbarinos have collected on their European travels, and a well-stocked library. A fire burns in the hearth evenings as well as mornings, when guests gather for breakfast in the adjoining dining room. The table

LARKMEAD COUNTRY INN

1103 Larkmead Lane,
Calistoga, California 94515

Telephone: (707) 942-5360

Accommodations: four rooms with twin or queen-size beds; private baths with stall showers; no telephones; no television; air-conditioning.

Rates: moderate, breakfast included.

No credit cards.

Open all year.

is formally set with sterling silver and floral-patterned porcelain on which Joan arranges grapes and slices of watermelon, oranges, pears, peaches, kiwis—whatever is in season. Individual baskets of croissants, scones, and french rolls are served with crocks of sweet butter.

European etchings and oil paintings grace the dining and living rooms, as well as the four bedrooms. The rooms are named after various wines and command spectacular views of the vineyards. Chablis features an enclosed sun porch off the bedroom; Beaujolais has private use of the open porch over the loggia. Chenin Blanc is feminine and flowery, and Chardonnay has an Art-Deco look, with old brass bedsteads that came from a Parisian hotel. Fresh flowers are placed in all the rooms.

Larkmead Inn is surrounded by wide verandas and lawns shaded by sycamores, magnolias, and cypresses. It's a peaceful haven you will be reluctant to leave—but you don't have to go far for wine touring. Just walk next door to the Hanns Kornell Champagne Cellars, where members of the Kornell family will explain in detail the process of making bottle-fermented champagnes.

Getting There: From Napa, take Highway 29 past St. Helena and turn right on Larkmead Lane.

RUSSIAN RIVER VALLEY

From its origin in Mendocino County, the Russian River winds over two hundred miles through the lush vineyards of northern Sonoma County and the redwood-forested coastal mountains to the Pacific. The first settlers here engaged in agriculture and logging, but in the last quarter of the nineteenth century vineyards began to appear. They stretched from Guerneville in the south, where the Korbel cellars were established in 1886, to Cloverdale in the north, home of Italian Swiss Colony since 1887. Until recently, however, most of the other wineries in this area produced bulk wines. Then in the late 1960s, winemakers began to realize that the climate and soil of this area (particularly the Alexander and Dry Creek valleys) were capable of producing premium grapes to rival those of nearby Napa.

Today some sixty wineries are bottling varietals from the vineyards alongside the Russian River, among them such prestigious names as Davis Bynum, Simi, Trentadue, and Dry Creek. Many have tasting rooms, winery tours, and picnic areas. (Specific information on these wineries, a map showing their locations, and schedules of forthcoming events such as fairs, musicals, art shows, and barrel tastings can be obtained by sending one dollar to The Russian River Wine Road,

Box 127, Geyserville, California 95441.) The advent of the premium grape in the Russian River Valley was followed inevitably by the appearance of country inns in the towns along the river.

Getting There: North of San Francisco, Highway 101 passes through Santa Rosa and Healdsburg. Guerneville is reached by turning westward on River Road just north of Santa Rosa. From the Napa Valley, Highway 29 leads from Calistoga to Geyserville.

In the sleepy town of Geyserville, Bob and Rosalie Hope offer an escape back to the nineteenth century in two authentically restored Victorian houses and a trek through the vineyards in an 1882 stagecoach. Before moving to Geyserville in 1980, the Hopes operated a resort farther down the Russian River while Rosalie passionately pursued her hobby of collecting Victoriana. Her assemblage of period furniture and bric-a-brac formed the nucleus for decorating their inn complex.

Their first project was a 1904 Queen Anne cottage built from a pattern book by the Bosworth family, pioneers in the area. Rechristened Hope-Bosworth, the inn is papered with reproductions of Victorian wall coverings, but the furnishings in the cozy parlor, dining room, and four upstairs bedrooms are genuine. A rear sun porch opens to a pretty garden with a grape arbor.

The Hope-Merrill House, across the street, is a stately century-old Eastlake-Stick that stands on land once occupied by a Wells Fargo stage stop. In the house the wallpapers are magnificent custom-made replicas of fin de siècle patterns, complete with a frieze around the ceilings. The hall wainscoting is an original Lincrusta Walton pattern, unpainted and in mint condition. The pride of the high-ceilinged formal living room is a five-piece Eastlake walnut parlor set, with chairs upholstered in cranberry velvet. And the dining room is distinguished by Tudor-style furnishings and a massive 1871 cast-iron chandelier with its original shades.

But back to those stagecoach rides. On weekends from May through October, the Hopes cosponsor "Stage-A-Picnic" for their guests and others. The old stage, drawn by teams of Belgian draft horses, rambles through the vineyards for several hours, stopping at small wineries for a tipple along the way. The tour concludes at the grape arbor of Trentadue Winery for a grand picnic featuring the famed cheeses, sausage, and produce of Sonoma.

After lunch it's back to the inn for a dip in the Hopes' pool or a nap in one of the cozy bedrooms, where visions of vineyards peek through lace-curtained windows. Some of these rooms contain pieces of museum quality, such as an 1865

HOPE-MERRILL HOUSE

21253 Geyserville Avenue,
Geyserville, California 95441

Telephone: (707) 857-3356

Accommodations: seven rooms with double or queen-size beds; private baths with showers or tub/showers, some with whirlpool tubs; no telephones; no television.

Rates: moderate, breakfast included. No smoking.

Cards: MC, V

Open all year.

HOPE-BOSWORTH HOUSE

21238 Geyserville Avenue,
Geyserville, California 95441

Telephone: (707) 857-3356

Accommodations: five rooms with double or queen-size beds; two private baths with showers, two shared baths with tub/showers; no telephones; no television.

Rates: moderate, breakfast included. No smoking.

Cards: MC, V

Open all year.

STAGE-A-PICNIC

Advance reservations must be made by calling (707) 857-3619 or either of the inns. The morning tour departs at ten; an afternoon tour is preceded by the picnic lunch, which starts at one.

Hope-Merrill House

walnut and burl headboard and an 1850 child's crib. And if you need some reading material, you're likely to find on the bedside table some gems from Rosalie's collection of Victorian-era books. The Hopes have recently added two new rooms with showers for two, and have outfitted two other bathrooms with oversized whirl-pool tubs.

Homemade preserves and breads, along with fruit and juice, start the day at both Hope houses. Refreshments are offered in the evening. With advance notice and a party of at least ten, the Hopes will also prepare catered dinners at either of the houses. But you need not worry about going hungry in Geyserville; the area boasts several good restaurants.

Getting There: From Highway 101, take Geyserville exit, which leads north into Geyserville Avenue.

Many things set this inn apart from the typical small B&B. First, there's the hilltop setting: The inn sits on thirty-five wooded acres, with a spectacular view of hillside vineyards rising to a forested ridge and a glimpse of Geyser Peak beyond. Then there's the swimming pool, the spa, and the tennis court. So much else to do, too: horseshoes, table tennis, and bikes to ride. Or you may just want to relax on the terrace and admire the gardens that Mary Jane and Jerry Campbell manage to keep in bloom most of the year—azaleas, rhododendrons, and pansies in springtime; marigolds and stock in the summer months.

Four guest rooms occupy the split-level ranch house that was the Campbells' home before they became innkeepers. Three of these bedrooms open to balconies. One room even has a piano, and all are bedecked with fresh flowers, fruit, and ample reading material. Indoors, you'll find much to do as well: a jigsaw puzzle is always in the works in the homey family room, which is also equipped with a television set, cards, and almost every game imaginable. A fire usually burns in the brick see-through hearth that also opens to the formal living room. Wander into the kitchen where lemonade, iced tea, and other refreshments are stashed in the fridge. "Help yourself to anything," the Campbells tell their guests.

Instead of the usual early-evening social hour, the Campbells offer a late-evening snack when you return from dinner: most likely a pie that Mary Jane has made from the peaches, apples, or pears that grow on the ranch. Before retiring you'll be asked to select your breakfast from a quite varied menu: a choice of juices or fresh fruit; entrées that range from fried eggs and potatoes to the Campbell

CAMPBELL RANCH INN

1475 Canyon Road,
Geyserville, California 95441

Telephone: (707) 857-3476

Accommodations: four rooms with king-size beds; some private baths with showers, some shared baths with tub/showers; no telephones; one room with television.

Rates: moderate, breakfast included. No smoking.

Cards: MC, V

Open all year.

Ranch egg puff, loaded with mushrooms and jack cheese; and muffins or coffee cake or a miniloaf of freshly baked zucchini or honey-wheat bread. In the morning you'll find robes in your room so you can start the day with a dip in the pool and breakfast on the lovely terrace.

Getting There: From Highway 101, take Canyon Road exit north of Geyserville and head west 1.6 miles to the ranch.

In 1881 San Francisco financier John Paxton spared no costs in building a three-story mansion with a gabled mansard roof on a wooded knoll overlooking the Russian River valley. Even though the manor was to be only a summer home, he constructed it lavishly with fourteen-foot ceilings, ten fireplaces inlaid with brightly painted tiles, and floors of Italian mosaic, and furnished it with massive pieces of carved walnut and mahogany.

When Carol and John Muir (a distant cousin of the naturalist) discovered this country estate a century later, they knew it was the perfect site for the inn they had dreamed of when John was serving as a Bechtel executive in Saudi Arabia. Although the mansion needed a lot of repair, the original furnishings were still in place and the Muirs added only the fine Persian carpets they had acquired on their travels. On the lower floors, five guest rooms contain hundred-year-old, ten-foot-high four-posters or carved headboards, gigantic armoires, and marble-topped dressers. You almost feel as though you are sleeping in a museum. Each of these rooms also has a fireplace and private bath. The third floor shelters four cozy rooms under the eaves, also with fireplaces.

Behind the mansion Paxton had built a Carpenter Gothic carriage house. The Muirs reconstructed its interior, which houses a large common room with fireplace and game tables as well as eight guest rooms. These rooms are furnished with carved rosewood tables and chairs that the Muirs had commissioned in Nepal for their then nonexistent dream inn. Although the carriage-house rooms—with twin or queen-size beds and modern baths—are more comfortable than those in the main house, they lack the opulent style of the manor rooms. Two other outbuildings have been remodeled as two-room suites, each with its own sitting room.

Yet the sleeping accommodations are only half the story of Madrona Manor. The food reaches a quality that even Paxton, with all his millions, probably never enjoyed. The chef is the Muirs' son Todd (a graduate of the California Culinary Academy), who plans his menus to utilize the seasonal bounties of Sonoma County.

MADRONA MANOR

1001 Westside Road (Box 18), Healdsburg, California 95448

Telephone: (707) 433-4231

Accommodations: eighteen rooms and two suites with twin, double, queen-, or king-size beds; private baths with tub/showers; one room fully equipped for the handicapped; no telephones; no television.

Rates: expensive, breakfast included. Restaurant open to the public for dinner and Sunday brunch. Children and pets welcome.

Cards: AE, MC, V

Open all year.

The Carriage House at Madrona Manor

Breakfast consists of fresh fruit, platters of smoked meats and local cheeses, soft-boiled eggs, toast, and churros (little deep-fried pastries), served with housemade preserves such as mandarin marmalade. The restaurant is open to the public for dinner and features unusual pastas, meats, mesquite-grilled poultry, seafood, and smoked salmon, trout, and duck from the manor's own smokehouse. A Sunday brunch is served on the terrace when weather permits.

Madrona Manor sits on eight acres of orchards and gardens studded with oaks, redwoods, and the palms that Paxton planted a century ago. But the Muirs have added one luxury that the nabob never dreamed of—a swimming pool.

Getting There: From the south, take second Healdsburg exit off Highway 101 and follow Healdsburg Avenue north to Mill Street, which becomes Westside Road. From the north, take Westside Road exit from Highway 101.

Behind a rose-covered picket fence on a quiet side street in Healdsburg, this 1912 Queen Anne exudes the warmth and charm of a well-run country home. You would never guess that three decades of housing a convent, then a boys' home, and eventually a rest home had taken their toll on the place. But innkeepers Joanne and Richard Claus painstakingly removed all traces of institutional wear and tear. Now the gleaming natural fir floors contrast splendidly with pastel dhurrie rugs, handmade in India. The six second-floor bedrooms are decorated with French and American antiques, custom-made down quilts that match the bed linens, baskets of mixed dried and silk flowers, lots of plants, and a menagerie of teddy bears and Raggedy Ann dolls. Not all the rooms have private baths, but three have claw-foot tubs set out in the bedrooms.

The most sought-after accommodations, however, are the two stunning new rooms in a Victorian Gothic carriage house behind the lovely gardens. Rotating fans are suspended from the high, vaulted ceilings; the plank floors are constructed of Vermont pine; and each room has a private bath with a double whirlpool tub set under skylights. The queen-size bed in one room has a handsome wicker frame; next door a four-poster is crowned with a canopy of Battenberg lace.

Joanne is particularly proud of her buffet breakfasts, served in the large, sunny dining room off the comfortable double parlor. The menu varies, but a typical repast includes freshly squeezed orange juice, fresh pineapple and a compote of seasonal fruits, two frittatas (one meatless and one with sausage), a freshly baked

HAYDON HOUSE

**321 Haydon Street,
Healdsburg, California 95448**

Telephone: (707) 433-5228

Accommodations: eight rooms with double or queen-size beds, additional sofabed in one room; some shared, some private baths, two with whirlpool tubs; no telephones; color television in parlor.

Rates: moderate, breakfast included. No smoking.

Cards: MC, V

Open all year.

coffee cake, and apple, bran, or blueberry muffins. Many guests return just for the breakfasts, but Haydon House itself is a place people want to come back to. Even the nuns from the convent drop in to see their former home.

Getting There: From Highway 101, take second Healdsburg exit to the plaza, turn right on Matheson. Drive three blocks to Fitch and turn right. Drive another two blocks to Haydon and turn left.

From Healdsburg the Russian River flows west through more vineyards and wooded mountains to the Pacific. Although this is wine country now, a century ago much of this rich acreage was planted in hops. One of the major hop growers was Raford W. Peterson, who built in the 1880s a spacious house, flanked by broad verandas, on the hillside overlooking his land. Today the grounds are covered with grapevines and prune trees, and all that remains of the hop ranch are the Victorian farmhouse and the foundation of the hop kilns. In 1980 Alan Baitinger and Beth Foster bought the thirteen-room residence from the Peterson family and converted it into an inn.

Giant palms and gardens rife with roses and other flowers surround the building. On chilly mornings, a cheery fire burns in the parlor, where guests are served a simple Continental breakfast at a long oak table. A big grandfather clock in the corner is a hint of the owners' hobby. Antique clocks of all sizes are found throughout the bedrooms, which are handsomely appointed with turn-of-the-century furnishings. Quaintness, however, ends with the beds (all new mattresses) and the modern baths. Each room has its own distinctive decor and special features. Some have wood-burning fireplaces, others have private patios. Then there is a shared-bath suite of two bedrooms, one light and airy in champagne tones, the other one dressed up in deep burgundy hues with a brass bedstead; a small game room with a garden view opens off this room. The best view in the house is from the broad veranda—a perfect spot to while away an afternoon in a wicker rocker, gazing out over the vineyards.

Getting There: From Highway 101, take River Road exit (north of Santa Rosa) and drive west seven miles to Wohler Road; turn right.

RAFORD HOUSE

**10630 Wohler Road,
Healdsburg, California 95448**

Telephone: (707) 887-9573

Accommodations: seven rooms with double beds; most rooms have private baths with tub/showers; one room with wheelchair access; no telephones; no television.

Rates: inexpensive to moderate, breakfast included. No smoking in bedrooms.

Cards: MC, V

Open all year except Christmas.

Former New Yorker John Duffy is a nuclear physicist. His wife, Francisca, is a European-born trilingual interpreter. How did this couple wind up as vineyardists and innkeepers in Sonoma County? It started in the mid-1970s, when they began to seek "the ultimate life-style" and bought a century-old, fifty-acre prune ranch four miles north of Santa Rosa. After replanting the fields with premium grapes, they built among their vineyards an inn inspired by the villages of Provence.

Five stucco buildings with pitched red-tile roofs cluster around a plaza complete with bubbling fountain and French streetlights. The interiors, designed by Francisca, have an elegant, understated French-country aura with delicate multiflora wallpapers and woven cotton prints. Except for the custom-made beds, the pine furnishings are European antiques, as are the old farm implements scattered around the inn. The guest rooms have beamed ceilings, comfortable seating areas, and French doors opening to balconies or patios; some have wood-burning fireplaces. In each room an armoire conceals a color television, and portable VCRs are available for viewing films, old and new, from the Duffys' large collection.

So you're not a movie buff. Well, the handsome library in the main building is well stocked with books and games. But on balmy days you'll be tempted outside by the twelve-foot spa and its surrounding sun deck on the edge of the vineyard. If you're looking for more strenuous recreation, inn guests have swimming, golfing, and tennis privileges at a nearby country club. Also popular here are murder-mystery weekends, when you can be the sleuth—or even the suspect.

As in Provence, food plays an important role at Vintners Inn. In the pretty, tile-floored dining room, a bountiful breakfast buffet of fruits, jams, croissants, and cereals is laid out; a waffle iron is provided so you can make your own waffles. In the afternoon and evening, light snacks are available through room service. You don't have to travel far for an exquisite meal, however: One of the buildings in the inn complex houses the restaurant of John Ash, one of America's most talented and highly acclaimed young chefs.

Getting There: From San Francisco, take Highway 101 north past Santa Rosa to the River Road/Guerneville exit. Cross back over the freeway and take the first left onto Barnes Road.

VINTNERS INN

4350 Barnes Road,
Santa Rosa, California 95401

Telephone: (707) 575-7350,
in California (800) 421-2584

Accommodations: forty-four rooms with queen-size beds; private baths with tubs and showers; some rooms fully equipped for the handicapped; telephones; television.

Rates: moderate to expensive, breakfast included. Children and pets welcome.

Cards: AE, CB, DC, MC, V

Facilities for small conferences. Open all year.

As the Russian River approaches the Pacific it widens and its banks are lined with vacation cabins and rustic resorts. The hub of this hurly-burly is the town of Guerneville. Though only a few minutes out of town, The Estate offers elegance and secluded comfort among the redwoods. Built in 1922 on sixty acres for Guerneville's first bank president, the imposing Spanish-style house on its sylvan hillside was converted to a B&B in the 1980s.

Owners Jim Caron and Darryl Notter are among the most dedicated innkeepers in the business. They both love to cook (Darryl specializes in pastries and Jim in savories), so breakfast here is a big deal. Besides freshly squeezed juices and hot beverages, a creative entrée is offered, such as french toast stuffed with cream cheese and almonds, topped with strawberries, and accompanied with apple syrup, sausages, and orange sections. Breakfast is served at tables for two in the formal dining room on gray days, but if the weather is nice, you're seated out back by the pretty swimming pool and spa. This area is a pocket of sunshine amid the redwood forests, and overlooks a meadow where a sway-backed horse and an old sign are remnants of an abandoned rodeo ground.

On weekends the innkeeper-cooks whip up hors d'oeuvres—perhaps little pizzas or a caviar pie—for a social hour. The appetizers are served beside the enormous stone fireplaces in the living room and in the skylighted solarium, where a bay of multipaned windows offers more woodsy views. With advance notice, Jim and Darryl will do lunches and dinners, too.

Those omnipresent redwoods are also glimpsed from the bedrooms, where down quilts and a sextet of pillows grace the queen-size beds. In some of the bedrooms, French doors open to private patios or covered porches; the largest room has a pleasant sitting area in a large, windowed bay. The furnishings are handsome, solid, and comfortable without too many frills. "We spent our budget on quality pieces," Darryl explains. "We'll add the embellishments, later."

Getting There: From Highway 101, take River Road (north of Santa Rosa) westward to Guerneville, then head south on Highway 116.

THE ESTATE

13555 Highway 116, Guerneville, California 95446

Telephone: (707) 869-9093

Accommodations: ten rooms with queen-size beds; private baths with tub/showers; one room completely equipped for the handicapped; telephones; remote-control color television.

Rates: moderate to expensive, breakfast included. No smoking in bedrooms.

Cards: AE, MC, V

Facilities for small conferences. Open all year.

THE REDWOOD EMPIRE

**THE NORTH COAST
THROUGH MENDOCINO
TO EUREKA**

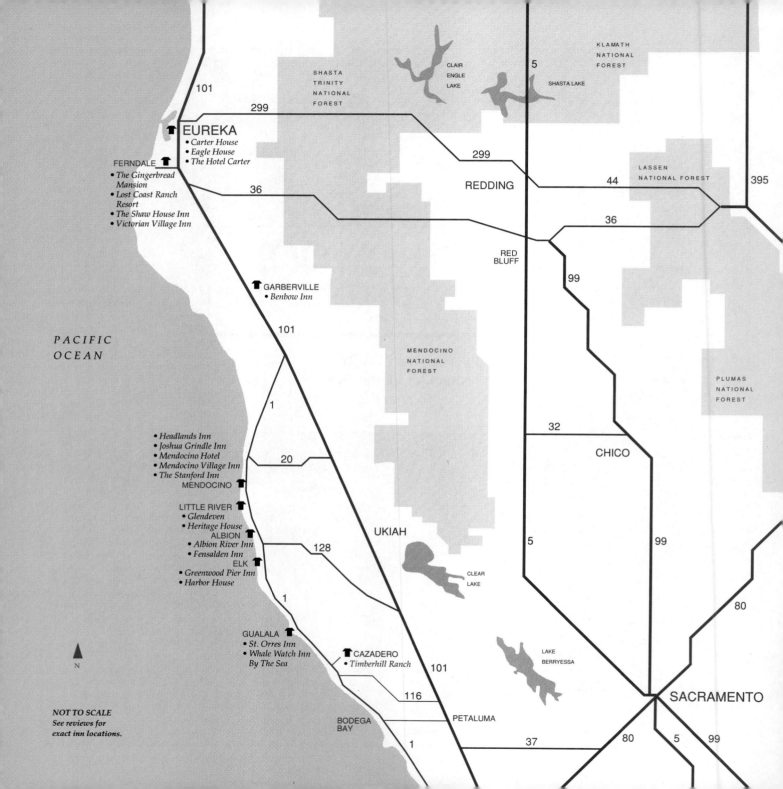

PACIFIC
OCEAN

EUREKA
• *Carter House*
• *Eagle House*
• *The Hotel Carter*

FERNDALE
• *The Gingerbread Mansion*
• *Lost Coast Ranch Resort*
• *The Shaw House Inn*
• *Victorian Village Inn*

GARBERVILLE
• *Benbow Inn*

• *Headlands Inn*
• *Joshua Grindle Inn*
• *Mendocino Hotel*
• *Mendocino Village Inn*
• *The Stanford Inn*
MENDOCINO

LITTLE RIVER
• *Glendeven*
• *Heritage House*
ALBION
• *Albion River Inn*
• *Fensalden Inn*
ELK
• *Greenwood Pier Inn*
• *Harbor House*

GUALALA
• *St. Orres Inn*
• *Whale Watch Inn By The Sea*

CAZADERO
• *Timberhill Ranch*

SACRAMENTO

CHICO

UKIAH

RED BLUFF

REDDING

SHASTA TRINITY NATIONAL FOREST

CLAIR ENGLE LAKE

SHASTA LAKE

KLAMATH NATIONAL FOREST

LASSEN NATIONAL FOREST

MENDOCINO NATIONAL FOREST

PLUMAS NATIONAL FOREST

CLEAR LAKE

LAKE BERRYESSA

BODEGA BAY

PETALUMA

101
299
299
44
395
36
36
99
32
5
99
80
5
99
80
37
1
101
128
20
1
116
1

N

NOT TO SCALE
See reviews for exact inn locations.

THE NORTH COAST

North of Jenner, where the Russian River meets the Pacific, Highway 1 soars upward, switchbacking through mountainous terrain, then stretches north along the craggy coast to Mendocino. This awesomely beautiful drive through mostly isolated countryside takes you past the reconstruction of Fort Ross, the site of a Russian seal- and otter-trapping settlement in the early 1800s. It also passes by numerous coves where weathered pilings and abandoned cemeteries are the only testimony to the once-thriving lumber towns that dotted the coast in the last century. In the forested mountains that rise from the sea, millions of redwood trees were hewn to build the Victorians of San Francisco.

Getting There: To reach Highway 1 from San Francisco, take Highway 101 north to Petaluma; take Washington Street exit to the road leading to Bodega Bay, then proceed north on Highway 1. Alternative routes are Highway 116, north of Petaluma, west to Highway 1; or River Road, north of Santa Rosa, west to Highway 1.

A mid eighty acres of pines, redwoods, and live oaks on a ridge eleven hundred feet above the Pacific, Timberhill Ranch provides an idyllic retreat for those who enjoy the great outdoors yet like to live in style. The property is both an inn and a working ranch where horses, goats, rabbits, and llamas are raised. Timberhill is also the home of Barbara and Frank Watson and Tarran and Michael Riordan, who opened this unique vacation getaway in 1984. Doing most of the work themselves, they transformed an old ranch house into a splendid lodge with skylights in the pitched ceilings, stone fireplaces in the dining and living rooms, and redwood decks. They also built ten guest cottages spaced far apart among the trees and added a lovely swimming pool, an outdoor whirlpool spa, and two tennis courts.

A stay at Timberhill is designed so you need never leave the ranch. Included in the rate are three meals a day, which are prepared by professional chefs and are not exactly your typical ranch food. A six-course dinner is served at candlelit tables for two, set with fresh flowers, family silver, china, and crystal—even silver napkin rings. A typical meal starts with carpaccio, cream of broccoli soup, California waldorf salad, and pink grapefruit sorbet. You have a choice of five entrées ranging from loin of lamb with garlic cream to mahimahi in coconut-ginger cream, and a selection of four or five sumptuous housemade pastries and desserts. If you're on a diet, however, Timberhill will prepare any kind of special menu with advance notice.

TIMBERHILL RANCH

35755 Hauser Bridge Road, Cazadero, California 95421

Telephone: (707) 847-3258

Accommodations: ten cottages with queen-size beds; private baths with stall showers; one room with wheelchair access; no telephones; no television.

Rates: expensive, three meals included. Smoking and nonsmoking rooms.

Cards: MC, V

Facilities for weddings if entire inn is booked. Open all year.

Coffee is often served by the fire in the living room, where you can while away the evening at the chess board or jigsaw puzzle or with a book from a library of leather-bound volumes.

Although the cottages look rustic from outside, the interiors are luxuriously appointed in a charming country style. Pitched ceilings and walls are sheathed with knotty cedar, glass doors open to a private deck, a wood fire is ready to light in the raised hearth, and the bed is covered with a handmade patchwork quilt. Flowers are everywhere: in bouquets on the table, on the pillows of the turned-down bed, even tucked atop the towels and the toilet paper in the tiled bathroom.

In the morning, many guests like to help feed the animals before breakfast, which is brought to the cottages. Lunch (sometimes a buffet and sometimes a simple meal like lovash sandwiches, salad, and soup) is served in the dining room or out on the deck. You'll find plenty to do here during the day: tennis, swimming, or just watching the wild ducks and geese swim in the pond. If you want to venture into the adjacent redwood forests or down to the beach, the chefs will pack a picnic in a wicker basket; for serious hikers, a knapsack lunch is also provided.

Getting There: From Highway 1, about five miles north of Jenner, turn right onto Meyers Grade Road, which becomes Seaview. When you reach the turnoff to Plantation, swing right onto Hauser Bridge Road. The ranch is exactly 13.7 miles from Highway 1.

Turrets capped with onion-shaped domes frame this amazing architectural sculpture emblazoned with leaded-glass windows and hand-carved balconies overlooking the ocean. Is this miniature palace a relic of the coast's Russian past? No. Eric Black, a carpenter of extraordinary skills and patience, built the inn in the 1970s on property once owned by the St. Orres family, who homesteaded the area. The inn is surrounded by forty-two acres of redwood-forested hillsides where nine guest cottages now nestle.

You enter the inn through a trellis-covered terrace; on your arrival you can enjoy a glass of wine in a plant-filled solarium or beside the fire in a pretty parlor where oval windows offer peeks at the Pacific. Beyond is the spectacular dining room where light filters down from stained-glass clerestories in the domed tower fifty feet above; three tiers of mullioned windows provide glimpses of forest and sea through a cascade of hanging plants.

St. Orres has one of the best restaurants on the north coast. Its menu changes seasonally, but you can usually count on fresh local seafood along with entrées

ST. ORRES INN

Highway 1 (Box 523),
Gualala, California 95445

Telephone: (707) 884-3303

Accommodations: in the main building eight rooms with double beds share three baths with showers; nine cottages with double or queen-size beds have private baths; no telephones; no television.

Rates: inexpensive to expensive, breakfast included. Children welcome in cottages.

Cards: MC, V

Facilities for weddings and small conferences. Open all year.

St. Orres Inn

such as rack of lamb, medallions of venison, and breast of duck. A complimentary breakfast of juices, fruit, house-baked breads, and coffee is served here to guests of the inn.

Overnight accommodations vary widely from the small, inexpensive, and rather spartan upstairs rooms in the main building to the delightful cottages hidden away in the redwoods. Some of these have fully equipped kitchens or wet bars; many have fireplaces or cast-iron stoves, private decks, and ocean views. Everywhere you will find visual surprises—a skylight in an unexpected spot, handcrafted wood rafters or balustrades, perhaps a bed on a raised platform, a sunken bathtub, or a Japanese soaking tub.

Three older cottages are sited beside a meadow behind the inn. The newer Creekside units, in a separate complex to the north, are clustered around a turreted spa building that contains a hot tub, sauna, deck, and kitchen facilities—an ideal spot for small conferences. St. Orres Inn has its own private beach across the road. The area offers steelhead fishing in season, and on weekends flea markets and arts and crafts festivals are popular events.

Getting There: St. Orres Inn is located on Highway 1 between Gualala and Anchor Bay.

Perched on sheer cliffs some fifty feet above the Pacific, this striking inn of contemporary design offers spectacular views of the ocean and the craggy coast. On this magnificent site Irene and Enoch Stewart built a summer home in the 1970s, added some guest cottages, and by the 1980s their romantic inn had grown to eighteen rooms in a complex of five buildings.

Whale Watch, the original building, is now the center for those who want to socialize at the inn. It has a huge hexagonal living room paneled in redwood and glass with a freestanding fireplace in the center, its flue soaring up to the high, pitched ceiling. A wide deck surrounds the ocean side of the building, with stairways leading down to smaller decks with chairs for two—glorious spots to admire the view on sunny days. But even when rain or fog shrouds the coast, this beautiful room provides a convivial spot to relax by the fire; you'll find game tables and a good assortment of books, puzzles, games, and taped classical music. Two of the guest rooms are also in this building.

The four newer buildings were designed with privacy in mind. All have their own fireplaces, sitting areas, breakfast tables, and decks for enjoying the view. If you wish, you need never see another person at Whale Watch, except the innkeepers

WHALE WATCH INN BY THE SEA

35100 Highway 1, Gualala, California 95445

Telephone: (707) 884-3667

Accommodations: eighteen rooms with twin or queen-size beds; private baths with tub/showers; no telephones; no television.

Rates: expensive to very expensive, breakfast included.

Cards: AE, MC, V

Open all year.

when they bring around the breakfast trays laden with fresh fruit, freshly baked bread, and coffee or tea.

Pacific Edge, the newest building, offers the most luxurious accommodations, with skylights in the second-floor rooms and double or single whirlpool tubs throughout. One two-story suite provides the ultimate in bathing experiences: A spiral staircase ascends to a skylighted room that has an enormous spa tub for two and an ocean view. Units in one of the older outbuildings have kitchens that are fully equipped—even down to cookbooks and herbs.

Wooden steps scale the perpendicular cliff below the inn's flower-edged lawns, leading to a sandy, sheltered beach. In winter and spring the favorite pastime here is watching the great gray whales swim by on their annual ten-thousand-mile migration between the Arctic seas and the warm water of Baja California. February through April, when they return with their babies, is the best time to spot the swimming mammals.

Getting There: The Whale Watch is on the ocean side of Highway 1 just north of Anchor Bay, which is five miles north of Gualala.

In 1916 the Goodyear Redwood Lumber Company built this stately house on the cliffs above Greenwood Landing as an executive residence. In those days the small port below was heavily trafficked by schooners coming for their rich cargoes of lumber from the nearby forests. In fact, the house itself is an enlarged replica of a model redwood house designed by Louis Christian Mullgardt for the 1915 Pan American Exposition in San Francisco. When the lumber boom came to an end in the 1930s, Harbor House became an inn.

The walls, vaulted ceiling, and fireplace of the gracious living room are entirely paneled with hand-carved and hand-fitted redwood, still preserved by its original finish of polished hot beeswax. Furnishings are comfortable and eclectic: overstuffed chairs, a large Persian rug, a Steinway piano, Chinese chests and tables, bookcases bulging with reading matter, jigsaw puzzles, and the like. When Helen and Dean Turner bought Harbor House from longtime innkeeper Patricia Corcoran, they kept the furnishings pretty much intact, but they made some welcome improvements such as modernizing the bathrooms and adding showers, some with tiles hand painted by a local artist.

The Turners have also carried on Corcoran's tradition of providing substantial home-cooked meals, leisurely served in the dining room, where picture windows

HARBOR HOUSE

Highway 1 (Box 369),
Elk, California 95432

Telephone: (707) 877-3203

Accommodations: ten rooms with twin, double, or king-size beds; private baths with showers or tub/showers; no telephones; no television.

Rates: expensive, breakfast and dinner included.

No credit cards.

Open all year.

frame a view of the Pacific and the tunneled rocks in the harbor below. A typical dinner, which is included in the room tariff, might start with a homemade tomato-basil soup, and include a salad of greens just picked from the inn's garden, a main course (often local lamb or seafood), homemade breads, and a fruit cobbler for dessert; guests may purchase wine from an extensive list of California bottlings. Breakfasts are bountiful, too, focusing on a main course that might be spinach quiche, an oven-baked Gruyère omelet, or perhaps a waffle made from freshly ground flour.

Six spacious bedrooms occupy the main house, five with fireplaces and one with a private deck. Many have ocean views, and all are comfortably furnished in the style of an Edwardian country house. Next door, four cottages perch on the edge of the bluff; though small and somewhat rustic, these rooms do offer privacy as well as ocean views.

Harbor House is only twenty minutes by car from Mendocino's interesting shops and art galleries. But most guests choose to spend their time exploring the inn's private beach.

Getting There: Harbor House is on the ocean side of Highway 1 just north of Elk, which is six miles south of the intersection of Highway 1 and Highway 128.

I n eight buildings, old and new, on the top of a cliff above the Pacific, Isabel and Kendrick Petty have created a beguiling inn. Both artists, the Pettys moved here twenty years ago, before the north coast became a popular getaway area. But as the traffic grew along Highway 1, so did their inn. The Pettys started renovating old buildings on their property as guest rooms, as well as building new ones. They run a roadside café and country store, too. The entire complex has a spontaneous feeling, as does the decor of the rooms.

All but two of the rooms are built smack on the edge of the cliff, above the long-gone Greenwood Pier that was built by an erstwhile lumber company next door; this property is now a state park. In addition to their spectacular ocean views, these rooms also have decks and fireplaces or wood-burning stoves. Each is decorated according to a theme determined by the hand-painted tiles in the shower—Whale, Hummingbird, Starfish, and so forth. Goldfish shelters fifty-three finny creatures in one form or another: A carved goldfish decorates the windowsill, appliquéd ones swim on a pillow, and needlepointed fish hang on a wall. Much of the artwork in the rooms is the Pettys' own, and Isabel made all the quilts, curtains, and ruffled covers for the many pillows on the beds. She also lavishes the rooms with flowers cut fresh from her gardens, and lots of books.

GREENWOOD PIER INN

Highway 1 (Box 36),
Elk, California 95432

Telephone: (707) 877-9997

Accommodations: twelve rooms with double, queen-, or king-size beds; private baths with showers, some tubs; no telephones; no television.

Rates: moderate to very expensive, breakfast included. Children and pets welcome.

Cards: AE, MC, V

Open all year.

The inn's newest building, which Kendrick designed and constructed, contains a pair of two-story units with a colonnaded Romanesque entry. Each of these rooms has a skylight that opens over the bed and a spiral staircase to a loft where you can soak in a double bathtub and gaze out to sea.

The daily routine at Greenwood Pier starts with a breakfast tray that Isabel brings to your room, with fruit, a hot dish such as waffles or plum-filled crêpes, coffee cakes, and freshly ground coffee. If you wish, she will also deliver dinner to the room any night, even though the café is open only two evenings a week. And if you want a picnic during the day, she'll whip that up, too.

Getting There: The inn is on the ocean side of Highway 1 in the town of Elk.

MENDOCINO AREA

Cabrillo discovered Cape Mendocino in 1542 and named it after Don Antonio de Mendoza, first viceroy of New Spain. But except for its name, nothing about the coastal village of Mendocino is Spanish. Situated on a rocky bluff projecting into the Pacific, the town looks like a movie set for a New England village, which reflects the heritage of its founders. (In fact, a number of "New England" films have been shot here, including the television series *Murder, She Wrote.*) Except for fresh paint, time has not touched the clapboard Victorians set among windmills, water towers, and windswept cypress trees. Behind the town rise the redwood-covered mountains of the Coast Range.

It was this precious timber that attracted the early settlers. Harry Meiggs, a San Francisco lumberman, brought the first sawmill to Mendocino from the East aboard the brig *Ontario,* and the lumber boom began. Others harvested seafood from these northern waters and started a fishing industry that still flourishes in the nearby harbor of Noyo. In the late nineteenth century, some 3,500 people lived in Mendocino, which then boasted eight hotels, seven saloons, and as many bordellos.

Today the population is only eleven hundred, and includes many artists and craftspeople who sell their wares in the numerous galleries and shops that line the picturesque streets. Within the area are tennis courts and a nine-hole golf course. The surrounding waters offer deep-sea and stream fishing, as well as canoeing.

Just north of Mendocino—but a continent away in atmosphere—is Fort Bragg, which looks like a typical western town and is still an active lumber center for the Georgia-Pacific Company. Fort Bragg is also the departure point for the Skunk Trains, which carry passengers on scenic journeys inland through the redwoods. Advance reservations may be made by writing California Western Railroad, Box 907, Fort Bragg, California 95437.

All along this coast, a favorite winter pastime is watching the migration of the great gray whales from the Arctic to Baja California and back. From December into April, you can spot these thirty-ton mammals by the ten-foot water sprays they eject into the air. But the whale watch culminates during the last two weeks of March, when an annual whale festival is conducted in Mendocino and Fort Bragg. An even closer look is possible from charter boats operating out of the port of Noyo. Another favorite pastime in this area—year-round—is eating: A number of excellent restaurants dot the coast from Albion to Fort Bragg.

Getting There: Driving time from San Francisco to Mendocino via Highway 1 is about five hours. A much shorter route is the inland approach: From San Francisco, take Highway 101 north to Cloverdale and Highway 128 west to the coast where it joins Highway 1 just south of Albion and north of Elk.

For many years the Albion River Inn was a restaurant only, overlooking the inlet where the Albion River flows into the sea. In 1987 the restaurant owners constructed nine handsome cottages along the cliffs above the Pacific, containing sixteen luxuriously appointed ocean-view rooms and suites. They also refurbished four rooms in an older building. Not only can you enjoy the view here, you are also treated to a constant serenade from the foghorn and the waves breaking on the rocks below.

The rooms are individually decorated with pretty flowered wallpaper or wood paneling, furnishings of rattan or wicker or upholstered traditional pieces, well-tended palms or scheffleras, and down comforters on the beds. Most have fireplaces, and several have oversized tubs for two or whirlpools.

A breakfast of fresh breads and fruit is served in the lobby, and coffee makers are provided in the rooms. The restaurant is open for dinner.

Getting There: The inn is on the ocean side of Highway 1, north of the Albion River bridge.

ALBION RIVER INN

Highway 1 (Box 100),
Albion, California 95410

Telephone: (707) 937-1919

Accommodations: twenty rooms with queen- or king-size beds; private baths with tub/showers or showers, some with double tubs or whirlpool tubs; one room fully equipped for the handicapped; telephones; no television.

Rates: moderate to very expensive, continental breakfast included.

Cards: MC, V

Open all year.

For over a century, this lovely house on a cypress-studded hillside overlooking the Pacific has been dispensing hospitality to north-coast travelers. Built as a stagecoach way station in the 1860s, this hostelry, after an enormous amount of renovation, is now a bed-and-breakfast inn. The current owners, Scott and Frances Brazil, took it over in 1986 and have made improvements of their own, such as converting the old water tower into two attractive guest units.

In the main house, the spacious common room is particularly inviting, with a fireplace and a view of the sea through multipaned windows. A grand piano is well used; Frances is a professional pianist and former music professor at the University of Oklahoma. If you can coax her to the piano, you're in for a treat. But she says she doesn't play much anymore because she's so busy whipping up hors d'oeuvres and breakfasts for her guests.

The house also contains four bedrooms, with ocean or mountain views; you can enjoy both these vistas from an upstairs suite that has a fireplace, too. The water-tower rooms also have fireplaces, as well as dramatic cathedral ceilings; one unit is actually a mini-apartment with a loft bedroom and a kitchenette. But you need not worry about cooking at Fensalden Inn. It's only a short drive from the many good restaurants along the Mendocino coast.

Getting There: Just after Highway 128 joins Highway 1 (south of Albion), take Navarro Ridge Road east. The inn is on the left.

FENSALDEN INN

Navarro Ridge Road (Box 99), Albion, California 95410

Telephone: (707) 937-4042

Accommodations: seven rooms or suites with queen- or king-size beds; private baths with showers or tub/showers; no telephones; no television.

Rates: moderate to expensive, breakfast included. Children over twelve welcome. No smoking.

Cards: MC, V

Open all year.

This handsome New England–style farmhouse—flanked by two acres of cypress trees, lawns, and flower gardens—stands on a headland overlooking the bay of Little River. Built in 1867 by Isaiah Stevens, an early settler from Maine, the house was acquired in 1977 by Dutch-born designer Jan de Vries and his wife, Janet. They lavished improvements on it over the years, including a charming addition next door and a stunningly renovated barn, until they now have one of the north coast's most distinguished inns.

The de Vrieses have skillfully decorated the rooms with a mix of good contemporary art and European antiques. Bright paintings, ceramics, prints, and handmade quilts contrast with Louis XV bedsteads and marble-topped tables. The large living room is splashed with light from a bank of mullioned windows that look into the garden. In the evening refreshments are served by the fireplace and, if you're lucky, a guest might play the baby grand piano. In the morning fresh fruit, juices, and homebaked breads are served here or, if you like, in your room.

GLENDEVEN

8221 North Highway 1, Little River, California 95456

Telephone: (707) 937-0083

Accommodations: nine rooms and suites with queen-size beds, plus barnhouse suite; private baths with tub/showers or stall showers; no telephones; no television.

Rates: moderate to expensive, breakfast included. Children over eight accepted by special arrangement. No smoking.

Cards: MC, V

Facilities for small conferences. Open all year.

Glendeven

Accommodations in the farmhouse include two suites with fireplaces. Atop the house, a garret room has skylights and a terrific view of the bay. The four units in the new building are more lavishly appointed; all have fireplaces and sitting areas, some have private decks or balconies, and the top-floor rooms have vaulted ceilings and skylights. The barn was the de Vrieses' own home for a number of years and is now rented as a suite. It contains two bedrooms and a spacious living area with fireplace and deck—a super spot for small conferences.

Getting There: Glendeven is north of Little River on the inland side of Highway 1.

This ivy-covered inn, with its many cottages rambling over hillsides, meadows, and gardens that reach down to a private beach, has been a favorite haven of visitors to Mendocino for the past four decades. New Englander John Dennen constructed the inn's main building in 1876, intending it as a home for rancher Wilder Pullen. During Prohibition, neighbors started to eye the former Pullen house with suspicion: Baby Face Nelson was using the cove below the house for his bootleg operations. As recently as the early 1940s, Chinese immigrants were smuggled into the country here.

In 1949 L. D. Dennen bought the house his grandfather had built and turned it into an inn. Over the years, he added cottages on the meadows below the original house, building some and moving others from elsewhere in the countryside. Each has a name: Firehouse, Barbershop, Ice Cream, Schoolhouse. The latter was built with lumber salvaged from the Greenwood School in Elk; the school's sign serves as a headboard and the children's desks as bedside tables. An old water tower, brought down from Mendocino, is now a two-story unit with a circular stairway leading from a living room to a balconied bedroom. Some of the seventy units have brick fireplaces or Franklin or potbellied stoves; all have private baths; and a few have whirlpool tubs and wet bars.

The original building now houses the lobby and a restaurant; adjoining is a bar and lounge, which was once an apple-storage house at a nearby farm. These rooms have wonderful views and are open to the public for breakfast, lunch, and dinner. Heritage House operates on semi-American plan only: Breakfast and dinner are included in the rates. This inn is more formal than most north-coast places; jackets and ties are encouraged at dinner.

Getting There: Heritage House is on the ocean side of Highway 1 between Albion and Little River.

HERITAGE HOUSE

5200 Highway 1,
Little River, California 95456

Telephone: (707) 937-5885

Accommodations: seventy rooms with twin, double, or king-size beds; private baths with showers or tub/showers; some rooms with wheelchair access; no telephones; no television.

Rates: moderate to very expensive, breakfast and dinner included. Children welcome.

No credit cards.

Open February through November.

BUILT 1877 A D

Heritage House

The Old West facade of this historic hotel probably looks about the same as it did a century ago when Ben Bever started taking in lodgers here. But old Mendocino hands who have not been around in recent decades wouldn't recognize the present interior.

In 1973 San Diego businessman R. O. Peterson bought the hotel and brought it to a level of luxury that had never existed before. Even in its prime, the hotel had been nothing fancy, just a comfortable hostelry for loggers and traveling salesmen. Peterson invested the place with the elegance of the Victorian era. Polished dark woods and wainscotings, Oriental rugs, and Tiffany-style glass were installed in the lobby and dining room. A spectacular dome of genuine Tiffany, found in Philadelphia, was suspended over the carved wooden bar. (Founder Bever surely wouldn't approve of the goings-on today. He once named the place The Temperance House, decreeing that "no liquor shall be served.") Off the lobby, an attractive dining room is open to the public for dinner; breakfast and lunch are served in a plant-filled addition to the hotel.

Upstairs, twenty-six bedrooms have been renovated to mint condition, with an eclectic turn-of-the-century ambience. Hand-painted porcelain sinks from France and European armoires are combined with replicated American wallpapers and Victorian brass and carved-wood bedsteads. Many of the rooms have ocean views and private balconies.

Then in the 1980s Peterson nearly doubled the hostelry's capacity with four cottages clustered around a formal garden in the block behind the hotel. One of these, now elegantly refurbished, was the home of the Heeser family, early settlers of the area. The other garden cottages, though newly constructed, also have the look of old Mendocino. The rooms in the cottages are more lavishly appointed than most of those in the hotel; many have wood-burning fireplaces or stoves, all have television and private bathrooms, and many have their own verandas. Each guest room is named after a pioneer Mendocino family, and yellowed photos of family members hang on the walls, making you feel as though you're a part of the town's early history, too.

Getting There: From Highway 1, turn left on the Mendocino exit to Jackson Street, which becomes Main Street.

MENDOCINO HOTEL & GARDEN COTTAGES

45080 Main Street (Box 587), Mendocino, California 95460

Telephone: (707) 937-0511, (800) 548-0513

Accommodations: fifty-one rooms and suites with twin, double, two double, queen-, or king-size beds; most rooms have private baths with tub/showers; in the hotel some have shared baths with stall showers; some rooms fully equipped for the handicapped; telephones in all rooms; television in garden cottages.

Rates: moderate to very expensive, no meals included. Dining rooms open for breakfast, lunch, and dinner. Children welcome.

Cards: AE, MC, V

Facilities for conferences. Open all year.

In the 1860s Joshua Grindle came to Mendocino from Maine, and had become the town banker by 1879, when he built a fine house overlooking the village and the ocean. In 1977 Bill and Gwen Jacobson, who had been searching the state for a B&B site, bought the house, its imposing water tower, and the surrounding two acres. In keeping with Grindle's New England heritage, they decorated the rooms with Early American furnishings, many from their own collection of antiques.

On the first floor, one bedroom is papered with historic scenes of Philadelphia, boasts a handsome maple four-poster, and overlooks a patio shaded by a giant rhododendron tree. Another is decorated with pale yellow woodwork, a peony-patterned quilt on a queen-size bed, and comfortable chairs around a fireplace. An upstairs room has a nautical theme and a fine ocean view. Joshua Grindle's former bedroom, with its dormered windows, is large enough for three, with a queen-size bed and a studio couch. An adjacent saltbox cottage contains two rooms with Franklin stoves, and the water tower has been remodeled to create another three units, two with fireplaces.

Yet another fireplace, decorated with hand-painted English tiles, distinguishes the paneled living room. A baby grand piano is also there for the guests' enjoyment, as are jigsaw puzzles and backgammon and chess sets. In the cheerful dining room an antique pine refectory table, a handsome old hutch, and a grandmother's clock catch the eye. Here Gwen serves a full breakfast of homemade bread or coffee cake, fresh fruits, eggs, coffee, and tea. The Jacobsons will be happy to brief you on activities in the area, but if you want to be left alone, they won't intrude. That's one of the reasons travelers return again and again to this exemplary inn.

Getting There: From Highway 1, take Jackson Street exit into Mendocino. Turn right on Lansing to Little Lake.

JOSHUA GRINDLE INN

44800 Little Lake,
Mendocino, California 95460

Telephone: (707) 937-4143

Accommodations: ten rooms with double or queen-size beds; private baths with tub/showers; one room with wheelchair access; no telephones; no television.

Rates: moderate, breakfast included. No smoking.

No credit cards.

Open all year.

Joshua Grindle Inn

Shortly before you cross Big River into the village of Mendocino, you see a handsome lodge sitting on the hillside. Flowers burst from its balconies, and manicured lawns and gardens slope down to a barn and a pasture where llamas graze and ducks splash in a pond. This place, long known as Big River Lodge, was built in the 1960s. In 1980 Joan and Jeff Stanford transformed the motel-like structure into a lovely inn, doing most of the work themselves.

Some of the rooms have walls of knotty pine or barnsiding; all have beamed ceilings, fireplaces, and multipaned French doors leading to private patios or balconies with magnificent views of the town and the ocean. Each room is individually decorated with antiques, four-posters, down quilts, and the like. Coffee and other refreshments await your arrival.

The Stanfords' ten acres extend north to the wooded river bank, where a cottage contains three suites. There's a boat house here, too, where you can rent canoes to paddle around, or fish for salmon and steelhead in the winter months. If you feel energetic, ten-speed and mountain bikes are also available for exploring the redwood forests behind the inn.

In the mornings, fruit, juices, hot danish pastries, coffee cake, and a basket of fresh fruit are set out in the recently enlarged lobby, which opens out to a terrace behind the inn. But most guests prefer to take their breakfasts back to their beautifully appointed rooms.

Getting There: From Highway 1, just south of Mendocino, head east on Comptche-Ukiah Road. The inn is on the left.

THE STANFORD INN BY THE SEA (BIG RIVER LODGE)

Comptche-Ukiah Road (Box 487), Mendocino, California 95460

Telephone: (707) 937-5615

Accommodations: twenty-five rooms and three suites with queen- or king-size beds, some rooms with hide-a-beds and trundle beds as well; private baths with showers or tub/showers; wheelchair access; telephones; television.

Rates: expensive to very expensive, breakfast included. Children and pets welcome.

Cards: AE, CB, DC, MC, V

Open all year.

Surrounded by a picket fence and a flower-filled English garden, this three-story, nineteenth-century shingled house looks across the whitecapped bay to the tree-covered mountains beyond. Rich champagne-colored carpeting flows throughout the rooms, which are painted and papered in cream, soft blue, and restful earth tones. All rooms have wood-burning fireplaces, most have ocean views, and one has Dutch doors leading to a private deck; another unit is in a little cottage situated behind the house. All are appointed with handsome English and American antiques, comfortable couches or chairs, magazines, plants, and flowers just picked from the garden.

Headlands has long been one of Mendocino's loveliest B&Bs, but after former San Franciscans Pat and Rod Stofle purchased the inn in 1986, they added some

HEADLANDS INN

Howard and Albion Streets (Box 132), Mendocino, California 95460

Telephone: (707) 937-4431

Accommodations: five rooms with queen- or king-size beds; private baths with tub/showers; no telephones; no television.

Rates: moderate to expensive, breakfast included. No smoking.

No credit cards.

Open all year.

improvements of their own. You now enter the inn through a gracious living room with a fireplace and an 1824 square baby grand piano. Refreshments await newly-arrived guests in a second-floor sitting room that's stocked with books and games. The Stofles have added many family heirlooms: an antique sewing machine in one of the bedrooms, a grandfather clock in the parlor, and a church pump organ in the sitting room.

Breakfast is brought to the rooms on wooden trays bedecked with edible flowers, colorful linens, and the morning paper. Pat loves to cook, and in addition to serving freshly baked muffins and fresh fruit, she prepares a special entrée each day. Some of these creations are truly spectacular, such as a basil-seasoned tomato basket containing a baked egg topped with Gruyère cheese. "I don't paint or sew," she says. "Cooking is my way of being creative."

Getting There: Take Jackson Street exit off Highway 1. Turn right on Howard Street to Albion Street. The inn is on the corner.

When you enter the village of Mendocino, one of the first sights you see, behind a pretty garden and a white picket fence, is an 1882 Queen Anne Victorian that houses the Mendocino Village Inn. Sue and Tom Allen bought this older inn in 1986 and gave it a much-needed facelift and an entirely new life. They furnished the rooms with eclectic abandon. Some have a traditional look with flowered papers and old four-posters; others are decked out with Navajo rugs and Indian art. The Captain's Quarters boasts nautical memorabilia, and the Roosevelt Room displays trophies that might have been Teddy's. Many of the rooms have wood-burning fireplaces, others have views, and a few have private garden entrances. Two inexpensive garret rooms provide a perfect spot for older children or young budget travelers who don't mind having to share a bath down a steep flight of stairs.

The Allens are engaging hosts with interesting backgrounds. They have lived in New York, Japan, and San Francisco, where she managed an architectural office and he was in advertising. They have made the homey first-floor common room the hub of the inn, joining their guests in the evening for refreshments and lively discussions of politics or the arts. They serve a hearty breakfast: fresh fruit, homemade breads, and main dishes such as herbed cheesecake or blue-cornmeal pancakes. Large tables are provided for those who feel sociable, as well as tiny tables for two. Or if you like, take your coffee out to the redwood deck and listen to the taped music that's an integral part of a stay here. In the morning it's classical

MENDOCINO VILLAGE INN

Main Street (Box 626),
Mendocino, California 95460

Telephone: (707) 937-0246

Accommodations: twelve rooms with double or queen-size beds; all have private baths except two, which share a bath; tubs, showers, and tub/showers; no telephones; no television.

Rates: inexpensive to expensive, breakfast included. Children welcome in some rooms. No smoking.

Cards: MC, V

Open all year.

and in the evening, jazz—perhaps Brubeck, the Manhattan Transfer, or Jean-Luc Ponty. If the tapes run out, don't worry. There's a guitar and a piano here, too.

Getting There: At Mendocino, exit from Highway 1 on Jackson Street, which becomes Main Street.

I n a remote valley surrounded by forests of giant redwoods, the Benbow family built a small resort hotel on the banks of the Eel River in 1926. The four-story English Tudor manor house of half-timbered construction is an incongruous sight in this mountain setting. The baronial lobby—with its high, coffered ceiling, carved woodwork, massive fireplace of sculptured stone, and French doors leading to a formal terrace—was a gathering place for the elite of the era. John Barrymore, Charles Laughton, President Herbert Hoover, and Mrs. Eleanor Roosevelt were among early guests. But even they would be astounded if they could see the elegance of Benbow today.

In the 1940s this fine old inn slid into a period of genteel shabbiness. Nostalgia was almost all it had going for it in 1978, when Patsy and Chuck Watts rescued the aging dowager and transformed her into the empress of the Redwood Empire. Now the lobby is resplendent with carved period furniture, Oriental rugs, and an impressive array of antique clocks, paintings, and prints. The terrace and gardens are a blaze of color with over three dozen varieties of flowering plants. And the bedrooms boast every conceivable luxury—air-conditioning, modern tiled bathrooms—and a lovely country look, with matching floral bedspreads, draperies, and wallpaper. A coffeepot and a basket of paperback mysteries are provided with the inn's compliments. In the deluxe rooms, small refrigerators are stocked with beverages.

The second- and third-story rooms of the Benbow have views of the surrounding terrain from large windows or bays. These used to be the choice rooms, but that distinction now belongs to two stories of rooms under the terrace overlooking the river. These were rebuilt from the ground up with wood-burning fireplaces in some and private terraces or balconies adjacent to all. A rebuilt cottage offers a whirlpool tub as well. Despite Benbow's isolation, there's no lack of things to do. The inn houses one of the finest restaurants in the Redwood Empire, with a

BENBOW INN

445 Lake Benbow Drive,
Garberville, California 95440

Telephone: (707) 923-2124

Accommodations: fifty-six rooms with twin, queen-, or king-size beds; private baths; no telephones; color television in terrace rooms; central air-conditioning.

Rates: moderate to very expensive, no meals included. Dining room open to the public for breakfast, lunch, dinner, and Sunday brunch. Children over three welcome.

Cards: MC, V

Open April through November, and December 18 through January 2.

Benbow Inn

sophisticated menu. In the lounge just off the lobby, a jukebox is filled with big-band favorites—Glenn Miller, Freddy Martin, Artie Shaw—and a piano player entertains nightly. In another salon, old-time movies from a library of some hundred classics are shown each night. And there's always the possibility of a game of chess or a jigsaw puzzle in the lobby. Special events are staged at certain times of the year: a Halloween masquerade ball, a November tasting of Napa Valley wines, a nut-cracker Christmas celebration, and a New Year's Eve champagne dinner-dance.

A plethora of daytime activities is available as well. In the summer the Eel River is dammed into a lake, offering swimming from the inn's private beach, canoeing, and paddleboating. Nearby are tennis courts, a nine-hole golf course, fishing, hunting, and horseback-riding trails. Seven miles south of Benbow is Richardson Grove State Park, one of California's most important redwood preserves, and to the north is the Avenue of the Giants, a road that winds through dense groves of sequoias, the world's largest and oldest trees.

Getting There: Benbow Inn is two hundred miles north of San Francisco and two miles south of Garberville on Highway 101. From the Mendocino coast, Benbow may be reached by taking Highway 1 to Leggett and Highway 101 north. The inn will send a car to Garberville airport for guests arriving by private plane.

EUREKA AND FERNDALE

Eureka shares its name with California's motto: I have found it! It wasn't gold that the city's founders discovered in 1850, but rather a large bay at the mouth of the Eel River. This was a convenient harbor for ships awaiting a cargo almost as precious as gold: the redwoods hewn in the great sequoia groves through which the Eel flows. Ferndale's first settlers were not seeking gold either; they were dairy farmers attracted by the verdant pastureland along the river's broad delta. Today, however, another kind of treasure lures visitors to this area: Both Eureka and Ferndale are gold mines of well-preserved Victorian architecture.

Eureka, the Humboldt County seat, is the largest California port north of San Francisco and a bustling commercial center for the lumber and fishing industries. Yet the city is preserving its heritage in Old Town. Many of the historic buildings near the waterfront have been restored, and the streets are partially paved with brick and banked by flowers. Ferndale, on the other hand, remains a sleepy community that has changed little since the nineteenth century. Its Main Street is lined with brightly painted Victorian buildings that now house a bevy of shops, arts and crafts galleries, restaurants, and the Village Theatre, home of the Ferndale Repertory Company. The entire town, which is dubbed "The Victorian Village," has been designated a historical landmark by the state of California.

The drive to this area follows the Eel River from the redwood-forested mountains down to the sea. Beyond Garberville, you will see a number of turnoffs to the Avenue of the Giants. This is the old road that winds through the dense groves of sequoias, some of which are over 3,000 years old and as tall as 350 feet. It's worth the detour for the awesome experience of being among some of the world's oldest living things.

Getting There: Eureka is 277 miles north of San Francisco on Highway 101. The turnoff to Ferndale is clearly marked shortly before the highway reaches Eureka.

Every architectural gewgaw known in the 1890s was lavished on this showplace. Its gables and turrets were festooned with intricately carved spoolwork, brackets, finials, and friezes and painted in flamboyant tones of peach and gold. Flanked by a formal English garden where brick walkways lead through a maze of manicured boxwoods and topiaries, The Gingerbread Mansion makes a stunning sight on this quiet side street of Ferndale. The same Victorian spirit pervades the inside of the house. The rooms are papered with colorful replicas of Victorian patterns and furnished with period pieces: carved headboards in the bedrooms, an Empire couch and Eastlake parlor set in one of the four parlors, an ornately carved sideboard in the adjoining library with an abundant supply of books, games, and even a jigsaw puzzle depicting the inn.

Ever since they acquired the house in 1981, innkeepers Wendy Hatfield and Ken Torbert have continually improved it. All nine of the bedrooms now have private baths, and the Gingerbread Suite also has two old-fashioned claw-foot tubs right in the bedroom; bubble bath and tubside reading lamps are also provided. But the most deluxe room in the house is the two-hundred-square-foot bathroom in the Fountain Suite where two claw-foot tubs sit side by side in splendor on a raised platform in front of a Franklin fireplace. Guests may read on the chaise or enjoy "his and hers" bubble baths by the fire.

Wendy, who was formerly in the travel business, treats her guests with a hospitality as lavish as the gingerbread facade of the house. Late afternoon tea and cake are served at fireside, beds are turned down at night, and a hand-dipped chocolate is placed on the bedside table. In the morning, trays of coffee and tea are set

THE GINGERBREAD MANSION

400 Berding Street,
Ferndale, California 95536

Telephone: (707) 786-4000

Accommodations: nine rooms with twin or queen-size beds; private baths with showers, some with claw-foot tubs; no telephones; no television.

Rates: moderate to expensive, breakfast and tea included. Children over ten welcome. No smoking.

Cards: MC, V

Open all year.

The Gingerbread Mansion

out upstairs so guests can have an eye-opener before proceeding to the formal dining room for a breakfast of fruit, cheeses, hard-boiled eggs, and homemade muffins, breads, and cakes. The inn even provides rubber boots for rainy days and bicycles for exploring the village. These are painted the same gold and peach as the house, so the shopkeepers can recognize guests from The Gingerbread Mansion.

Getting There: Proceed into town on Main Street, turn left at the Bank of America building, and go one block to Berding. The inn is on the corner.

Dominating a corner at the end of Main Street is Ferndale's biggest building—a tall two-story Victorian with many elaborate bays. This was originally the town's bank, later a tractor showroom, and in recent years a restaurant with apartments upstairs. In 1988 real estate developer Merv Phelan converted the handsome structure into an elegant little hotel, with twelve rooms upstairs and a bar, restaurant, and antique car museum on the first floor. But this is only half the story. Phelan has also turned his thousand-acre cattle ranch on the "Lost Coast" south of Ferndale into a secluded retreat and conference center, operated in conjunction with the hotel.

In town, the guest rooms at the Victorian Village Inn have twelve-foot ceilings, intricate woodwork, and large sunny bays. They've been done up with stunning Victorian-style wallpapers, brass beds, wood armoires, skirted tables, and Oriental rugs on the carpeted floors. Complimentary candies are placed in the rooms. Several packages offer options of a Continental breakfast in the room or a full morning meal in the downstairs dining room.

Phelan is an old-car buff. He has turned one area of the hotel into a museum displaying his large collection of Packards, Model As, and Model Ts; auto memorabilia is scattered around the bar and dining room, too, and he even has a vintage wood-paneled station wagon to drive his guests around town.

In contrast to the flurry of activity around the hotel, the ranch offers total tranquility. The three-story Georgian Colonial mansion is perched amid landscaped gardens high on a wooded ridge above the Pacific. Phelan built the place eight years ago as a hideaway for himself, then added another wing of rooms to make it a resort and executive retreat. The rooms have a rustic country look with whitewashed walls and polished fir floors with rag and Oriental rugs scattered about. Bedroom furnishings tend toward Shaker four-posters and patchwork quilts; an elk's head

VICTORIAN VILLAGE INN

400 Ocean Avenue (Box 1028), Ferndale, California 95536

Telephone: (707) 786-9400

Accommodations: twelve rooms or suites with twin, double, queen-, or king-size beds; private baths with tub/showers; telephones and television on request.

Rates: inexpensive to expensive, no meals included. Guests at the inn do not have ranch privileges. Children welcome.

Cards: AE, MC, V

Open all year.

LOST COAST RANCH RESORT

Reservations should be made through the Victorian Village Inn.

Accommodations: eighteen rooms with twin or queen-size beds; private baths with tub/showers; telephones and television on request.

Rates: moderate to expensive.

Facilities for small conferences. Open to groups all year; open to individual guests only in the summer.

keeps watch in the living room, which boasts a big brick fireplace and a piano. Adjoining is a dining area where guests are served family-style breakfasts and dinners at a long refectory table.

Despite the isolation of the ranch, guests will find plenty to keep them busy: a billiards room, horseback riding, trout fishing in a stocked pond, skeet shooting, hay rides, and barbecues. Because the road to the ranch house passes through open cattle range, guests are not permitted to drive their own cars in; instead, a van offers shuttle service several times a day to and from the Village Inn in Ferndale. But who wants to leave the Lost Coast?

Getting There: In Ferndale, proceed down Main Street to Ocean.

I n the early 1850s, Seth Shaw and his brother Stephen were the first settlers of the rich farmlands south of the Eel River, replacing jungles of twelve-foot-high ferns with orchards and cultivated fields. Seth chose a spot on the banks of Francis Creek to erect a gabled Carpenter Gothic mansion for his bride, and named the estate Fern Dale. But as other farmers populated the area, the town name was contracted to Ferndale. In 1980 the old Shaw house with its acre of wooded grounds became an inn, now owned and operated by Norma and Ken Bessingpas.

The mansion is distinguished by an abundance of bays and coffered ceilings, even under the sloping roof of the second-story gables. Four of the guest rooms are located upstairs. Two of them have Gothic doors opening to private balconies, and a third holds the Shaws' honeymoon bed with its handsome six-foot headboard. Norma has decorated the rooms with quilted spreads, flowered wallpapers, and fresh flowers from the gardens. In the rear of the house, downstairs, another two rooms share a private parlor that opens to a deck filled with tubs of hydrangeas and pelargoniums. A path leads from here down to Francis Creek.

Norma offers afternoon tea on the deck in warm weather, or by the fire in the double parlor if the day is chilly. Breakfast is served at a long lace-covered table in the formal dining room. Norma prepares an egg entrée in addition to breads, cheeses, fruit, and juice.

Getting There: The house is on the right side of Main Street just before you reach town.

THE SHAW HOUSE INN

703 Main Street (Box 1125), Ferndale, California 95536

Telephone: (707) 786-9958

Accommodations: seven rooms with double, queen-, or king-size beds; private and shared baths with tub/showers; no telephones; no television.

Rates: moderate, breakfast included.

Cards: MC, V

Open all year.

The Shaw House Inn

This Stick-style four-story Victorian hotel, built in 1888, was a popular water-ing hole for sailors and lumbermen in days past. Now colorfully restored, it's still a lively spot. The first-floor is literally a three-ring circus with a restaurant, bar and grill, and a theater where professional entertainers and musicians perform. Things are quieter on the top three floors, which have been con-verted into an elegant B&B.

Owners John and Shirley Lipscomb searched Europe for the furnishings, and some of the carved headboards, wooden armoires, and marble-topped dressers rightfully belong in a museum. Windows are draped with lace and velvet. And the beds—some canopied, some tucked into alcoves—are picture-pretty with down comforters and piles of pillows. The best rooms by far are on the top floor, with views of Old Town or Humboldt Bay; one of these has a working fireplace, too. Also on the top floor is a lovely breakfast room where a buffet of juices, fruit, and past-ries is set out. Guests can enjoy this repast at formally set tables while admiring a grand view of the bay. That same view may also be enjoyed in a cozy little spa.

Getting There: From Highway 101, turn west on C Street.

EAGLE HOUSE

Second and C Streets,
Eureka, California 95501

Telephone: (707) 442-2334,
in California (800) 522-8686

Accommodations: twenty-four rooms with twin, double, queen-, and king-size beds; private baths with showers, tubs, or tub/showers; one room fully equipped for the handicapped; telephones; television.

Rates: moderate, breakfast included. Smoking and non-smoking rooms.

Cards: AE, MC, V

Facilities for weddings and conferences. Open all year.

Samuel and Joseph C. Newsom, architects of Eureka's famous Carson Mansion, also designed a number of other buildings in the city. One of their admirers is Mark Carter, who helped renovate some Newsom structures owned by his fa-ther. When Mark found an old book of Newsom house plans, he decided to build from scratch an 1884 San Francisco house that had been destroyed in the fire of 1906. Mark faithfully re-created the four-story structure on a hillside in Eureka's Old Town. It's a magnificent hand-crafted Victorian that offers views of the bay and of the nearby Carson Mansion from almost every room.

Unlike most Victorians, the entire house has a light and airy feeling of flowing space. Joseph Newsom himself wrote, "The lower portion of the house can be thrown open to form a very fine continuous room." And so it is today with the three parlors distinguished by two marble fireplaces and three large bays. Mark did depart, however, from the Victorian tradition of interior design by painting the walls stark white and eliminating the frills and clutter associated with the period. The decor is beautifully understated, with well-chosen and well-placed antiques, Oriental rugs scattered on the highly polished oak floors, no curtains or drapes to

CARTER HOUSE

Third and L Streets,
Eureka, California 95501

Telephone: (707) 445-1390

Accommodations: seven rooms with double, two double, or queen-size beds; four rooms with private baths, three rooms share a bath with tub/shower; one room fully equipped for the handicapped; no telephones; no television.

Rates: inexpensive to very expensive, breakfast included. No smoking in bedrooms.

Cards: AE, MC, V

Open all year.

Carter House

shut out the light, contemporary paintings and ceramics by local artists, and baskets of flowers and potted plants strategically set about.

Three guest rooms with high, pitched ceilings occupy the top floor. The third floor contains another guest room, as well as a two-room suite with a whirlpool bath for two. At street level, below the parlor, are two more rooms and a wine cellar.

Mark's wife, Christi, is an avid cook. One of her breakfast specialties is a recipe learned in classes with Jacques Pépin: a delicate tart with a ground-almond filling topped by very thin slices of apple. This might be accompanied with fresh orange juice, eggs Florentine or Benedict or a smoked salmon platter; a fruit dish is also served, such as fresh strawberries with zabaglione. In the late afternoon, the Carters serve brie and fruit, and at bedtime they offer tea and cookies.

Getting There: From the south, Highway 101 becomes Fifth Street. Turn left on L Street and proceed two blocks.

THE HOTEL CARTER

Mark Carter might wind up rebuilding Eureka if he keeps up his whirlwind pace of reconstructing Victorians. After turning the Carter House B&B (see preceding) into a smashing success, he built a hotel across the street, modeled after Eureka's Old Town Cairo Hotel. Working from an old photograph, he constructed a three-story Queen Anne–type building with a gabled roof, twenty bedrooms (many with fine views of the bay), wide hallways, and a lovely lobby. Here, in the evenings, a tray of brie and fruit and a decanter of wine are set in front of the marble fireplace for the guests' enjoyment.

An intimate dining room, with just twelve tables, has enormous windows that look out to the flower-filled streets of Old Town. Three nights a week, Christi Carter and her co-chef Linda Claasen prepare very special prix-fixe dinners for hotel guests and the public. The cooking is creative and highlights north-coast seafood and produce. Breakfast is also served here daily.

The Hotel Carter is oriented toward the business traveler. The rooms, decorated with English natural-pine furnishings, offer modern comforts such as private baths (some with whirlpool tubs), television, and telephones. Two rooms have fireplaces, too. The Hotel Carter also reflects Mark's passion for contemporary art, which is found throughout the place.

Getting There: From Fifth Street, turn left on L Street and proceed two blocks.

301 L Street,
Eureka, California 95501

Telephone: (707) 445-1390

Accommodations: twenty rooms with two doubles or one queen-size bed; private baths, six with whirlpool tubs; telephones; television.

Rates: inexpensive to expensive, with or without breakfast. Children welcome. No smoking in guest rooms.

Cards: AE, MC, V

Facilities for weddings. Open all year.

INNS IN ALPHABETICAL ORDER

The Little Inn on the Bay, 20
The Sherman House, 103
The Stanford Inn by the Sea, 204
The Union Hotel, 127
The Upham, 52
The Venice Beach House, 30
Victorian Village Inn, 211
Vintners Inn, 185
Washington Square Inn, 111
White Swan Inn, 118

FACILITIES FOR THE HANDICAPPED
Albion River Inn, 196
Auberge du Soleil, 172
Beazley House, 168
Casa Madrona, 119
City Hotel, 134
Eagle House, 214
Fallon Hotel, 134
Garden Court Hotel, 100
Gramma's Bed and Breakfast Inn, 125
Hanford House, 144
Heritage Park Bed & Breakfast Inn, 12
Highlands Inn, 78
La Mancha, 44
Madrona Manor, 181
Martine Inn, 91
Mendocino Hotel & Garden Cottages, 210
Pillar Point Inn, 102
Spindrift Inn, 86
Strawberry Creek Inn, 37
The Ballard Inn, 62
The Estate, 186
The Inn at Harris Ranch, 70
Vintners Inn, 185

PETS WELCOME
Auberge du Soleil, 172
Greenwood Pier Inn, 194
Madrona Manor, 181
San Ysidro Ranch, 51
Stonepine, 82
Swan-Levine House, 154
The Inn at Rancho Santa Fe, 17

The Stanford Inn by the Sea, 204
Vintners Inn, 185

SPECTACULAR VIEWS
Albion River Inn, 196
Auberge du Soleil, 172
Beach House, 67
Campbell Ranch Inn, 180
Carter House, 214
Casa Madrona, 119
Doryman's Inn, 22
Eagle House, 214
El Encanto Hotel and Garden Villas, 57
Fensalden Inn, 197
Greenwood Pier Inn, 194
Harbor House, 193
Heritage House, 199
Highlands Inn, 78
Loma Vista Bed and Breakfast, 19
Lost Coast Ranch Resort, 211
Madrona Manor, 181
Martine Inn, 91
Pillar Point Inn, 102
Portofino Beach Hotel, 22
Rock Haus, 15
Sandpiper Inn-at-the-Beach, 80
Spindrift Inn, 86
The Green Gables Inn, 88
The Hotel Carter, 216
The Inn at Morro Bay, 65
The Inn on Mt. Ada, 24
The Jabberwock, 87
The Parsonage, 61
The Sherman House, 103
The Spreckles Mansion, 114
The Stanford Inn by the Sea, 204
The Union Hotel, 127
Ventana Inn, 68
Whale Watch Inn by the Sea, 192

SPAS AND HOT TUBS ON THE PREMISES
American River Inn, 149
Blackthorne Inn, 123
Briggs House (sauna), 132

Campbell Ranch Inn, 180
Eagle House, 214
Highlands Inn, 78
La Residence, 169
Magnolia Hotel, 170
Mill Rose Inn, 100
Murphy's Inn, 155
Quail Lodge, 83
River Rock Inn, 152
St. Orres Inn, 190
Ten Inverness Way, 123
The Cheshire Cat, 59
The Estate, 186
The Glenborough Inn, 58
The Inn San Francisco, 115
The Knickerbocker Mansion, 34
Timberhill Ranch, 189
Union Hotel, 64
Ventana Inn, 68
Villa Rosa, 54
Villa Royale, 41
Vintners Inn, 185
Wine Country Inn, 174

PRIVATE WHIRLPOOLS
Albion River Inn, 196
Auberge du Soleil, 172
Beazley House, 168
Benbow Inn, 206
Captain Dillingham's Inn, 127
Carter House, 214
Doryman's Inn, 22
Garden Court Hotel, 100
Haydon House, 183
Heritage House, 199
Highlands Inn, 78
Hope-Merrill House, 178
Ingleside Inn, 40
La Maida House, 27
La Mancha, 44
Point Reyes Seashore Lodge, 122
Portofino Beach Hotel, 22
Saddleback Inn, 34
San Ysidro Ranch, 51
Stonepine, 82

NOTES